COOL STUFF
EXPLODED
GET INSIDE MODERN TECHNOLOGY

LONDON, NEW YORK, MELBOURNE, MUNICH, AND DELHI

For Tall Tree Ltd:
Editors Rob Colson, Jon Richards
Designer Ben Ruocco

For Dorling Kindersley:
Senior editors Victoria Heyworth-Dunne, Claire Nottage
Senior art editor Smiljka Surla
Managing editor Linda Esposito
Managing art editor Diane Thistlethwaite
Publishing manager Andrew Macintyre
Category publisher Laura Buller
Design development manager Sophia Tampakopoulos-Turner
Picture researcher Rebecca Sodergren
Senior production editor Vivianne Ridgeway
Jacket editor Mariza O'Keeffe
Jacket designer Yumiko Tahata
Production controller Pip Tinsley

Consultant Jon Woodcock
Illustrators Nikid Design Ltd

First published in Great Britain in 2008 by
Dorling Kindersley Limited,
80 Strand, London, WC2R 0RL

ISBN: 978-1-40531-877-8

Printed and bound by Hung Hing, China

**Discover more at
www.dk.com**

COOL STUFF EXPLODED

GET INSIDE MODERN TECHNOLOGY

written by
Chris Woodford

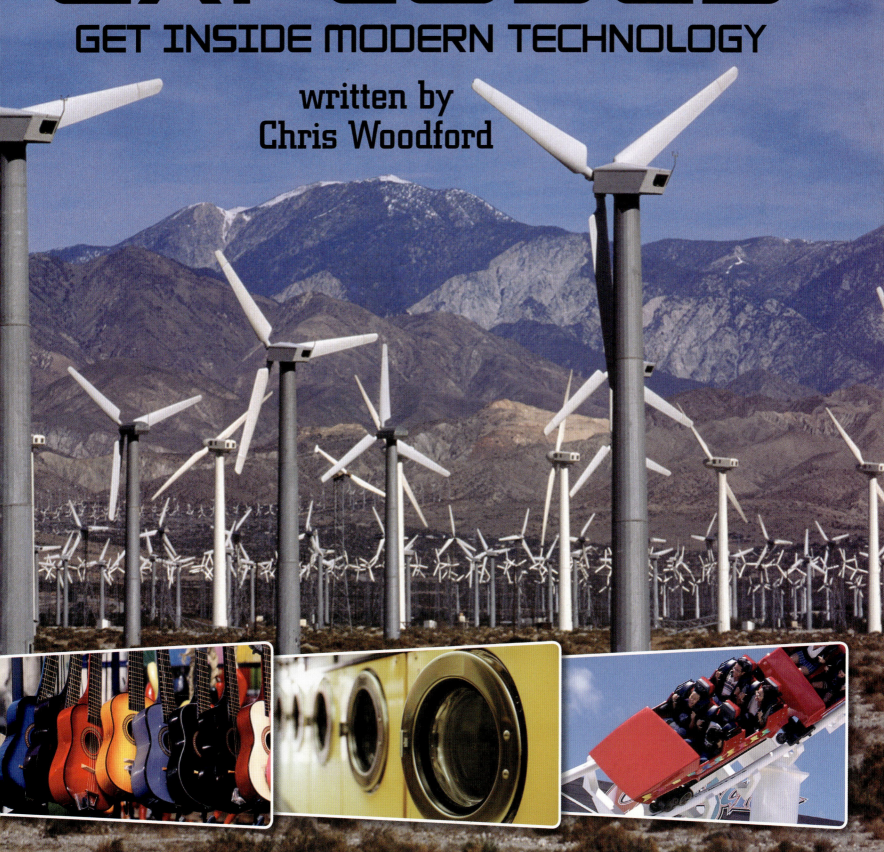

CONTENTS

ENTERTAINMENT AND LEISURE

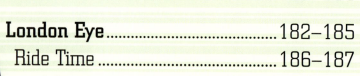

DIGITAL TECHNOLOGY

INTRODUCTION

This book reveals the secrets hidden inside the machines that surround us. Ever stopped to think how a jet plane can be so big and a laptop computer so thin? Have you wondered what makes a watch tick, or why a concert piano costs more than a car? In this book you'll find the answers. From helicopters to washing machines, cool vehicles, mean machines, and neat gadgets are blown apart to show the bits that make them work. You'll discover a motorbike that runs on hydrogen gas, a coffee machine that's under as much pressure as a deep-sea diver, and an amazing "eye" that's almost three times taller than the Statue of Liberty. If today's machines surprise you, the ones being planned will astound you, with bikes that can fly, 3-D TV, and electricity beamed down from space.

Hold tight... and step inside!

CD ROM When you see this symbol, it means this object is featured on the amazing animated CD-ROM. Just click and look.

Modelling

First the artist sets up the basic lighting, just as a photographer would do in a studio. Then he or she builds up the outer appearance of the model using photographs of real objects, and sketches. New parts are added and adjusted as necessary. For example, the artist added the engines to this hoverbike by starting with simple cylinders, then bending them into more complex shapes.

3-D MODELLING

The 40 objects featured in this book may look like photos, but they are actually detailed, 3-D models produced with cutting-edge computer graphics. Each one is like a sculpture that an artist has slowly built up on the computer screen. Unlike a flat picture, an artist can rotate a 3-D model in any direction, zoom in on its details, or explode it into hundreds of pieces.

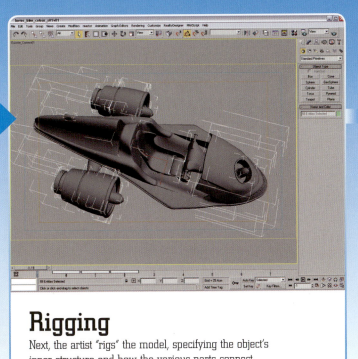

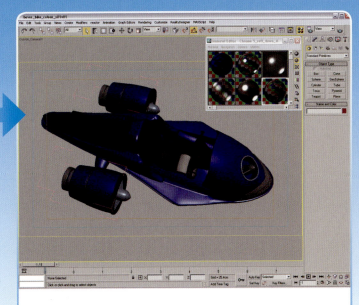

Rigging

Next, the artist "rigs" the model, specifying the object's inner structure and how the various parts connect together. Rigging is particularly important for computer animation. The end result is a "clay" – a dull-white version of the object, like an unpainted plastic model.

Texturing

In the final stage, the artist applies textures (surface finishes) and colours to the different parts of the object. The bodywork of this bike has been textured to look like shiny blue metal, while the handlebars are more like matt black plastic.

GETTINGABOUT

Trains are usually the fastest way of getting about on land –
and the French TGV (*Train à Grande Vitesse* – high-speed train)
is the world's fastest conventional train. A new experimental
version of the TGV set a speed record of 574.8kph (357mph)
on 3 April 2007, which is more than 160kph (100mph) faster
than a Formula One car!

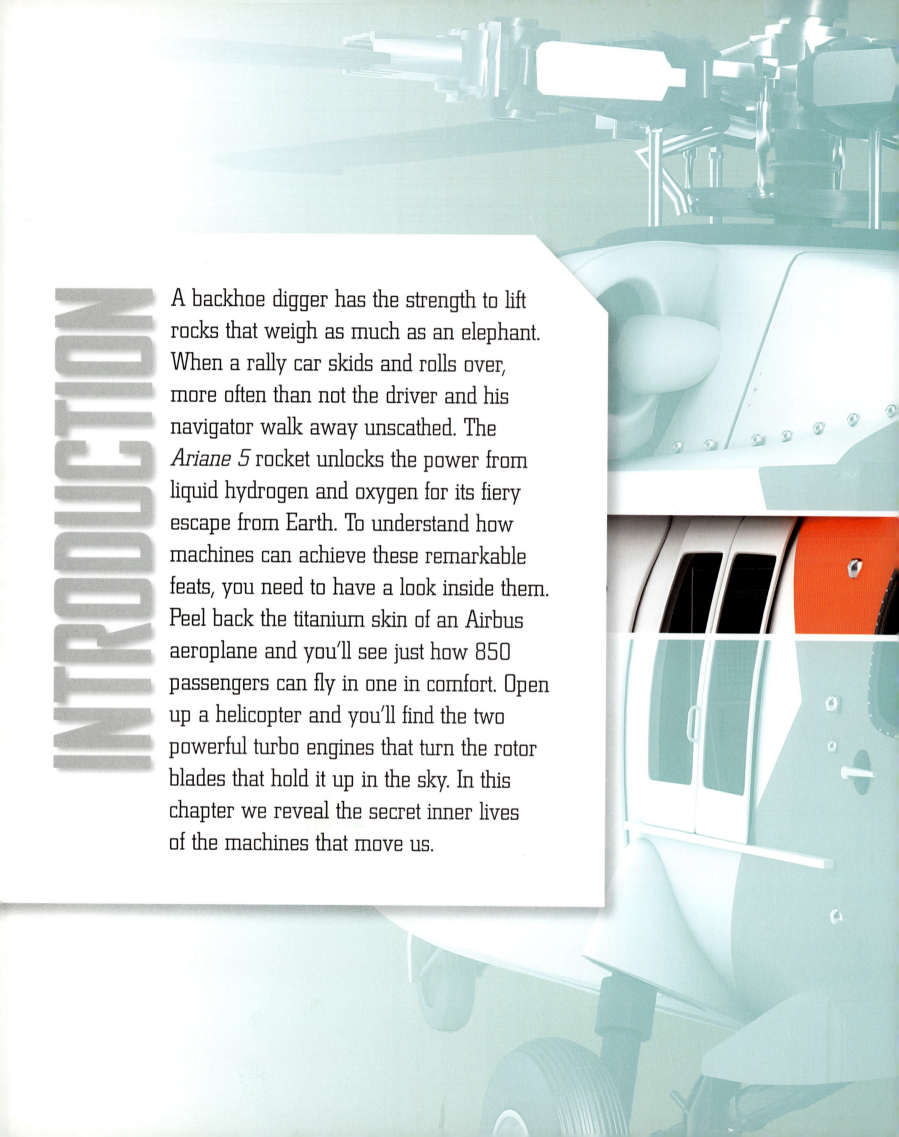

INTRODUCTION

A backhoe digger has the strength to lift rocks that weigh as much as an elephant. When a rally car skids and rolls over, more often than not the driver and his navigator walk away unscathed. The *Ariane 5* rocket unlocks the power from liquid hydrogen and oxygen for its fiery escape from Earth. To understand how machines can achieve these remarkable feats, you need to have a look inside them. Peel back the titanium skin of an Airbus aeroplane and you'll see just how 850 passengers can fly in one in comfort. Open up a helicopter and you'll find the two powerful turbo engines that turn the rotor blades that hold it up in the sky. In this chapter we reveal the secret inner lives of the machines that move us.

RALLY CAR

This may look like an ordinary car, but appearances can deceive. Rally teams buy a basic factory-made car, then spend 10 times more money toughening it up so that it can thump down rough roads at high speeds. It's inevitable that rally cars will crash, so the body joints are welded more securely and a rigid inner cage is added to protect the two people inside. After it has been modified, the car's body shell is so strong that it could support the weight of 10 cars standing on its roof.

Rough ride

The wheels suffer more punishment than any other part of the car. The wheel hubs and suspension are made from strong, lightweight titanium metal to survive high-speed jolts. Rally tyres last as little as 50km (30 miles), and a single car can get through 180 tyres in just one race.

FAST FACTS

Top speed	249kph (155mph)
Drive	4-wheel drive
Dimensions	441cm x 174cm x 143cm (174in x 69in x 56in)
Engine	Turbo-charged 4-cylinder

Ground hugger

Cars are shaped like aerofoils (aeroplane wings) – this makes the whole body lift up slightly at high speeds, which can make the car unstable and difficult to drive. Formula One racers and rally cars have spoilers (large air-deflectors) at the front and back to counteract this. By redirecting the airflow, the spoilers push the car down, increasing its grip on the road.

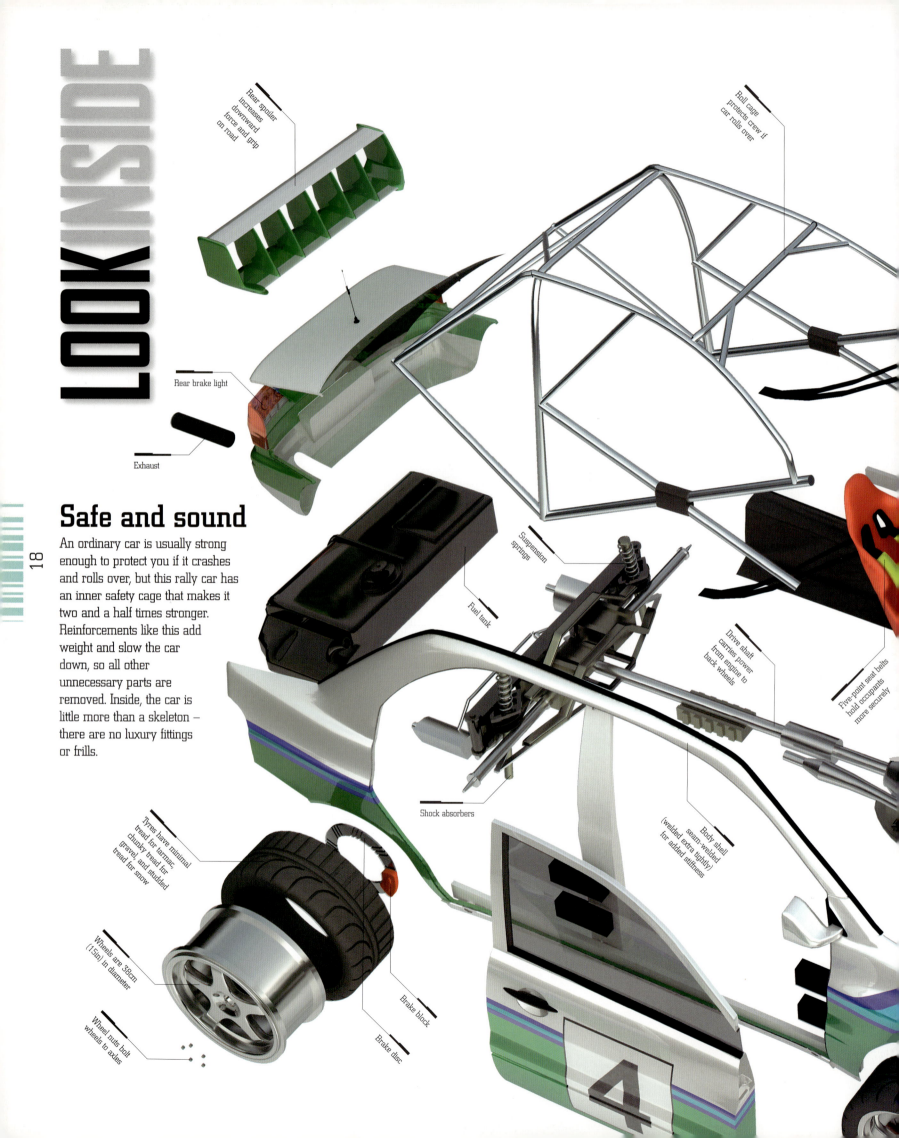

LOOK INSIDE

Rear spoiler increases downward force and grip on road

Roll cage protects crew if car rolls over

Rear brake light

Exhaust

Safe and sound

An ordinary car is usually strong enough to protect you if it crashes and rolls over, but this rally car has an inner safety cage that makes it two and a half times stronger. Reinforcements like this add weight and slow the car down, so all other unnecessary parts are removed. Inside, the car is little more than a skeleton – there are no luxury fittings or frills.

Suspension springs

Fuel tank

Drive shaft carries power from engine to back wheels

Five-point seat belts hold occupants more securely

Shock absorbers

Body shell seam-welded (welded extra tightly) for added stiffness

Tyres have minimal tread for tarmac, chunky tread for gravel, and studded tread for snow

Wheels are 38cm (15in) in diameter

Brake block

Wheel nuts bolt wheels to axles

Brake disc

Firing on all cylinders

The cylinders make power by repeating four steps over and over again. First, fuel and air enter through the valves at the top. Second, the piston moves up to squeeze the mixture. Third, a spark from the plug makes the mixture explode and this pushes the piston back down to power the car. Finally, the piston moves back up to clear out waste gases, which become the exhaust fumes.

How it works

An engine provides the energy that moves the car. This happens in metal canisters called cylinders. Pistons moving up and down the cylinders turn the crankshaft. The crankshaft drives the gearbox, which powers the drive shaft, which turns the wheels.

Valve

Spark plug

Cylinder

Piston

Crankshaft

Steering wheel has paddle control behind it for faster gear changes

Roof

Bucket seats are shaped to keep occupants in place during sharp turns

Front alloy wheel

Front brake disc

Bonnet

Fire extinguisher

Foglights

Air intake feeds oxygen to engine cylinders

Front bumper and spoiler made of lightweight composite material

Gearbox

Cylinders in engine

Battery

Four-cylinder engine needs servicing roughly every 800km (500 miles)

Axles hold and power wheels

Radiator helps to cool engine

Global warming

Carbon dioxide gas, made by burning fuels, is smothering Earth like an invisible blanket. The planet is warming and the poles are melting. Scientists think the North Pole could be ice-free in summer by 2013, pushing polar bears toward extinction.

Pollution

You breathe about 10 million times a year. If you breathe in car exhaust fumes, your lungs are inhaling a toxic cocktail of chemicals, including some that are known to cause cancer.

CAR CRAZY

People are crazy about cars. Since 1900, the number of people on Earth has roughly quadrupled to about 6.6 billion – but over the same period, the number of cars has increased by about 10,000 times. There's now about one car for every 10 people on the planet. Cars have brought a huge benefit: the freedom to travel when and where we please. But they've challenged society too, with environmental problems like pollution and global warming as well as major conflicts over limited supplies of oil. Will we soon have to choose between cars and our planet?

Milestones

Roman chariot
The sports cars of their day, chariots like this could reach speeds of up to 60kph (40mph) and were popular throughout Roman times (c.100BCE–400CE).

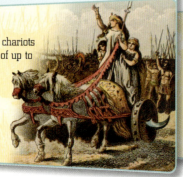

Benz car
Karl Benz (1844–1929) made one of the first cars in 1885 by putting a petrol engine onto a three-wheeled

Goodbye oil?

Oil companies are constantly discovering new reserves, but many people believe Earth's supplies of oil are limited. Nobody knows exactly how much oil is left, but some predict that most could be gone within decades. Oil will never completely run out, but it will become more expensive. People will slowly switch to other forms of energy, such as solar power or hydrogen gas, as they become cheaper.

Oil wars

Most of the world's oil is locked beneath the boundless deserts of the Middle East in such countries as Saudi Arabia, Iraq, and Iran. That is partly why this region has seen so much tension and conflict in recent decades.

Car growth

Developing nations like China and India are the fastest-growing markets for new cars. In China alone, car sales are increasing by 80 per cent a year. Car makers are trying to build better cars to stop global warming, but huge growth in car numbers in developing countries will hamper their efforts.

Price to pay

With a top speed of more than 400kph (250mph), the Bugatti Veyron is one of the world's fastest cars. It's also one of the most expensive to run – it uses up to three times as much fuel as a typical family car.

Ford Model T
American industrialist Henry Ford (1863–1947) made the first car that ordinary people could afford. He achieved this remarkable feat by building vehicles in enormous quantities. Each car was quickly assembled in a highly organized factory process called an assembly line.

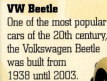

VW Beetle
One of the most popular cars of the 20th century, the Volkswagen Beetle was built from 1938 until 2003. "Volkswagen" is German for "people's car".

Green cars
Future cars may be like this Sunraycer. The back section is covered with solar panels that power an electric motor.

FUTURE INTELLIGENT CAR

Future cars will be packed with sensors and satellite navigation equipment so that they'll be able to drive themselves. Future "driving" will be more like taking a taxi: you'll recline in your seat listening to music, watching a film projected onto the windscreen, or reading a book – while the car does all the work!

Back of windscreen doubles as a widescreen TV for watching films as you travel

Driver's joystick control for manual driving

Radar system automatically guides car at night and in bad weather

Sensors built into front and back of car guide it through traffic

Whiz wheels

This tiny future car has more room inside than a conventional car. That's because there's no engine wasting space. Instead, there are four compact electric motors built into the wheel hubs. These hub motors give four-wheel drive for better grip in bad weather. They also give four-wheel steering, which makes the car very easy to move and park. The wheels even rotate 90° so that you can drive the car sideways!

PENDOLINO TRAIN

You've probably seen motorcyclists leaning into curves as they corner at high speed, but have you ever seen trains doing the same thing? The Pendolino is an Italian-designed train with tilting carriages that can sweep round curves 30 per cent more quickly than conventional trains, and just as safely. Tilting Pendolinos have slashed inter-city journey times, proving hugely popular in Europe. More than 430 of these new trains are now in use in 10 different countries.

Comfort zone

Pendolinos are designed with passengers in mind. They are fully air-conditioned, and each carriage is pressurized, so passengers don't feel uncomfortable when the train enters tunnels. Large windows make the carriages feel spacious, and the electric doors are wide enough for wheelchairs.

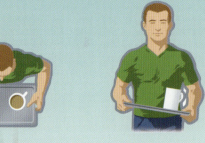

Flat tray
When you swerve the tray round a corner, the cup keeps moving in a straight line. It slides towards the edge of the tray.

Tilted tray
If you tilt the tray, the cup leans into the curve. The tilted tray now pushes the cup inwards so it follows a curved path. The cup stays in place instead of sliding.

How it works

Why is it easier for a train to go round a curve at high speed, without the passengers inside being tossed around, by tilting into the curve? Suppose you are walking down a corridor at speed carrying a cup of tea on a tray, and you turn a corner. A basic law of physics says that objects always keep moving in the same direction and at the same speed unless another force acts on them. Unless you tilt the tray, there is no force acting on the cup to make it turn with you. It will continue in a straight line and slide across the tray as you corner.

Windscreen wiper

Aerodynamic front roof

Windscreen

Crew seats

Driver cab desk

LOOKINSIDE

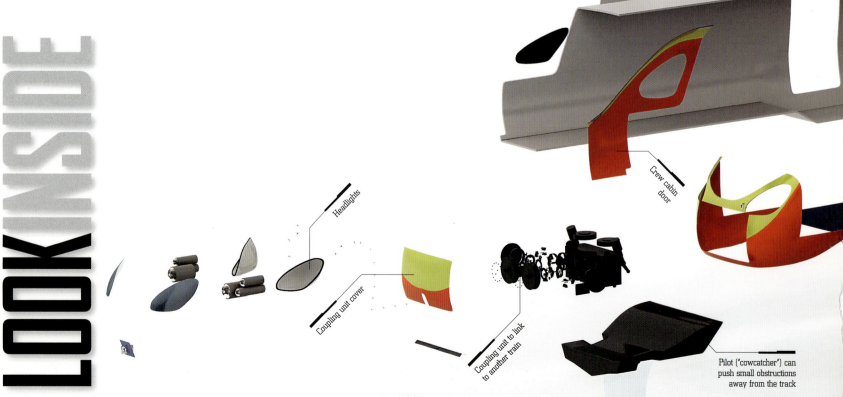

Headlights

Coupling unit cover

Coupling unit to link to another train

Crew cabin door

Pilot ("cowcatcher") can push small obstructions away from the track

Super-safe

Pendolinos travel faster than ordinary trains, so they need to have extra safety features. The driver is protected by a shell-like structure at the front. There are crumple zones at the ends of each carriage that protect passengers by absorbing most of the impact in a crash. The carriages are built from a single, tube-like aluminium structure called a monocoque, which is both lightweight and very strong.

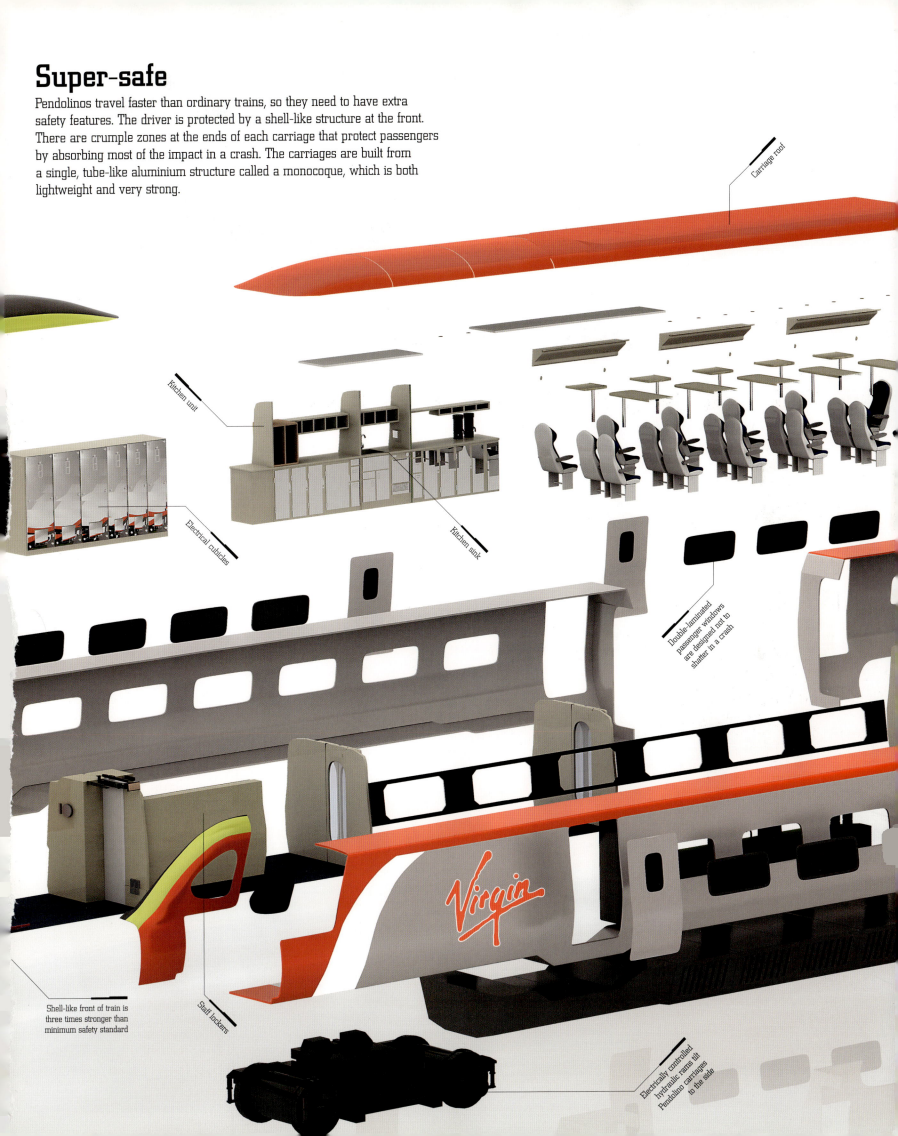

Carriage roof

Kitchen unit

Electrical cubicles

Kitchen sink

Double-laminated passenger windows are designed not to shatter in a crash

Shell-like front of train is three times stronger than minimum safety standard

Staff lockers

Virgin

Electrically controlled hydraulic rams tilt Pendolino carriages to the side

Moovie business

This futuristic concept car, the Peugeot Moovie, is how designers believe vehicles might look in 2020. The passengers sit inside a plastic bubble with two huge wheels running around it at the back. There are two more tiny wheels under the nose at the front. The car is made from lightweight materials, such as polycarbonate plastic, so it uses as little fuel as possible.

Hydrogen fuel tank built into back of car

Huge reclining seats can rotate to face in any direction

Electric doors open at the touch of a button

Hinge allows wheel to rotate 90°

Inner coils float inside outer magnets, giving automatic suspension and braking and powering the wheels

Hard-wearing puncture-resistant tyres last up to 10 years

Coils inside wheels work with magnets to power the vehicle

Magnets built in outside of wheel hub

390 027

FAST FACTS

Top speed	250kph (155mph)
Material	Aluminium body shell
Typical configuration	7 cars (with 1 power car at each end)
Passengers	Max. 432–494
Total weight	Approx. 450 tonnes (including passengers)
Total train length	187m (613ft)

Tilting power

When a Pendolino corners at speed, hydraulic (fluid-filled) pistons tilt the top of each car up to 8° into the curve. The bogies (wheel units) underneath do not tilt, but remain safely on the track. The pantograph (overhead electricity connector) swivels so that power to the train is uninterrupted.

Lighting

Plug sockets next to seats can power laptop computers and mobile phones

Seats are mounted on thin pedestals to give passengers more legroom

Vestibules at carriage ends work as crumple zones, absorbing energy in an accident

Aluminium body shell

Electrically operated passenger doors

Window made of toughened glass to prevent breakage

Electric motors under carriages power the train

Two bogies per carriage

Tilting carriages

A Pendolino's secret lies in the bogies (wheel units) under the carriages. The top part of the carriage is connected to the bogies by powerful hydraulic pistons, which are connected to an electronic control system. When the train corners at speed, the control system sends signals to the pistons. They push up on the side of the train facing the outside of the curve, and the carriage tilts slightly into the corner. This allows the train to corner more quickly and makes the ride more comfortable for passengers.

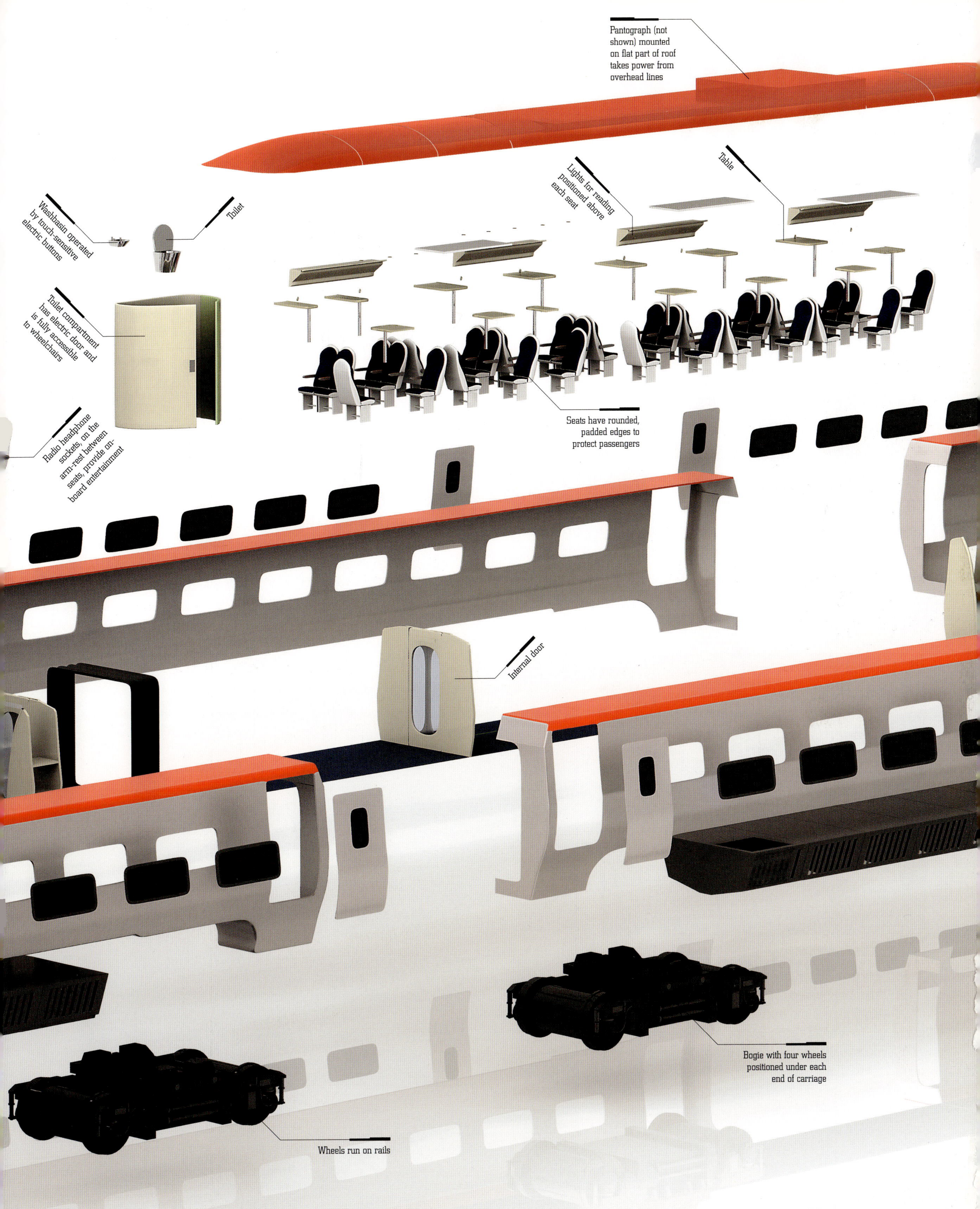

Pantograph (not shown) mounted on flat part of roof takes power from overhead lines

Washbasin operated by touch-sensitive electric buttons

Toilet

Lights for reading positioned above each seat

Table

Toilet compartment has electric door and is fully accessible to wheelchairs

Radio headphone sockets, on the arm-rest between seats, provide on-board entertainment

Seats have rounded, padded edges to protect passengers

Internal door

Bogie with four wheels positioned under each end of carriage

Wheels run on rails

MAKING TRACKS

After almost a century of decline, rail travel has recently been enjoying something of a revival. Steam-powered locomotives were invented in the early 18th century. In the decades that followed, tracks were built to carry steam trains between major cities, often cutting journey times from days to hours. Rail travel then gradually fell out of favour during the 20th century. Cars replaced rail for most individual journeys, lorries carried much of the freight once moved by rail, and aeroplanes revolutionized long-distance travel. Now, in the early 21st century, high-speed train services are winning back business from cars, lorries, and planes. They are a fast, safe, and convenient way to travel.

Meeting in the middle

On 10 May 1869, two tracks were joined at Promontory Summit in Utah, United States, completing a transcontinental railway that crossed North America, connecting the east and west coasts. As more long-distance lines were laid, markets for goods became much bigger. In this way, laying railway tracks was vital to the growth of business.

Tilting trouble

Trains can go faster around corners if they tilt. Helped by a lightweight aluminium body, this 1970s advanced passenger train (APT) could corner 40 per cent faster than a conventional train. Unfortunately, it tilted so steeply round curves that it made passengers feel sick. The train was scrapped, but some of its technology was used to make the Pendolino, which was first manufactured in Italy by Fiat in 1987.

Rush hour

As train travel becomes popular again, overcrowding is a growing problem – and it's not easy to solve. Train platforms are a fixed length, so trains can't always be made longer. Running trains more often causes congestion and can delay the network as a whole.

Trains versus planes

Engines give off carbon dioxide gas, a cause of global warming. Planes give off more than trains, especially on short journeys, because they need lots of fuel to take off. Taking a train instead of making a short flight cuts emissions by 90 per cent.

Tight corners

Roller coasters work the opposite way to tilting trains. With wheels under the track to stop the cars falling off, roller coasters tilt through seemingly impossible angles to make you feel excited. No-one would dare go on trains that tilted like this!

Bullet train

Japanese Shinkansen trains are nicknamed "bullets" for good reason: with sloping, aeroplane-style fronts, they can reach speeds of up to 300kph (186mph). This N700 Shinkansen tilting train was introduced in July 2007.

Floating into the future

Maglev trains float on powerful magnets and can reach speeds of up to 580kph (360mph). Some engineers have suggested tunnelling a magnetic railway under the Atlantic Ocean. Trains would go from London to New York in just 54 minutes!

BACKHOE LOADER

If there's earth to move or holes to dig, call in the backhoe loader. These amazingly versatile diggers are similar to tractors, only with hydraulic (piston-powered) digger buckets at the front and rear. Sit inside the cab and you're controlling a monster. The front bucket is strong enough to lift an elephant and big enough to move a cubic metre (35 cubic feet) of soil – about 60 spadefuls – in one go. You'll get the job done in no time with a backhoe!

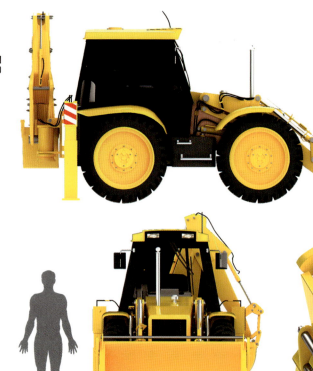

Metal muscles

Think of a backhoe as a giant extension of the driver's body. The rear digger has three separate joints similar to the shoulder, elbow, and wrist. The front bucket works like two arms outstretched and lifting together.

FAST FACTS

Dimensions	Approx. 7m x 2m x 3m (23ft x 6.5ft x 10ft)
Top speed	40kph (25mph)
Bucket swivel	Rear digger rotates through 200°
Cost	£45,000

Making tracks

Backhoe arms can dig deep below ground level: fully extended, a typical backhoe arm can go down more than 6m (20ft). A tracked excavator like this one (right) can dig even deeper – typically about 9m (30ft). The top of its body (the part above the giant caterpillar tracks) can swing through 360°, making it easy to dump spoil (waste rocks).

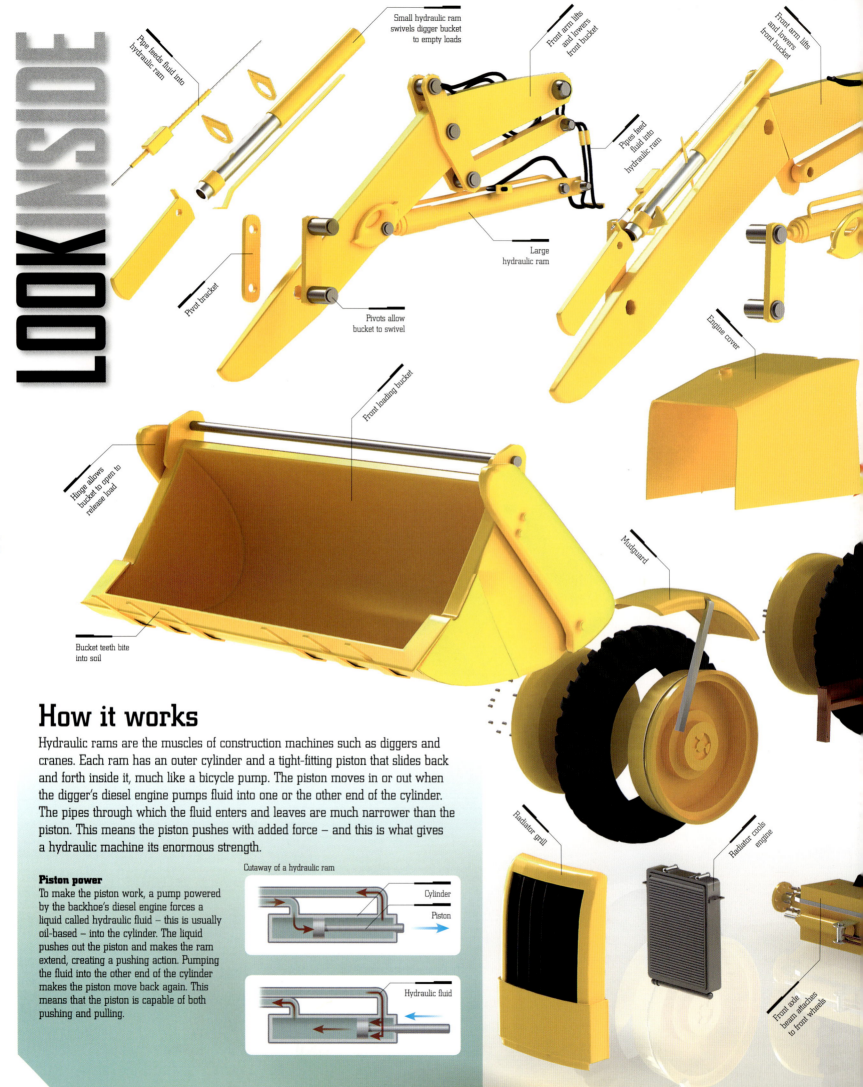

LOOK INSIDE

Pipe feeds fluid into hydraulic ram

Small hydraulic ram swivels digger bucket to empty loads

Front arm lifts and lowers front bucket

Front arm lifts and lowers front bucket

Pipes feed fluid into hydraulic ram

Large hydraulic ram

Pivot bracket

Pivots allow bucket to swivel

Engine cover

Front loading bucket

Hinge allows bucket to open to release load

Mudguard

Bucket teeth bite into soil

Radiator grill

Radiator cools engine

How it works

Hydraulic rams are the muscles of construction machines such as diggers and cranes. Each ram has an outer cylinder and a tight-fitting piston that slides back and forth inside it, much like a bicycle pump. The piston moves in or out when the digger's diesel engine pumps fluid into one or the other end of the cylinder. The pipes through which the fluid enters and leaves are much narrower than the piston. This means the piston pushes with added force – and this is what gives a hydraulic machine its enormous strength.

Piston power

To make the piston work, a pump powered by the backhoe's diesel engine forces a liquid called hydraulic fluid – this is usually oil-based – into the cylinder. The liquid pushes out the piston and makes the ram extend, creating a pushing action. Pumping the fluid into the other end of the cylinder makes the piston move back again. This means that the piston is capable of both pushing and pulling.

Cutaway of a hydraulic ram

Cylinder

Piston

Hydraulic fluid

Front axle beam attaches to front wheels

Radio aerial

Roof

Front cab lights

Rear digger arm

Digger arm struts

Pivots allow rear arm to swivel

Cab reinforced to protect driver if digger rolls over

Rear digger arm

Rear bucket

Pivots

Wing mirror

Rear digger hydraulics

Exhaust pipe

Pivot allows rear digger bucket to swivel up and down

Pivot

Air intake

Warning sign

Rear digger mounting

Diesel engine and hydraulic pump

Strong girders help to support weight of rear digger

Hydraulic pipe raises and lowers stabilizers

Stabilizers are lowered to support digger at rear

Rear axle beam

Outer part of wheel

Engine mounting

Wheel nuts

Inner part of wheel

Big, chunky tyres stop digger sinking into mud and give grip

Digging machine

Every moving part on a backhoe is powered by the diesel engine at the centre. Apart from driving the wheels, it also operates the hydraulic pump, steering the digger and raising and lowering the front and rear buckets.

DIGGING DEEP

Earth is a giant rock packed full of minerals – everything from sand and coal, to silver and gold. Since prehistoric times, human ingenuity has been finding uses for practically every mineral that has ever been discovered. Digging things out of the planet is often harder than it looks, however – minerals may be locked into Earth's surface or buried miles beneath it, and getting them out can be a real challenge. In ancient times, people had no choice but to dig and scrape out the minerals they needed by hand. These days, we use giant hydraulic machines to shift the dirt dozens of times faster, and far fewer people work in mines and quarries. We are also starting to recognize the harmful effects that such activity can have on our environment and the animals that live in it.

Ancient tools

Tools like these were the backhoes of the Stone Age. Masterpieces of design, they have stone blades attached to wooden handles by leather straps. They work scientifically, too – the long wooden handles enable the user to dig with much more force. The pointed tips concentrate the force in a smaller area, making it easier to chip through hard soil.

Dirty work

Mining is one of the world's most dangerous jobs. Fires and explosions are common, and mines sometimes collapse on the workers inside. Miners often have to breathe in large amounts of dust – even if this dust is not poisonous, long exposure to it can cause breathing difficulties and even death.

Mass consumption

We need giant mines because we use vast quantities of minerals. Those of us born in developed countries will consume about 1,600 tonnes of minerals during our lives – in fuel, housing, and all the products we buy and throw away.

Low tech

Despite the development of powerful machines to do the job, mining in some countries is still done by hand – and sometimes by children. The United Nations estimates that a million children as young as five work for up to eight hours a day digging and carrying heavy loads.

Big digger

This massive mechanical monster is designed to scrape coal from an opencast (surface) mine using the 18 buckets on the spinning wheel at the front. The world's biggest bucket excavator, a German machine called Bagger 288, is twice as tall as the Statue of Liberty. It can dig out 240,000 tonnes of coal per day – enough to fill more than 700 very large tipper trucks.

Danger signs

Construction machines are painted yellow for safety. Our eyes see yellow clearly, and it triggers warning signals in our brains – just as when we see wasps and bees.

Minerals

Minerals are the nonliving materials we dig from the ground. We use them for almost everything we do. We need coal and uranium to make energy, aggregates like sand and clay to build things, and metals like iron and aluminium to make machines.

Doing damage

Mining can harm our planet. By removing vegetation, it destroys important habitats, killing the animals who live there or forcing them to flee. Many species are threatened by human activities like this.

Shipping out

It's not just people who move around the planet. Countries transport vast amounts of goods to each other, much of it in giant metal containers. The world's biggest cargo ship can carry 11,000 containers, each bigger than a family car.

Busy streets

Streets choked with traffic in the day may be totally empty at night. We could ease transport problems if people worked from home or worked more flexible hours. Making more shop deliveries at night would also help.

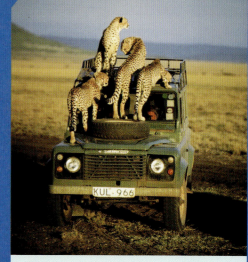

Ecotourism

Travel makes us appreciate the wonders of the world, but too many tourists can damage historic places and disturb wildlife. One solution is ecotourism, or green tourism. It means travelling in a more sustainable way, doing as little damage as possible to the area being visited.

PEOPLE AND PLANET

Every time you travel by car, bus, plane, or train, you hurt the planet. The engine that moves you uses oil and produces pollution. It also makes carbon dioxide gas, which causes global warming. People need to travel, but the planet is important, too. We need to get about more wisely, reducing our impact as much as we can.

Simple solutions

Saving the planet is a huge task, but people can work together to make a difference. Parents who drive children to school cause a quarter of rush-hour traffic. The "walking bus" is one simple solution to this problem. Instead of going by car, children dress up in high-visibility jackets and walk to school together in a crocodile. Ideas like this cut traffic, make roads safer, and make travel more fun.

Personal change

Whose job is it to save the planet? Governments can't solve problems unless people help them. We can all make a difference by using public transport for journeys wherever possible. Better still, walk, cycle, or skate. It uses no fuel and creates no pollution. It's good for your health, and it's fun, too!

FACTOIDS

- In 1950, 25 million people travelled internationally. In 2005, that figure was 760 million. ● More than 44 million new cars roll off the production lines worldwide each year. ● Food travels 25–50 per cent further from farm to table than it did 20 years ago.

Plane truths

Flying may be the fastest way to travel, but it's usually also the noisiest and dirtiest. Roughly half of all flights are short-haul (less than three hours and only a few hundred kilometres or miles). These journeys can often be made by train, which cuts the effect on global warming by 90 per cent.

Rough rescue

The SEAHAWK's cabin can be changed to suit different missions. For basic troop transporting, it can hold 14 seats. For search and rescue, the seats can be removed and replaced with a winch. The winching equipment takes up almost a quarter of the cabin space, leaving enough room for the crew and the casualties they save.

When there's trouble at sea, the world's navies often have to step in. Warships can move quickly to where they're needed, carrying tough helicopters like the Sikorsky SEAHAWK. Built for the rough and tumble of life at sea, it's packed with features that help it survive in the most demanding conditions.

SEAHAWK

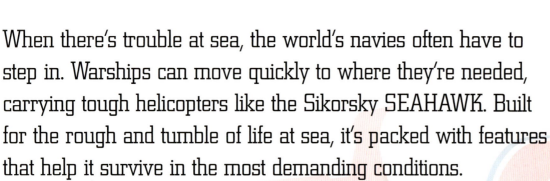

FAST FACTS

Cabin dimensions	3.8m x 1.9m x 1.3m (12ft 7in x 6ft 1in x 4ft 5in)
Maximum load	4,123kg (9,070lb)
Speed	284kph (153 knots)
Range	453km (245 nautical miles)
Power	2 turbo-shaft engines

Space saver

The SEAHAWK can fold its rotors to save space. Normally it is 16.4m (53ft 8in) wide. Folded, it is only 3.3m (10ft 8in) wide.

How it works

Unlike an aeroplane, a helicopter does not have to move forwards to fly. Its rotors work like small aerofoils that generate lift (upward force) as they spin round at high speed. The helicopter steers by tilting its rotor blades as they spin. This produces more lift on one side than the other, causing the whole craft to move in that direction.

In a spin

As the main rotor blades rotate, the whole body of the helicopter tends to turn the opposite way (red arrow). The small rotor at the tail of the helicopter pushes in the opposite direction to counteract this (blue arrow).

Main rotor blades

Tail rotor blades

Rotor blades designed to survive 23mm (0.9in) cannon fire

Rotor blade pitch control allows blades to swivel as they rotate

Second turboshaft engine

Sliding cargo door

Pilot's door

Hydraulic pitch control rods tilt rotors as they turn to steer helicopter

Hydraulic and electrical systems each have two backups

Energy-absorbing wheel makes it easier to land on ships

Toughened windscreen and cockpit designed to survive impacts

Pilot's seat

Co-pilot's seat

Cabin can be configured for troops, cargo, or equipment

Aerodynamic nose cone

Cockpit windows can be jettisoned in a crash

Electronic search system

Radio, radar, satellite navigation, and night vision, cockpit equipment

Four large digital monitors replace many conventional instruments

Radar equipment helps navigation at night and in bad weather

LOOK INSIDE

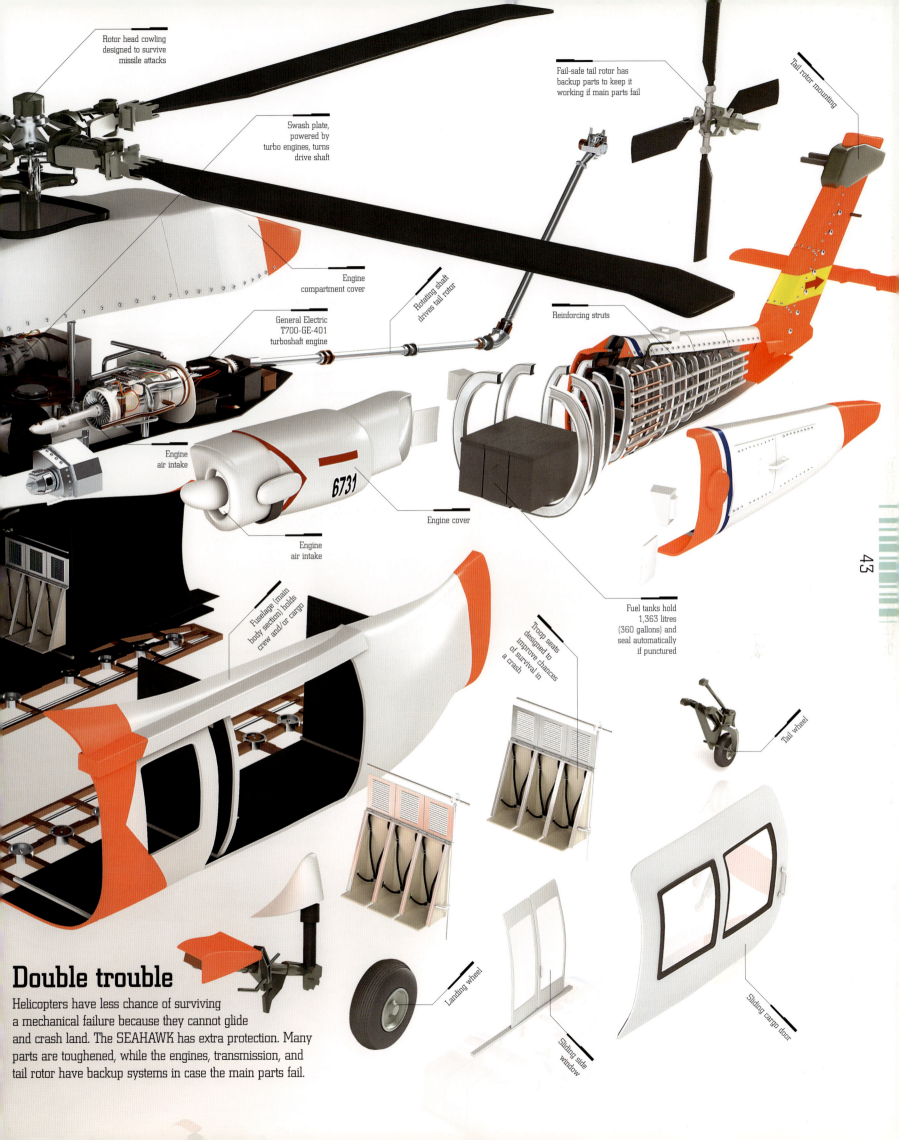

Rotor head cowling designed to survive missile attacks

Fail-safe tail rotor has backup parts to keep it working if main parts fail

Tail rotor mounting

Swash plate, powered by turbo engines, turns drive shaft

Engine compartment cover

Rotating shaft drives tail rotor

Reinforcing struts

General Electric T700-GE-401 turboshaft engine

Engine air intake

6731

Engine air intake

Engine cover

Fuel tanks hold 1,363 litres (360 gallons) and seal automatically if punctured

Fuselage (main body section) holds crew and/or cargo

Troop seats designed to improve chances of survival in a crash

Tail wheel

Landing wheel

Sliding side window

Sliding cargo door

Double trouble

Helicopters have less chance of surviving a mechanical failure because they cannot glide and crash land. The SEAHAWK has extra protection. Many parts are toughened, while the engines, transmission, and tail rotor have backup systems in case the main parts fail.

CHOPCHOP

If you're lost on a mountain or your ship's going down at sea, there's no more reassuring sound than the chop-chop of a helicopter swooping down to rescue you. Forwards or backwards, sideways, up, or down – a helicopter pilot can fly in any direction by tilting the rotor blades as they spin around. Helicopters can take off and land vertically, so they can reach places no aeroplane can go. That's why they're so useful in so many situations. When it comes to flight, helicopters really are the perfect all-rounders.

First flights?

These amazing patterns in the Nazca Desert, Peru, are visible only from the air. Some were created more than 2,000 years ago, suggesting flight may be far older than we think.

Nature's helicopter

Plants can improve their chances of reproducing by spreading their seeds. When these seeds fall from a maple tree, they spin and flutter away. Unlike helicopters, they cannot travel far because they have no on-board source of power.

Crop-dusting

Helicopters and aeroplanes can spray pesticides (insect-killing chemicals) onto crops more quickly than tractors. Some aircraft give the spray a static electric charge as it leaves the pipes. This makes it spread out and cover the plants more evenly.

Milestones

Leonardo's sketches

Italian inventor Leonardo da Vinci (1452–1519) sketched this mechanical helicopter in the 15th century. The screw-shaped rotor was supposed to be turned by the pilot. Sadly, scientists have calculated that it would not have had enough power to take off.

First helicopter

In 1907, four years after the Wright brothers first took to the skies, a French airman named Paul Cornu (1881–1944) made a 20-second flight in this twin-rotor helicopter.

Forest fires

Helicopters are the only way to tackle fires that break out in dense forests, far from the nearest road. This specially built fire-fighting helicopter uses a long dangling hose to suck up water from a lake or river, which it then drops on the fire. Its tank can hold as much water as three fire engines.

Air ambulance

Air ambulances can travel at least three times faster than road ambulances and, if accidents have happened on mountains, cliffs, or at sea, they may be the only option for a quick rescue. Most carry basic medical equipment and some even have on-board doctors.

Disaster relief

Helicopters don't need a runway or landing strip, so they are perfect for helping out after natural disasters like floods or earthquakes. The picture below shows emergency blankets arriving after a flood in Bangladesh.

Jumbo lift

The mighty Chinook is one of the world's most powerful helicopters. Its cabin is big enough to park a car inside. Using three hooks, it can lift loads up to 25 tonnes – the weight of three elephants!

Autogyro

This autogyro, built in 1933 by Spaniard Juan de la Cierva (1896–1936), could fly like a plane but take off or land like a helicopter. The pilot could tilt the rotors to move in any direction.

Igor Sikorsky

Always impeccably dressed, Russian engineer Igor Sikorsky (1889–1972) built the first practical, single-rotor helicopter in 1939. Aged 12, he'd built a rubber-band-powered flying machine – and he was obsessed with aircraft for the rest of his life.

Chopper plane

This US Navy Osprey has rotors on its wingtips that can point up, to fly like a helicopter, or forwards, to fly like a plane.

AIRBUS A380

It's hard to believe anything so huge could actually fly. The world's biggest passenger plane, the Airbus A380, is as long as nine double-decker buses parked end to end, and is even wider from wingtip to wingtip. From the outside it looks only a little bigger than a traditional jumbo jet, but it can carry more than twice as many passengers.

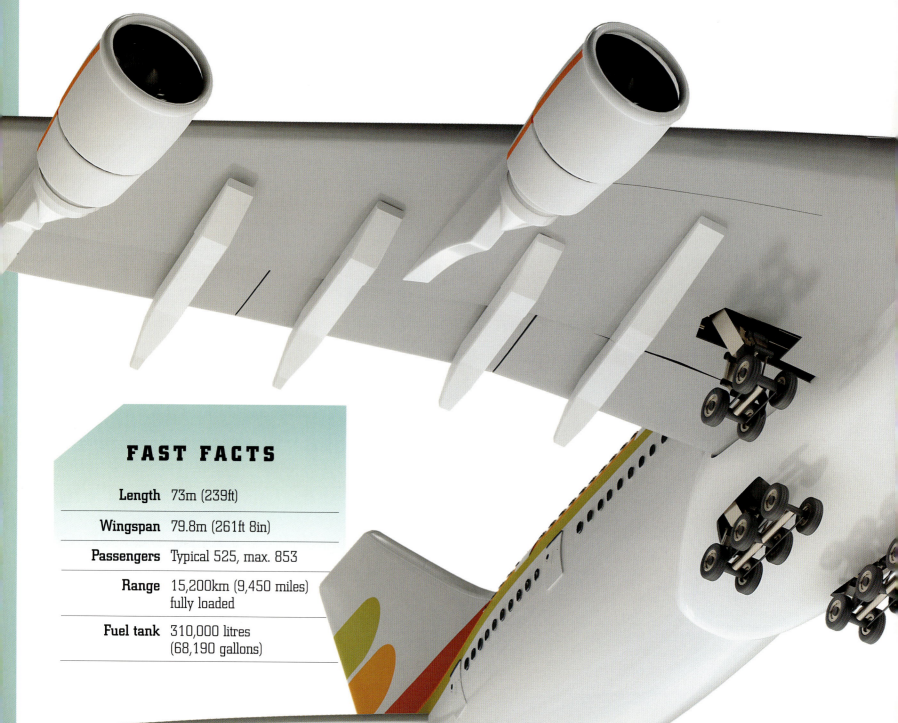

FAST FACTS

Length	73m (239ft)
Wingspan	79.8m (261ft 8in)
Passengers	Typical 525, max. 853
Range	15,200km (9,450 miles) fully loaded
Fuel tank	310,000 litres (68,190 gallons)

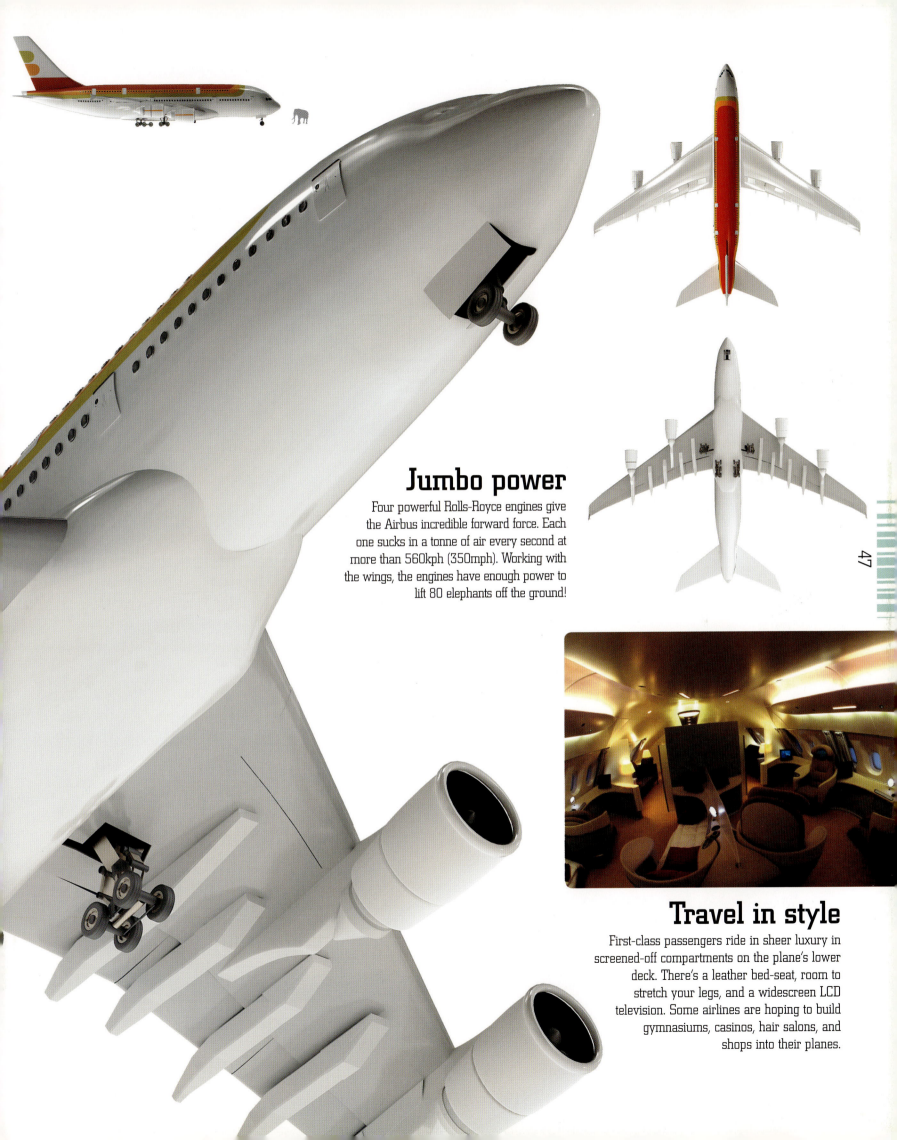

Jumbo power

Four powerful Rolls-Royce engines give the Airbus incredible forward force. Each one sucks in a tonne of air every second at more than 560kph (350mph). Working with the wings, the engines have enough power to lift 80 elephants off the ground!

Travel in style

First-class passengers ride in sheer luxury in screened-off compartments on the plane's lower deck. There's a leather bed-seat, room to stretch your legs, and a widescreen LCD television. Some airlines are hoping to build gymnasiums, casinos, hair salons, and shops into their planes.

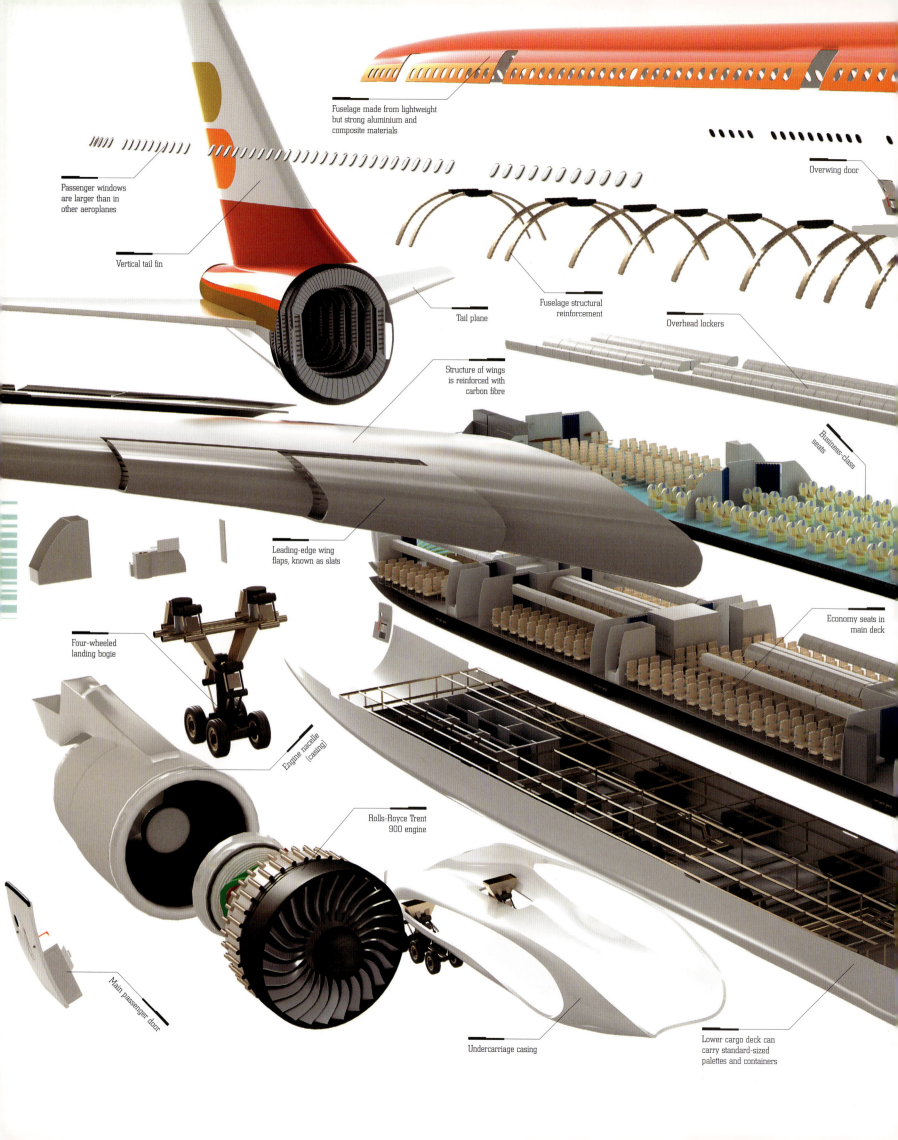

Fuselage made from lightweight but strong aluminium and composite materials

Overwing door

Passenger windows are larger than in other aeroplanes

Vertical tail fin

Tail plane

Fuselage structural reinforcement

Overhead lockers

Structure of wings is reinforced with carbon fibre

Business-class seats

Leading-edge wing flaps, known as slats

Four-wheeled landing bogie

Economy seats in main deck

Engine nacelle (casing)

Rolls-Royce Trent 900 engine

Main passenger door

Undercarriage casing

Lower cargo deck can carry standard-sized palettes and containers

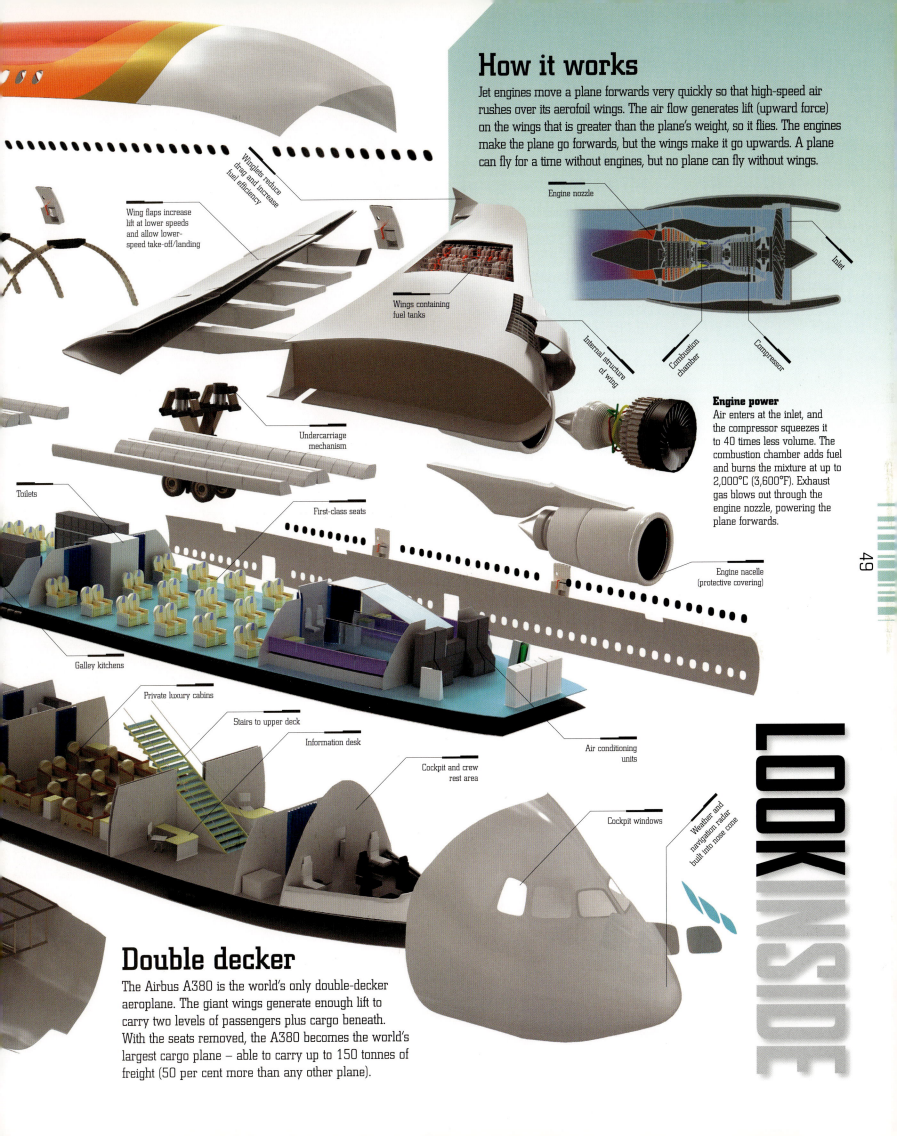

How it works

Jet engines move a plane forwards very quickly so that high-speed air rushes over its aerofoil wings. The air flow generates lift (upward force) on the wings that is greater than the plane's weight, so it flies. The engines make the plane go forwards, but the wings make it go upwards. A plane can fly for a time without engines, but no plane can fly without wings.

Engine nozzle

Inlet

Internal structure of wing

Combustion chamber

Compressor

Engine power

Air enters at the inlet, and the compressor squeezes it to 40 times less volume. The combustion chamber adds fuel and burns the mixture at up to 2,000°C (3,600°F). Exhaust gas blows out through the engine nozzle, powering the plane forwards.

Winglets reduce drag and increase fuel efficiency

Wing flaps increase lift at lower speeds and allow lower-speed take-off/landing

Wings containing fuel tanks

Undercarriage mechanism

Toilets

First-class seats

Galley kitchens

Engine nacelle (protective covering)

Private luxury cabins

Stairs to upper deck

Information desk

Air conditioning units

Cockpit and crew rest area

Cockpit windows

Weather and navigation radar built into nose cone

Double decker

The Airbus A380 is the world's only double-decker aeroplane. The giant wings generate enough lift to carry two levels of passengers plus cargo beneath. With the seats removed, the A380 becomes the world's largest cargo plane – able to carry up to 150 tonnes of freight (50 per cent more than any other plane).

LOOK INSIDE

FLYING HIGH

If you're looking for the fastest way to get around the planet, hop on a plane. There are thousands of these sleek metal "birds" soaring through our skies each day. It's easy to see why planes are so popular: roaring above mountains and soaring across oceans, jungles, and deserts, they can go almost anywhere. In the early 19th century, the fastest way to cross the Atlantic Ocean was by steamship – it took almost a month. By the late 20th century, planes could make the same journey in just three hours.

Faster than sound

With a top speed of 3,529kph (2,193mph), the Lockheed Martin SR-71 Blackbird (right) could travel three times faster than sound (and four times faster than an Airbus A380). It worked as a spyplane until the 1990s.

See the world

Flying opened up travel to exotic locations like Easter Island, in the Pacific Ocean off Chile (left). Few people had experienced such amazing places until air travel became popular in the 1950s.

Safer skies

You might not think it, but travelling by plane is 22 times safer than travelling by car. That's partly thanks to devices like these radar screens, which help pilots to land planes safely even in bad weather.

Milestones

Flying carpet

People were dreaming of flight long before they invented planes. In the famous Arabian Nights stories, written more than 1,000 years ago, Prince Ahmed travels on a magic carpet that flies and hovers like a helicopter.

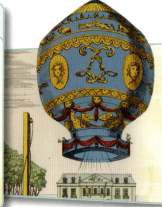

The Montgolfiers

Two French brothers called Montgolfier built the first practical hot-air balloons. On 21 November 1783, one of their balloons travelled 9km (5.5 miles) across Paris in a 23-minute voyage with a two-man crew.

Food miles

Even if you've never been in a plane, you still enjoy the benefits of flying. Our supermarkets are packed with fresh fruit and vegetables flown in from around the world, so we can enjoy all kinds of food all year round. Unfortunately, it takes lots of energy to transport food, which makes groceries more expensive and harms the environment.

Airport ordeals

Airports are hectic places. The world's busiest airport is Hartfield-Jackson International in Atlanta, United States. It handles around 80 million passengers on nearly a million flights each year.

Jumbo load

The specially designed Airbus Beluga Super Transporter pictured below is designed to carry parts of other planes around the world. When it takes off fully fuelled with a maximum load, it weighs 155 tonnes – as much as 22 large elephants. The cargo hold is big enough to carry more than 100,000 basketballs.

Look, no runway!

This plane has two large floats underneath it so it can take off and land on calm water near the coast. Seaplanes like this were very popular in the early 20th century, before most modern airports had been built.

The Wright brothers

Two more famous brothers, Wilbur and Orville Wright, made the first engine-powered flight in December 1903. Their flimsy wooden plane stayed in the air only 12 seconds – a short flight, but long enough to begin the age of the plane.

American hero

Millions fly across the Atlantic Ocean every year, but Charles Lindbergh (1902–1974) was the first person to make that journey alone. His 1927 solo transatlantic flight from the United States to France took a little more than 33 hours.

Jumbo jet

The Boeing 747 "jumbo jet" has been one of the world's most popular jet aeroplanes since it was introduced in 1970. Its wide body can carry 400–500 passengers.

FUTURE SPACE PLANE

Aerospace engineers are already designing planes that will climb 110km (70 miles) above Earth – 10 times higher than most planes go today. Those lucky enough to fly on these spaceplanes will be among the first space tourists.

Winglets improve control and efficiency of wing in atmosphere

Wing stores liquid hydrogen fuel and liquid oxygen for journey into space

Hybrid rocket engine

Hydrogen-powered main engines produce high thrust and no pollution

Pumps rapidly supply rocket engine with huge amounts of hydrogen fuel and oxygen

Fuel ignition ring initiates fuel burn

Hybrid rocket engine is cleaner and safer than traditional liquid-fuelled rocket engine

Fuel combustion cylinder

Hydrogen-powered main engine

Secondary engine, powered by oxygen and hydrogen, used only when plane has reached space

Heat disperser stops engine exhaust nozzle from melting

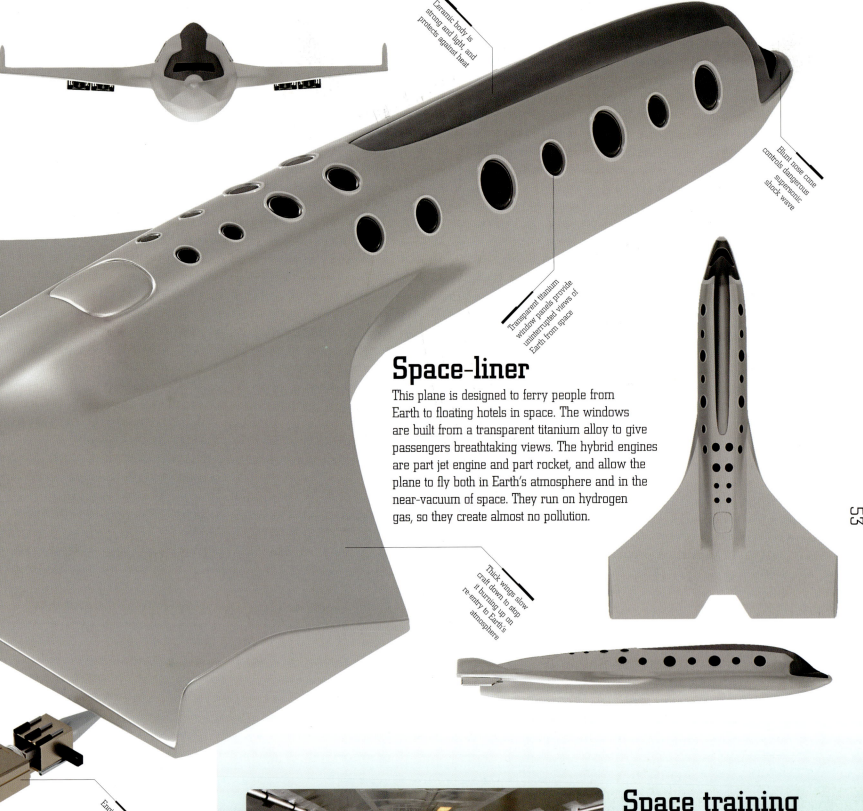

Ceramic body is strong and light, and protects against heat

Blunt nose cone controls dangerous supersonic shock wave

Transparent titanium window panels provide uninterrupted views of Earth from space

Space-liner

This plane is designed to ferry people from Earth to floating hotels in space. The windows are built from a transparent titanium alloy to give passengers breathtaking views. The hybrid engines are part jet engine and part rocket, and allow the plane to fly both in Earth's atmosphere and in the near-vacuum of space. They run on hydrogen gas, so they create almost no pollution.

Thick wings slow craft down to stop it burning up on re-entry to Earth's atmosphere

Engine's internal shape ensures air and fuel mix efficiently to give smooth operation

Space training

English physicist Stephen Hawking (1942–) is one of the world's experts on gravity and is training to become a space tourist. He is almost completely paralysed and normally uses a wheelchair. To celebrate his 65th birthday, in January 2007, he flew in a plane known as a "Vomit Comet". This soars to high altitudes before dropping suddenly to create periods of weightlessness for its passengers.

SPACESUIT

The human body is perfectly adapted for living on Earth, but travelling into space is something we were never designed for. Space is dark and dangerous, sometimes boiling hot, sometimes freezing cold, and there's no air to breathe. Without the help of a tough protective spacesuit – a one-person spaceship – you have no chance of survival.

Outer skin

Our bodies are machines with fleshy pipes, pumps, and all kinds of self-regulating mechanisms packed inside them to keep us alive. A spacesuit is similar. It's a bit like an adapter that allows the apparatus inside our bodies to carry on functioning in the challenging conditions of space.

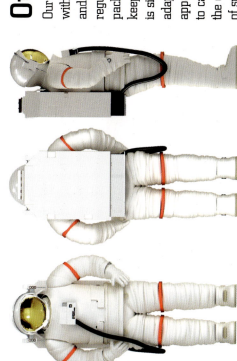

EVA

Most astronauts don't need space suits because they stay inside their craft. Space suits are worn for going outside for what is called extra-vehicular activity (EVA): a spacewalk or moonwalk. The longest ever spacewalk lasted eight hours, 56 minutes.

FAST FACTS

Weight	125kg (275lb) on Earth but feels like 21kg (46lb) on the Moon
Total parts	Approx. 18,000
Cost per suit	Approx. £6 million
Total thickness	9cm (3.5in)

LOOK INSIDE

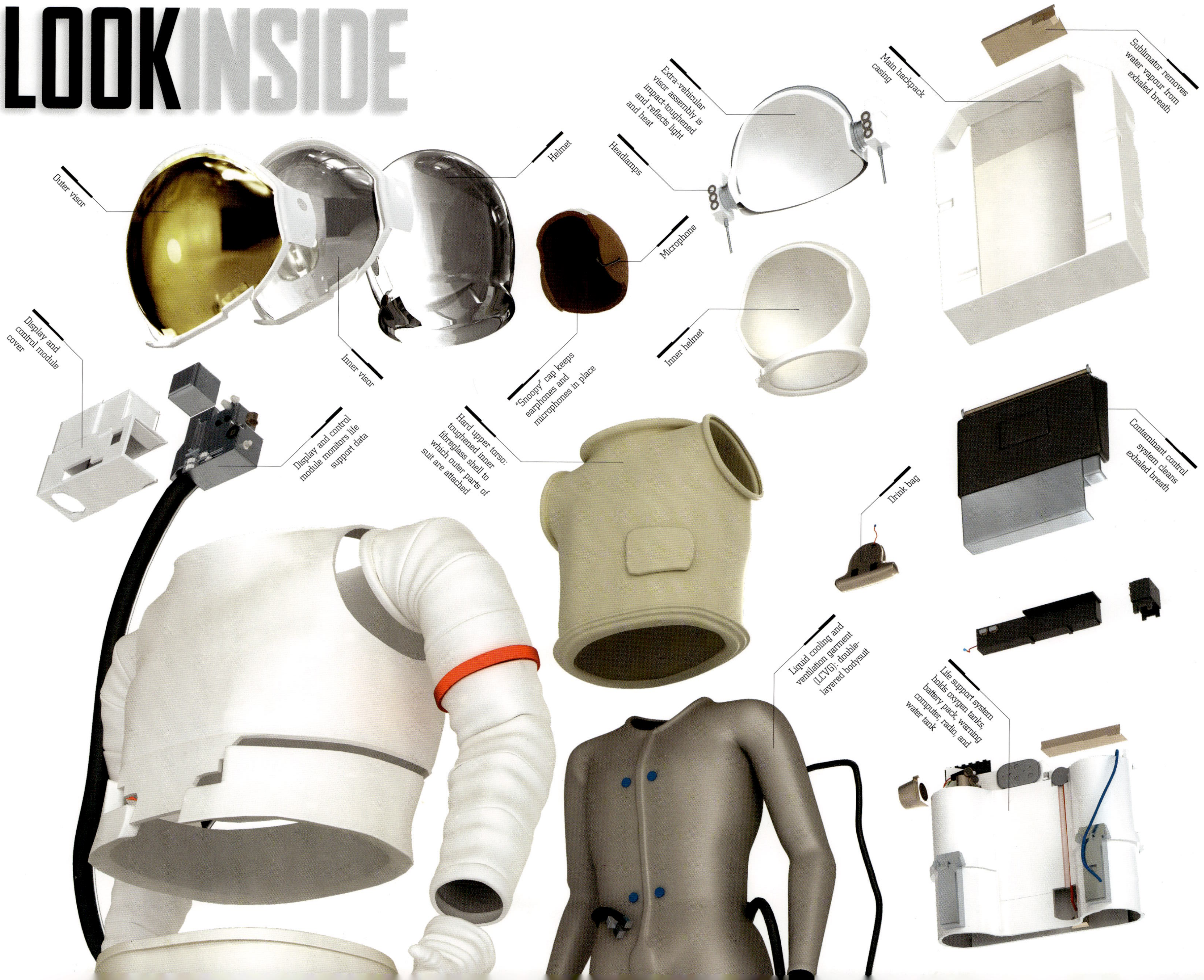

Sublimator removes water vapour from exhaled breath

Main backpack casing

Contaminant control system cleans exhaled breath

Life support system: holds oxygen tanks, battery pack, warning computer, radio, and water tank

Drink bag

Liquid cooling and ventilation garment (LCVG): double-layered bodysuit

Extra-vehicular visor assembly is impact-toughened and reflects light and heat

Headlamps

Microphone

Inner helmet

"Snoopy" cap keeps microphones and earphones in place

Helmet

Hard upper torso: toughened inner fibreglass shell to which outer parts of suit are attached

Inner visor

Display and control module monitors life support data

Outer visor

Display and control module cover

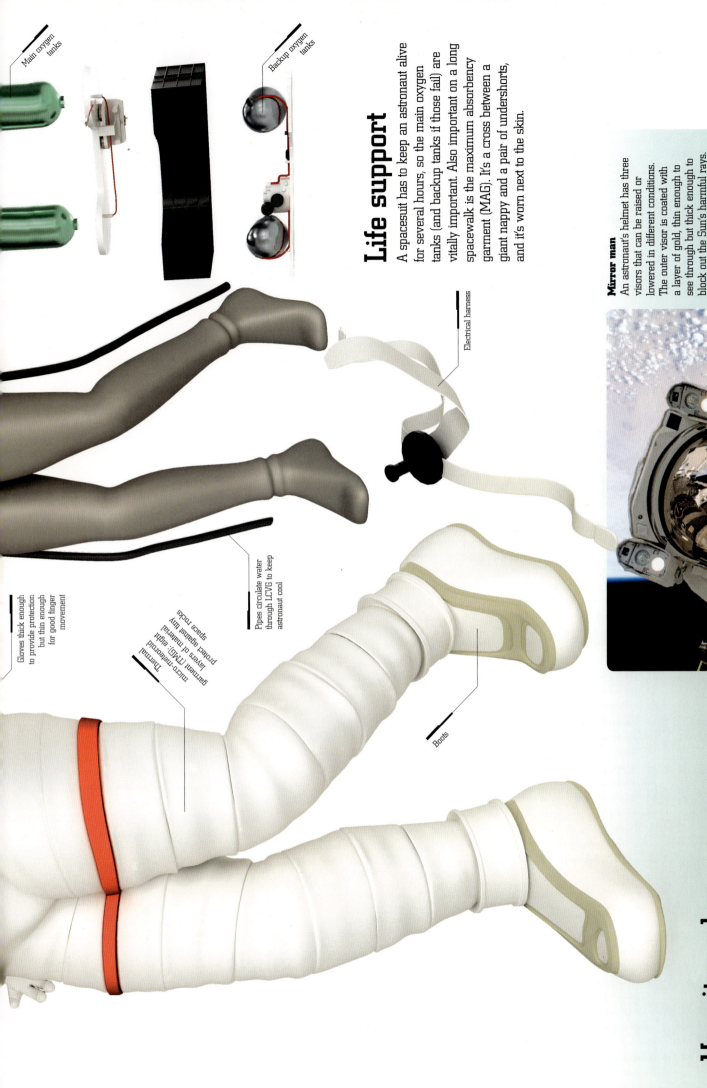

Main oxygen tanks

Backup oxygen tanks

Life support

A spacesuit has to keep an astronaut alive for several hours, so the main oxygen tanks (and backup tanks if those fail) are vitally important. Also important on a long spacewalk is the maximum absorbency garment (MAG). It's a cross between a giant nappy and a pair of undershorts, and it's worn next to the skin.

Electrical harness

Gloves thick enough to provide protection but thin enough for good finger movement

Thermal micro-meteoroid garment (TMG): eight layers of material protect against tiny space rocks

Pipes circulate water through LCVG to keep astronaut cool

Boots

Mirror man
An astronaut's helmet has three visors that can be raised or lowered in different conditions. The outer visor is coated with a layer of gold, thin enough to see through but thick enough to block out the Sun's harmful rays. Powerful headlamps on either side are for working in places where sunlight doesn't reach.

How it works

When astronauts step into space, suits like this are their only protection. A typical suit has 13–24 different layers, each of which does a specific job. The outer layer shields against micro-meteorites (tiny flying space rocks) and is fireproof, too. Inner layers protect against extreme heat (in sunlight) and cold (in shadow). The inside of the suit is pressurized like a jet plane cabin, so breathing and other body processes work much as they would back on Earth.

Sunglasses

Most sunglasses have plastic lenses. Thanks to space research, some are now coated with diamond-like carbon (DLC) that is 10 times harder to scratch. This very thin carbon film also makes the lenses smoother, so rain runs off more quickly.

Cold comfort

On the Moon, temperatures soar from a toe-tingling -157°C (-250°F) to a blood-boiling 120°C (250°F), so lunar astronauts wore suits with 24 insulating layers to protect them. Things are less extreme on Earth, but layers still help. Outer layers keep out the wind, while base (inner) layers carry moisture from your skin, trap air, and help your body retain heat.

Skid lid

Helmets used to be hot and heavy, but not any more. The aerodynamic shape and air vents on this cycling hat were developed through aerospace research. Helmets like this have a crunch-proof polycarbonate outer layer and shock-absorbing foam inside.

LESSONS FROM SPACE

You may not think of yourself as a space traveller, but that's exactly what you are. You live on a rock, spinning through space, often facing similar challenges to an astronaut. Even walking to the shops, you may have to wear glasses to block out the Sun's harmful rays or insulating layers to keep out the cold. Materials developed for space travel can often prove useful here on Earth. Look around you and you'll see cyclists wearing shock-proof helmets based on NASA technology, and joggers hitting the streets in shoes developed from moon boots!

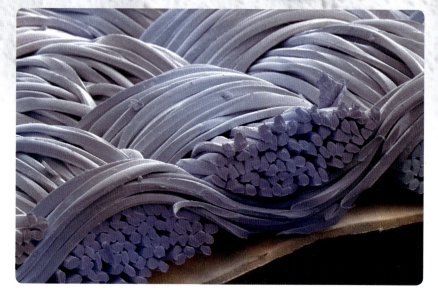

Fantastic fabric

Waterproof Gore-Tex, seen here under an electron microscope, is made from the slippery Teflon used in space suits. The fabric has microscopic holes 20,000 times smaller than a water drop. Rain cannot get in from outside, but sweat can escape. That's why Gore-Tex is waterproof and "breathable" at the same time.

ARIANE5

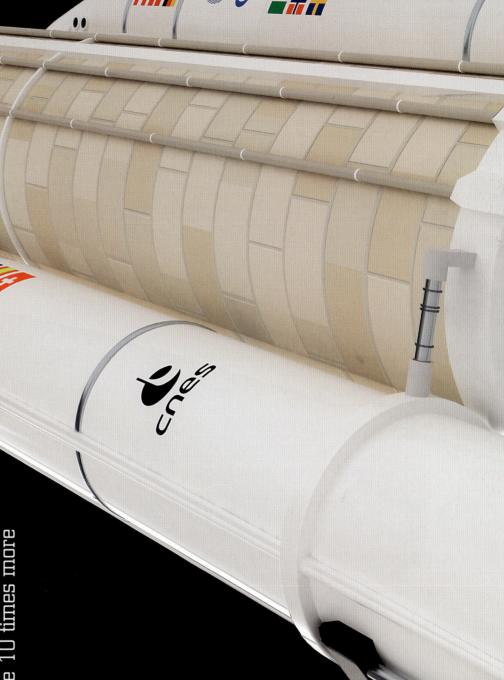

Blast-off! It's the biggest, boldest, fastest journey you can make – and it's literally out of this world. We think of rockets firing people to the Moon, but most just put satellites into space. The European *Ariane 5* rocket is 10 times longer than a family car and, at lift-off, its engines give 10 times more power than an Airbus jet.

Three in one

The central part of *Ariane 5* contains the main engine, powered by liquid fuel. On each side, there are two rockets powered by solid fuel. These solid rocket boosters (SRBs) are like giant fireworks that provide almost 90 per cent of the thrust at blast-off.

LOOK INSIDE

How it works

A rocket moves itself forwards like an aeroplane jet engine. The hot exhaust fires backwards to push the rocket forwards in exactly the same way. The biggest difference between a rocket engine and a jet engine is that a rocket has to work in space, where there is no air supply. Unlike a jet engine, it does not suck air in at the front. Instead, it carries its own oxygen supply in huge tanks inside.

Tanked up

A rocket makes power when oxygen from its upper tank mixes with hydrogen from its lower tank and burns in the engine beneath. *Ariane 5* carries 150 tonnes of liquid oxygen and 25 tonnes of liquid hydrogen.

Safe and sound

The satellites *Ariane* carries into space are often worth several hundred million pounds, so the shell that protects them, called a fairing, is extremely important. It is made of two half-shells of carbon fibre that break apart and fall away once the rocket has safely left Earth's atmosphere. The fairing is 5.4m (17.7ft) in diameter at the bottom – big enough to park a car inside.

Liquid oxygen

Liquid hydrogen

Hot gases provide thrust

Combustion chamber

Thermal blanket protects satellite from intense solar heat

Solar panels fold out to power satellite once in orbit

Absorbent material protects satellites from vibration during launch

Fairing protects satellite payload as *Ariane* blasts up through Earth's atmosphere

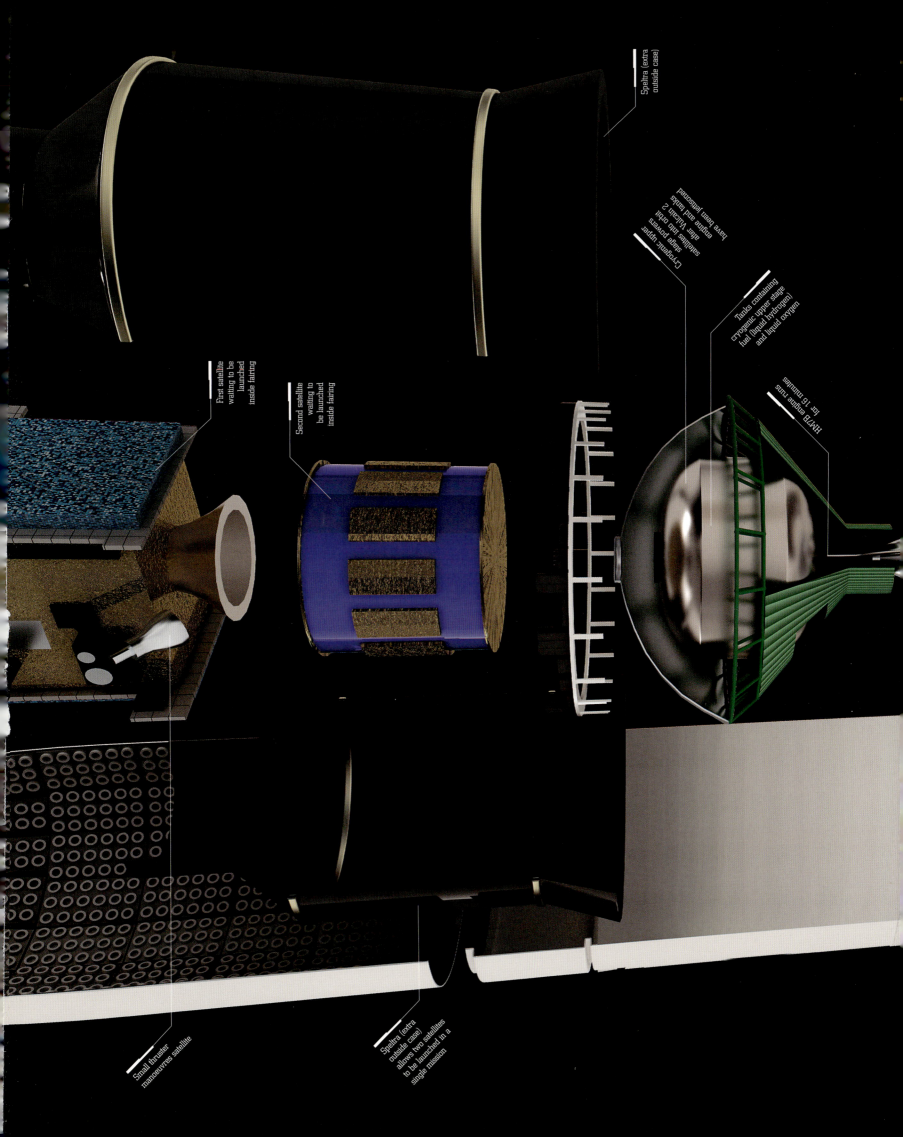

Spektra (extra outside case)

Cryogenic upper stage powers satellites into orbit after Vulcan 2 engine and tanks have been jettisoned

Tanks containing cryogenic upper stage fuel (liquid hydrogen) and liquid oxygen

HM7B engine runs for 15 minutes

First satellite waiting to be launched inside fairing

Second satellite waiting to be launched inside fairing

Small thruster manoeuvres satellite

Spektra (extra outside case) allows two satellites to be launched in a single mission

Water warmth

Water can suck heat from your body 40 times faster than air, which is why people can die in cold seas in a matter of minutes. Wetsuits are made from neoprene (synthetic rubber), with inner layers of metals like titanium or copper to reflect back heat. They fit tightly and trap water inside. The body quickly warms this water, which acts as an insulating layer. Space suits have neoprene layers, too.

Springy steps

Some shoes contain viscoelastic "memory foam" that softens and relieves pressure as it gets warmer. NASA scientists designed it in the 1970s for seats that would cushion astronauts from extreme forces during rocket blast-off. The shock-absorbing foam is also used in pain-relieving mattresses and pillows.

Fire away

Under their outer clothes, racing drivers wear fire-resistant inner suits made from a carbon-based material called Nomex. Some space suits and boots also have layers of Nomex for fire and heat protection. You may find Nomex in your own home – hi-tech oven gloves are often made from it.

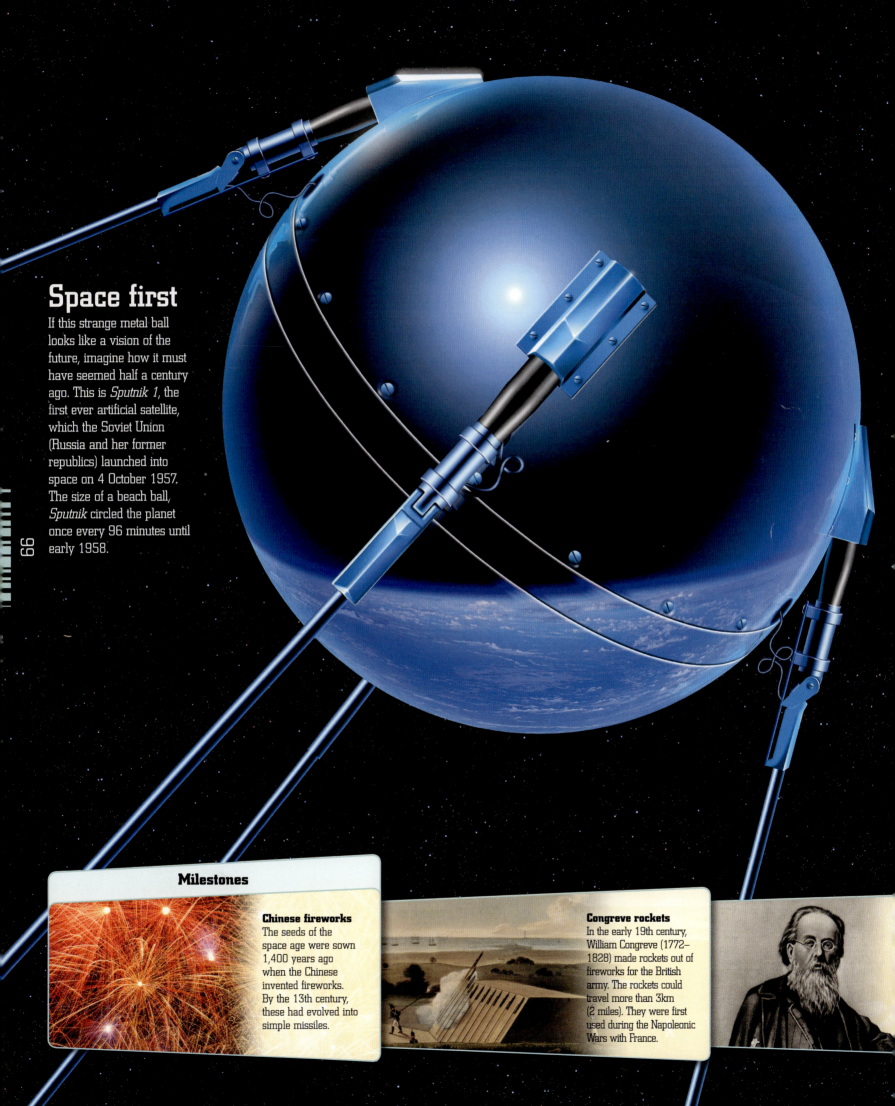

Space first

If this strange metal ball looks like a vision of the future, imagine how it must have seemed half a century ago. This is *Sputnik 1*, the first ever artificial satellite, which the Soviet Union (Russia and her former republics) launched into space on 4 October 1957. The size of a beach ball, *Sputnik* circled the planet once every 96 minutes until early 1958.

Milestones

Chinese fireworks
The seeds of the space age were sown 1,400 years ago when the Chinese invented fireworks. By the 13th century, these had evolved into simple missiles.

Congreve rockets
In the early 19th century, William Congreve (1772–1828) made rockets out of fireworks for the British army. The rockets could travel more than 3km (2 miles). They were first used during the Napoleonic Wars with France.

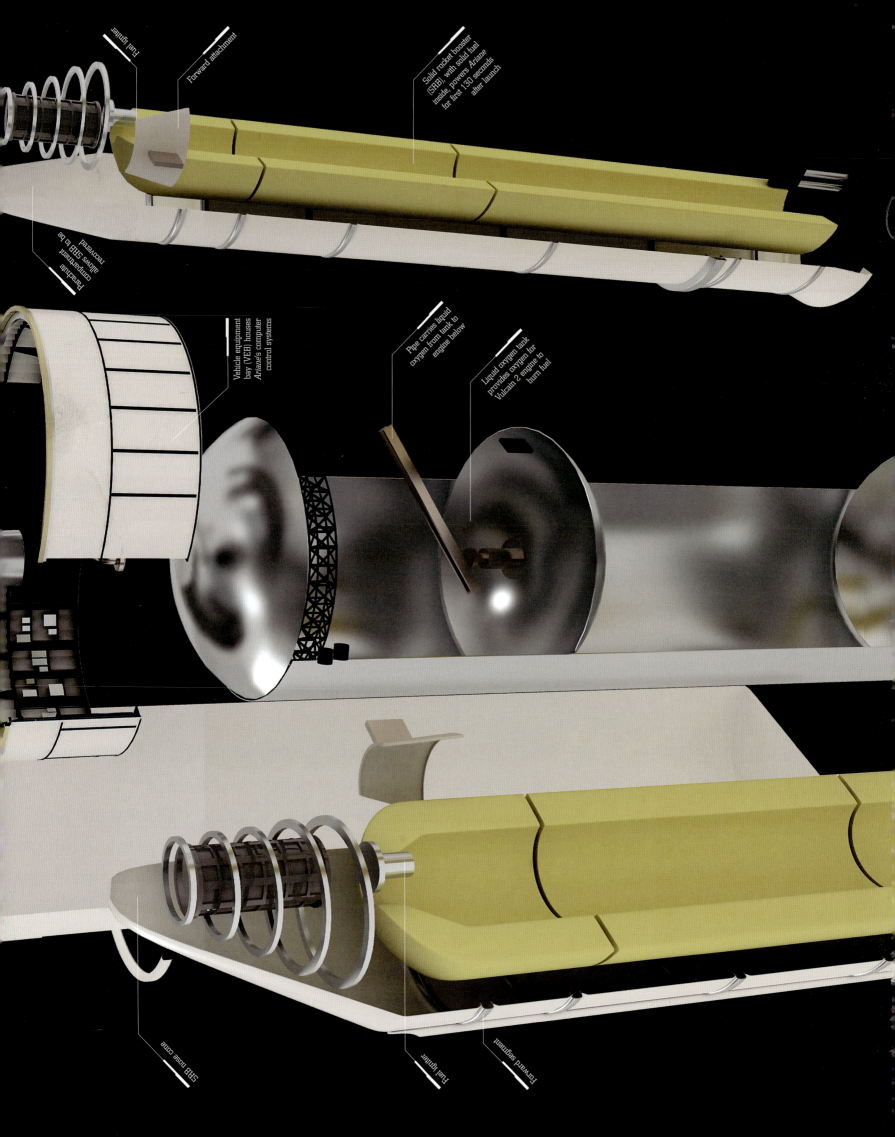

Fuel igniter

Forward attachment

Solid rocket booster (SRB), with solid fuel inside, powers *Ariane* for first 130 seconds after launch

Parachute compartment allows SRB to be recovered

Vehicle equipment bay (VEB) houses *Ariane's* computer control systems

Pipe carries liquid oxygen from tank to engine below

Liquid oxygen tank provides oxygen for Vulcain 2 engine to burn fuel

SRB nose cone

Fuel igniter

Forward segment

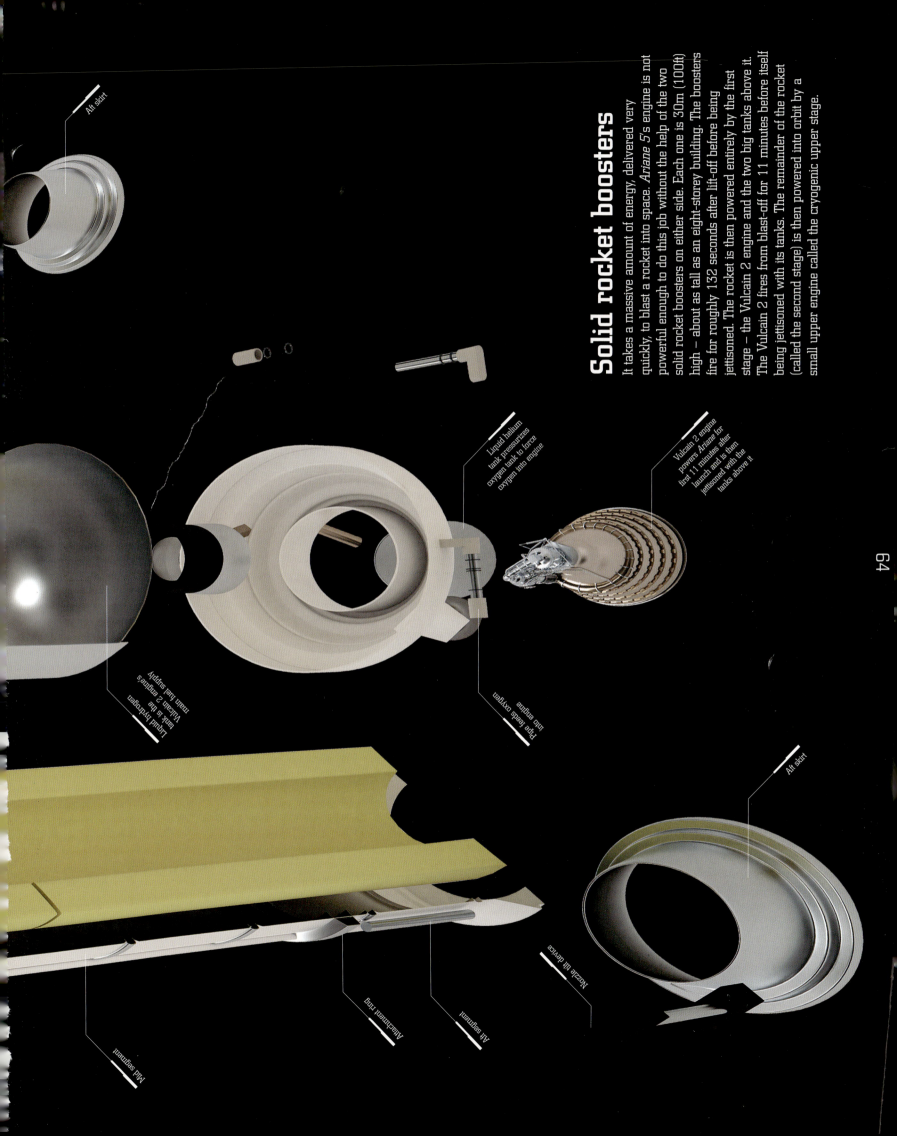

Solid rocket boosters

It takes a massive amount of energy, delivered very quickly, to blast a rocket into space. *Ariane 5*'s engine is not powerful enough to do this job without the help of the two solid rocket boosters on either side. Each one is 30m (100ft) high – about as tall as an eight-storey building. The boosters fire for roughly 132 seconds after lift-off before being jettisoned. The rocket is then powered entirely by the first stage – the Vulcain 2 engine and the two big tanks above it. The Vulcain 2 fires from blast-off for 11 minutes before itself being jettisoned with its tanks. The remainder of the rocket (called the second stage) is then powered into orbit by a small upper engine called the cryogenic upper stage.

Aft skirt

Liquid helium tank pressurizes oxygen tank to force oxygen into engine

Vulcain 2 engine powers *Ariane* for first 11 minutes after launch and is then jettisoned with tanks above it

Liquid hydrogen tank is the Vulcain 2 engine's main fuel supply

Pipe feeds oxygen into engine

Aft skirt

Nozzle tilt device

Mid segment

Attachment ring

Aft segment

Tanked up

It takes three huge engines and a massive amount of fuel to get *Ariane 5* into space. When it takes off, it weighs about 780 tonnes. Almost 90 per cent of this is fuel – less than 2 per cent is cargo.

EYES IN THE SKY

Next time you're walking down the street, look up at the sky and smile: there's every chance your photograph is being taken by a space satellite! There are thousands of these unmanned electronic spacecraft spinning round Earth. Some take photographs or make scientific measurements. Some help us beam phone calls, TV pictures, and Internet data from one side of the world to the other. Others tell us where we are and help us find our way around. The almost instant communication that we now take for granted is made possible by the satellites in orbit at various heights above our heads.

Always in touch

Communications satellites can transmit phone calls between any two places on Earth. Orbiting at exactly the speed Earth turns, they stay in the same spot above the planet, 35,900km (22,300 miles) over the equator.

Before and after

Satellites that take photos orbit about 250–1,000km (150–620 miles) above our heads. These pictures (left) were taken by the *Landsat 7* satellite. They show the city of New Orleans in the United States before (top) and after (bottom) the floods caused by Hurricane Katrina in August 2005.

Ariane crash

Ariane rockets have launched around 300 satellites, but not all of them made it into space. The very first *Ariane 5* launch on 4 June 1996 was a disaster. A software error meant the rocket crashed just after take-off, destroying the four science satellites on board.

Konstantin Tsiolkovsky
Russian schoolteacher Konstantin Tsiolkovsky (1857–1935) was decades ahead of his time. He predicted that one day rockets would carry people into space, and even drew designs for an early space station.

Robert Hutchings Goddard
American scientist Robert Hutchings Goddard (1882–1945) built his first liquid-fueled rocket in 1926. When he suggested that rockets could take people to the Moon, he was widely ridiculed. Since his death, many of his ideas have proved correct and he is now considered the father of modern rocketry.

Werner von Braun
During World War II, German engineer Werner von Braun (1912–1977) designed long-distance rocket bombs that terrorized much of Europe. After the war, he worked for NASA, helping to put men on the Moon in 1969.

MOUNTAIN BIKE

Tough stuff

Tough and lightweight, off-road mountain bikes first appeared in the 1970s. They are very different from racing bikes. Their smaller wheels produce less speed but give you more control on tricky terrain. Also, disc brakes give more stopping power than the rim brakes on a normal bike.

Brace yourself for a rough ride! If you're hurtling down a hill or churning through a field, you need a bike that's tough enough to survive. Mountain bikes have to be much stronger than racing bikes, but that can make them heavy, sluggish, and slow. This one is made from feather-light carbon fibre so you waste less energy reaching top speed. Chunky tyres bite the ground beneath you, while powerful front and rear suspension smooths away the rocks and knocks.

Lighter load

The bike weighs less than a conventional steel bike because it's made from carbon fibre. This composite material is a plastic that's reinforced with microscopic, rod-like strands of carbon, a bit like millions of tiny pencils.

FAST FACTS

Weight	11.9kg (26.2lb)
Gears	27-speed Shimano
Suspension	Front and rear shock absorbers
Brakes	Front and rear disc
Cost	Approx. £2,700

LOOKINSIDE

Lean machine

Bicycles use science to get you where you want to go. From the gears to the frame, virtually every part of a bike uses scientific principles to make riding quicker or easier. Apart from being great exercise, using a bicycle is one of the most energy-efficient forms of transport. Bicycles are around 90 per cent efficient, which means they turn virtually all the energy supplied by their power source – your legs – into kinetic energy to move you along. In contrast, a car is only

Shock absorbers
This canister behind the seat makes your ride smoother. A piston inside bounces up and down in thick oil, absorbing energy when you hit a bump.

Top stay (seat stay)

Rear suspension struts

Rear shock absorber

Tyres
Mountain bike tyres are designed for rough terrain. They're thicker and grip better than racing tyres. This bike's tyres are made from Kevlar, a tough, hard-wearing carbon-based fabric.

Spokes

Chain stay

Rear wheel and tyre

Rear disc brake

Brake and gear cables

Gears
Gears increase your bike's speed along a straight, or its climbing power up a hill. When the chain runs round one of the smaller gears, the back wheel goes faster each time you pedal, cranking up your speed. When the chain moves to a bigger gear, the back wheel slows down but turns with more force, enabling you to go uphill more easily.

Freewheel and rear sprockets (gear wheels)

Rear derailleur moves chain during gear changes and keeps it tight

Saddle

Rear brake lever

Handlebar grips

Front brake lever

Handlebar adjustment

Handlebar

Seat post

Top tube (crossbar)

Front shock absorbers

Seat tube

Front forks hold front wheel in place

Pedal

Pedal crank arm

Down tube

Front sprockets (gear wheels)

Front disc brake

Pneumatic inner tube

Rear axle

Chain

Tyre

Front axle supports front wheel

Rim of wheel

Frame
A bike's strong triangular frame supports your weight and spreads it more or less evenly between the front and back wheels.

Disc brakes
When you brake, rubber blocks press against small perforated discs on the wheels and slow you down. Friction turns the bike's energy into heat.

Wheels
Bigger wheels cover ground faster than smaller ones, so large bike wheels help to increase your speed. Spokes make the wheel lighter and more aerodynamic.

PEDAL POWER

Simple is often best – but simplicity is only one of the reasons why bicycles are still popular more than a century after their invention. They're very affordable, easy and great fun to ride, cost nothing to run, and sometimes last for decades. They're also perfect for city travel because they create no pollution and you can park them almost anywhere.

Green machines

In Paris, France, people are encouraged to leave their cars at home and use one of a new fleet of 10,000 hire bikes. You simply buy a swipe card, unlock a bike from one of 750 locations, and cycle away. The bikes clocked up four million rides in their first two months of use.

Spreading the load

Bicycles are incredibly versatile machines. In countries such as China and India, where fewer people have cars, bikes are widely used for transporting goods. In more industrialized countries, bikes can cut through heavy traffic to deliver smaller loads much faster than cars or vans.

Handcycles

This bicycle is designed for a disabled rider who cannot pedal with his legs. Instead, he powers the bike by turning hand-operated gears. The hand mechanism also controls the brakes and steering.

Milestones

Draisienne
One of the first bicycles, the Draisienne or "hobby horse", invented in 1817, was designed to help people walk more quickly. It had wooden wheels, but no gears, chain, or pedals.

Penny Farthing
Before bikes had gears, they had huge front wheels, like this 1870 Penny Farthing, to help them go faster. They were very hard to climb onto – and very easy to fall off!

Speed machines

Olympic cyclists try to make their bodies and bikes work together as a single machine. Special handlebars mean these riders can keep their arms in a very streamlined position. Their skin-tight clothes and pointed helmets also help to minimize drag (air resistance). The bikes themselves are made of carbon composites. These materials are as strong as metals but much lighter, giving extra speed.

Bicycles of tomorrow

Future bicycles will be better in every way. They could have aerodynamic covers like this to help them go faster, automatic gears, and tyres made of puncture-proof materials. Some bikes will have solar panels and electric motors on the wheels to help you climb hills with less effort.

Rickshaws

Rickshaws (bicycle taxis) are an environmentally friendly alternative to petrol-powered taxis. Originally developed in Asian countries, they are now being used as tourist taxis in western countries to help reduce pollution and congestion.

Dunlop bike
The next big advance came in 1888, when John Boyd Dunlop (1840–1921) made more comfortable bicycles with pneumatic (air-filled) tyres. Bicycles like this were much like modern ones. They had similar-sized wheels, gears, a comfortable saddle, and safety grips on the handlebars.

Folding bike
This odd-looking frame folds out to make a complete bicycle in under 10 seconds. Made of lightweight aluminium and fibreglass, it weighs just 5.6kg (12.6lb) and is light enough to carry on a bus or train.

Future bikes
Electric bicycles could be the future of transport. Using rechargeable batteries and lightweight electric motors, they can travel 48km (30 miles) at speeds of up to 24kph (15mph).

FUEL CELL BIKE

A motorbike might look small and efficient as it weaves in and out of stalled city traffic, but it makes up to 16 times more air pollution than a car. While cars are packed with pollution-scrubbing technologies such as catalytic converters, motorbikes pump their dirty fumes straight into the air. All that could change if bikes swapped petrol power for electricity. Intelligent Energy's ENV (emissions-neutral vehicle) bike has an electric motor instead of a petrol engine. It runs on clean, efficient hydrogen gas and the only waste product it makes is harmless steam.

Vroom vroom

Originally called the Cityhopper, the ENV was designed to cut the noise and pollution that traditional motorbikes make in busy streets. Its electric motor is virtually silent – but not everyone agrees this is a good thing. Silent motorbikes could be dangerous to pedestrians and other traffic, so the ENV's manufacturers are now fitting an artificial "vroom" noise, for safety, so people can hear it coming!

FAST FACTS

Weight	80kg (176lb)
Power source	6,000-watt, 48-volt electric motor
Top speed	80kph (50mph)
Acceleration	0–80kph (50mph) in 12.1 seconds
Range	160km (100 miles) on 1 tank of hydrogen
Cost	Approx. £3,000

The CORE

There's no petrol tank in the ENV bike. Instead, it uses a power source called the CORE: a box, the size of a desktop computer, containing a fuel cell and a tank that you fill up with hydrogen gas. The fuel cell works a bit like a battery; as long as there is hydrogen in the tank, it keeps making electricity.

How it works

All the power the ENV bike needs comes from the fuel cell inside the CORE. This takes hydrogen from its internal tank and oxygen from the air, and produces a chemical reaction between the two to make electricity. The only waste product is steam, which passes out harmlessly into the environment. It takes less than five minutes to refill the hydrogen fuel tank.

Future fuel

Fuel cells driving electric motors have many advantages over the engines we use today. They are light and compact, and are good for the environment because they are silent and pollution-free. Since they have no moving parts, they are also reliable and long-lasting.

Aerodynamic front cover improves fuel consumption

Hydrogen tank contains enough fuel for 160km (100 miles) of travel

Brake lever

Headlights

CORE side cover

Main chassis holds the CORE

Telescopic front forks

Chunky front mountain-bike tyre

LOOK**INSIDE**

The CORE (removable fuel cell and hydrogen tank)

Fuel cell creates power from hydrogen gas

Top panel hinges up to release the CORE

Seat with built-in rear lights

Pedal-free

The ENV is a bit like a mountain bike that you don't have to pedal. Power is generated in the CORE, stored in the batteries, then fed to the electric motor that drives the back wheel. The batteries help to ensure a steady power supply to the electric motor.

Stay supports rear wheel

Toothed belt carries power from electric motor to back wheel

CORE side cover

Rear suspension

Rear brake

Structure and body work provide support

Spokes keep back wheel strong but light

Sprocket is driven by belt from electric motor

Electric motor (6kW, 48-volt) powered by four batteries

Electronic circuits and controllers

Aerodynamic side cover

Stand folds down to park bike

Four 12-volt lead-acid batteries store power made by the CORE

ENV

OUTOFBREATH

Air quality has been a major problem since the Industrial Revolution. The coal-driven machines that powered us through the 18th and 19th centuries also choked our cities with smoke. Factories are now cleaner than ever, but with more than 600 million engine-powered vehicles on the planet the air is still dirtier than it needs to be, especially in cities. Pollution isn't just a nuisance: it makes lung problems like bronchitis and asthma much worse, kills trees, and even damages buildings. Fuel-cell vehicles, powered by electricity, offer one way to clear the smog.

Dirty diesels

This electron microscope photo shows tiny grains of soot and unburned fuel from a car exhaust. Diesel engines use less fuel than petrol engines, but produce more soot. The tiny particles they make, called PM10s, are linked to many health problems.

Monitoring pollution

This scientist (right) is studying pollution by firing a LIDAR (light detection and ranging) laser beam into the air. Different gases affect laser light in different ways, so when the beam reflects back from the sky it reveals what the pollution contains.

Smog

Mexico City is one of the world's most polluted places. Many of its factories have closed, but traffic fumes still choke the 25 million inhabitants. The filthy air over cities is called smog because it's like a cross between smoke and fog. Smog lingers when a layer of warm air above traps it like a lid.

Milestones

Fire
The basic technology inside engines is fire. Our ancestors discovered how to control fire between one and two million years ago. Nothing ever burns perfectly, so fires always make some pollution.

Steam engine
Steam engines were developed in the early 18th century, but the coal they burned made huge clouds of smoke. They powered industry but made cities really filthy.

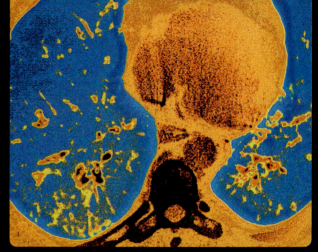

Bad breath

This medical scan of a person's lungs shows how smoke and air pollution cause a problem called bronchitis. The patient's lungs (the blue areas either side) become inflamed and fill with mucus (coloured brown), causing shortness of breath and wheezing that can last months or even years.

Wearing away

When rain mixes with pollution from factories and power stations, it can become 1,000 times more acidic. Known as acid rain, this can kill forests, turn lakes into acid baths too toxic to support fish, and even wear away stone statues.

Petrol engine
Petrol engines were invented in the mid-19th century. Although each one is far cleaner than a steam engine, there are now hundreds of millions of them in the world – together, they produce a great deal of pollution.

Jet engine
Jet engines need to burn an enormous amount of fuel very quickly to lift a plane off the ground. They don't make much pollution at ground level, but gases from their exhausts damage Earth's atmosphere and add to global warming.

Electric motors
Electric motors are the clean engines of the future. If the electricity they use comes from a clean source, such as a solar panel or a wind turbine, they make no pollution.

FUTUREHOVERBIKE

Everyone hates sitting in traffic jams. With more cars on the roads and fewer places to put them, jams will happen much more often in future – unless we start taking to the air. In the future, people may swap motorbikes and cars for hoverbikes, powered by mini jet engines, that leave the city streets struggling far below.

Handlebars control computer that keeps bike flying safely at all times

Front fan keeps the bike stable as it flies

Stereo system

Air intake

Hover bird

Birds are brilliantly designed flying machines. They use wind and thermals (rising pockets of warm air) to help them stay airborne. Hummingbirds have an extra trick: they can hover on the spot by flapping their wings around 50 times a second. They can also fly in any direction by changing the angle, or pitch, of their wings as they flap, just like helicopter blades.

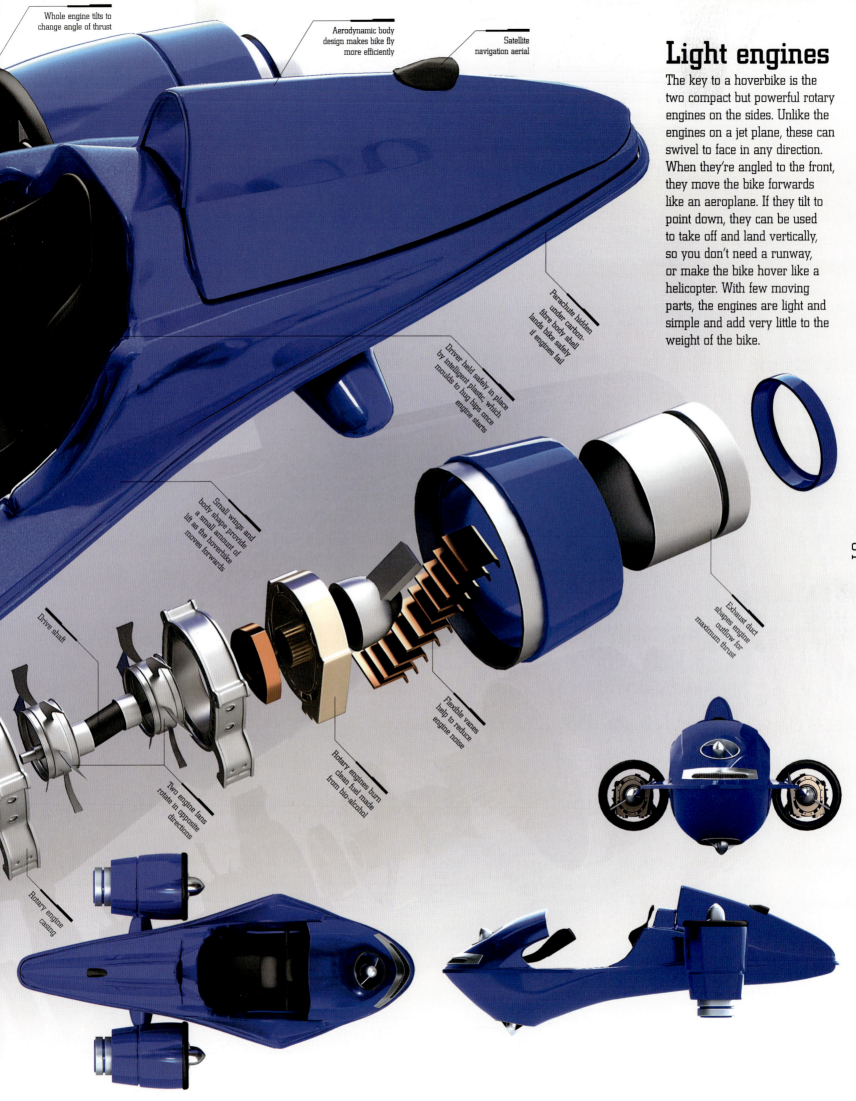

Whole engine tilts to change angle of thrust

Aerodynamic body design makes bike fly more efficiently

Satellite navigation aerial

Light engines

The key to a hoverbike is the two compact but powerful rotary engines on the sides. Unlike the engines on a jet plane, these can swivel to face in any direction. When they're angled to the front, they move the bike forwards like an aeroplane. If they tilt to point down, they can be used to take off and land vertically, so you don't need a runway, or make the bike hover like a helicopter. With few moving parts, the engines are light and simple and add very little to the weight of the bike.

Parachute hidden under carbon-fibre body shell lands bike safely it engines fail

Driver held safely in place by intelligent plastic, which moulds to hug hips once engine starts

Exhaust duct shapes engine outflow for maximum thrust

Small wings and body shape provide a small amount of lift as the hoverbike moves forwards

Drive shaft

Flexible vanes help to reduce engine noise

Two engine fans rotate in opposite directions

Rotary engines burn clean fuel made from bio-alcohol

Rotary engine casing

Solar panels catch the Sun's rays and turn them into electricity. If we covered just 1 per cent of the Sahara Desert with panels like these, we could generate enough electricity to power the entire world.

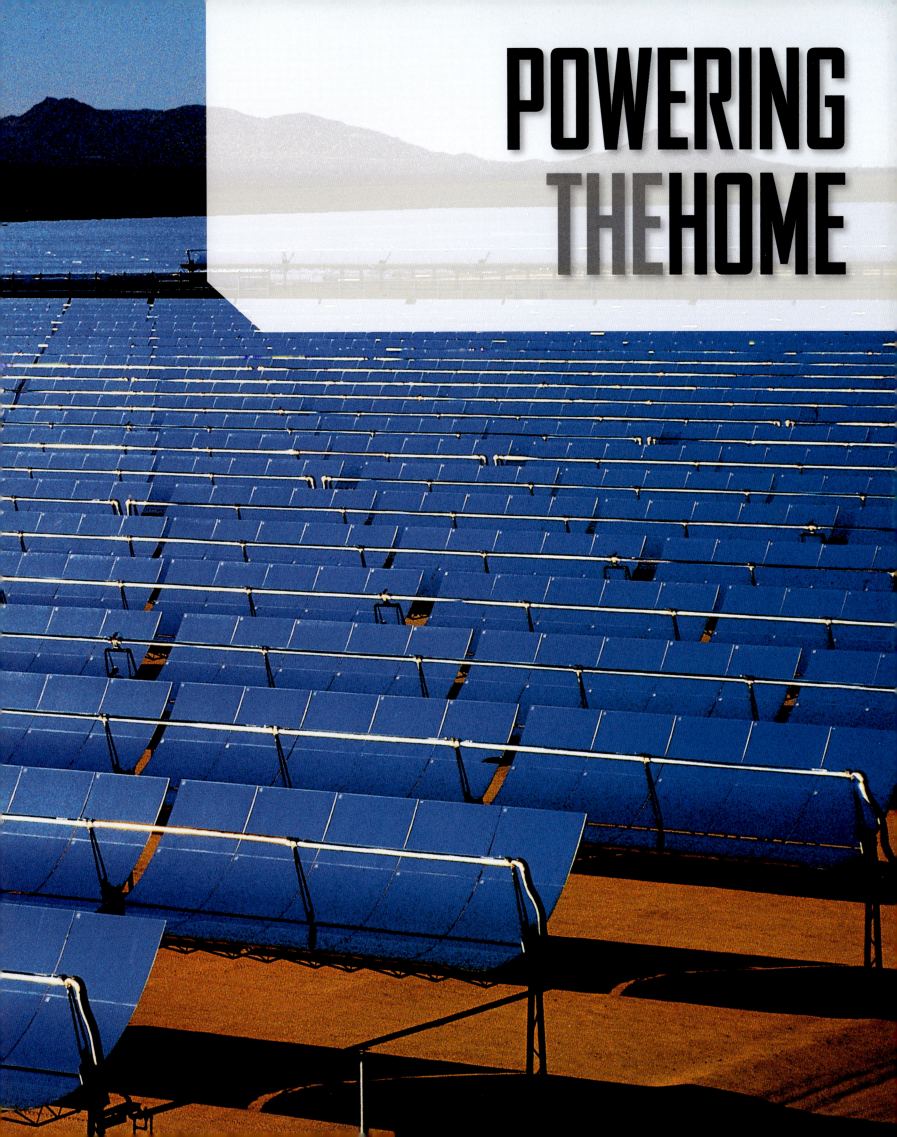

POWERING
THE HOME

Look down on Earth from a spaceship at night and you'll see small pinpricks of light where cities are burning with life. Zoom in on one of those cities and you'll find thousands or even millions of homes. If you could lift the roof off just one home, you would find that it is packed with ingenious gadgets and extraordinary appliances. Inside each gadget, hard-won scientific discoveries are being put to work to make our lives easier. Have you ever stopped to wonder how something as simple as an espresso machine can flush every last drop of flavour from a coffee bean? Or how a microwave oven cooks your dinner without ever getting hot itself? There's only really one way to find out, and that's to take a look inside.

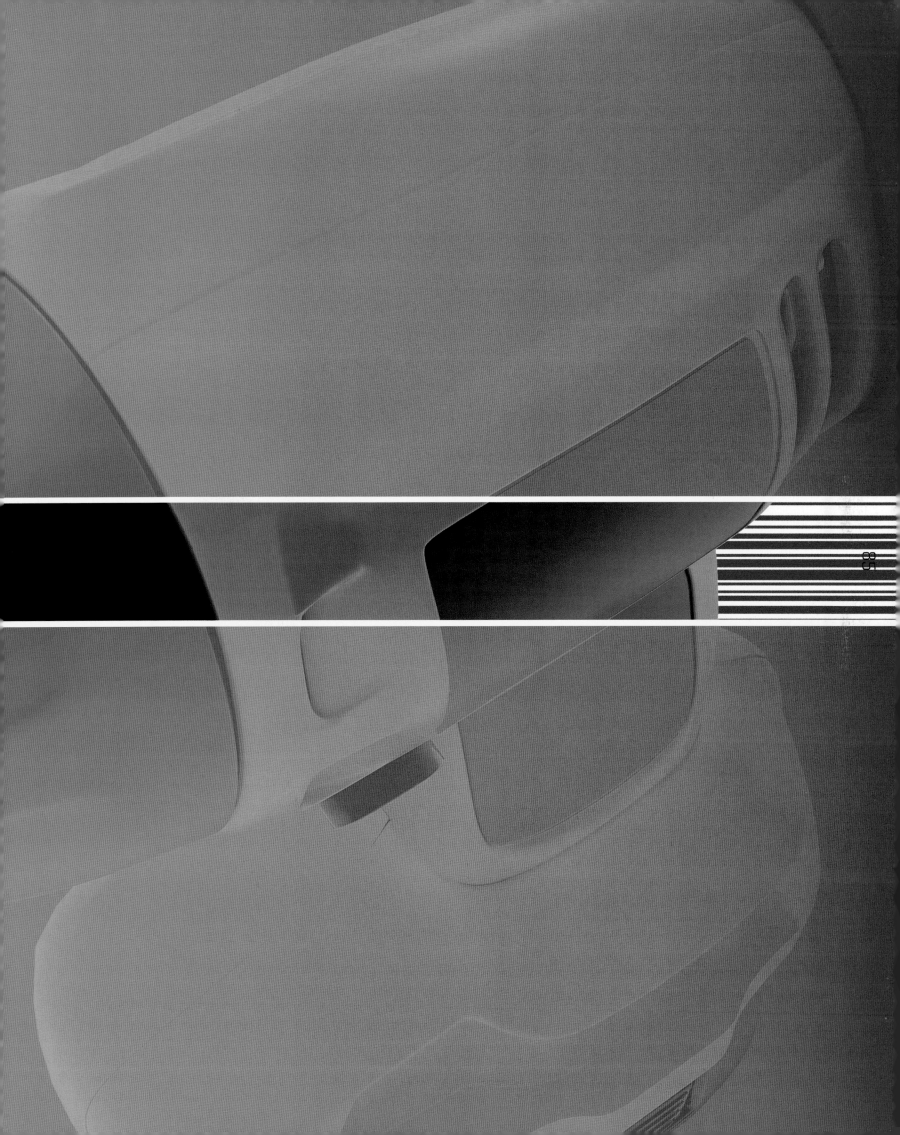

Wind farms

A big coal-fired or nuclear power station makes about 2,000 megawatts (a megawatt is a million watts) of electricity – enough to power a million toasters all at the same time! You need about 1,000 wind turbines to make this much power, which is why turbines tend to be placed together in large groups called wind farms.

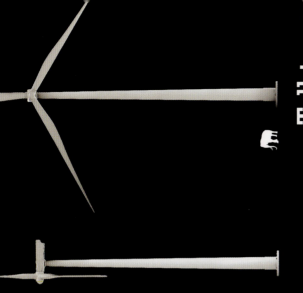

Tall towers

Wind moves faster high up than a[t] ground level. Doubling the height of a[...] wind turbine increases the energy i[t] can produce by more than a third[...]

FAST FACTS

Tower height	80m–105m (262ft–344ft)
Rotor diameter	Up to 90m (295ft)
Maximum wind speed	90kph (55mph)
Blade material	Fibreglass and carbon fibre
Turbine weight	110 tonnes
Tower weight	175 tonnes (80m height) 275 tonnes (105m height)
Power output	Up to 3 megawatts

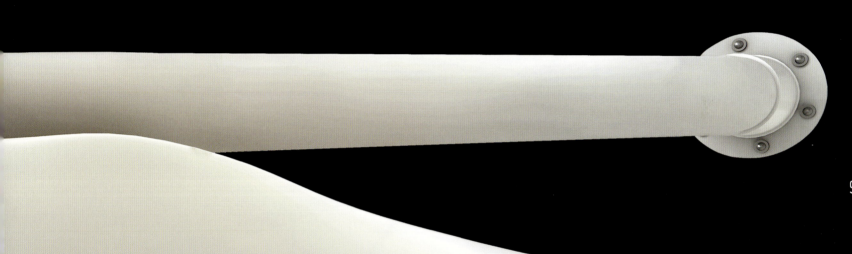

Our landscapes are flowering with elegant towers that produce energy from nothing but the wind. Just as well, because the oil and gas we rely on now may well be gone within decades. Coal, though plentiful, is too dirty to burn, and nuclear power produces dangerous waste. But soon we'll catch enough of the wind whistling round our planet to supply 10–20 per cent of our energy. Slowly spinning in the breeze, each wind turbine generates enough electricity to supply 1,000 homes, creates no pollution, and helps us tackle global warming.

VESTAS WIND TURBINE

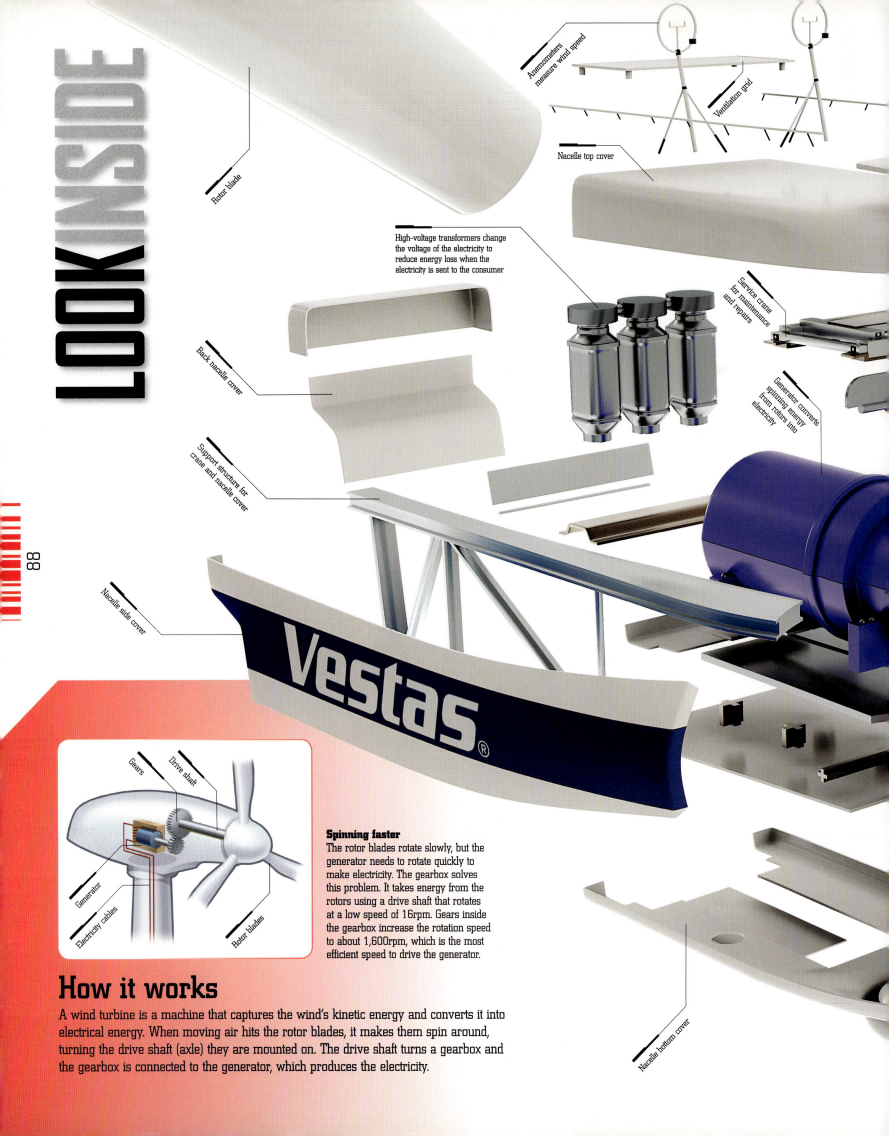

Rotor blade

Anemometers measure wind speed

Ventilation grid

Nacelle top cover

High-voltage transformers change the voltage of the electricity to reduce energy loss when the electricity is sent to the consumer

Service crane for maintenance and repairs

Back nacelle cover

Generator converts spinning energy from rotors into electricity

Support structure for crane and nacelle cover

Nacelle side cover

Vestas®

Nacelle bottom cover

Spinning faster

The rotor blades rotate slowly, but the generator needs to rotate quickly to make electricity. The gearbox solves this problem. It takes energy from the rotors using a drive shaft that rotates at a low speed of 16rpm. Gears inside the gearbox increase the rotation speed to about 1,600rpm, which is the most efficient speed to drive the generator.

Gears   Drive shaft

Generator

Electricity cables

Rotor blades

How it works

A wind turbine is a machine that captures the wind's kinetic energy and converts it into electrical energy. When moving air hits the rotor blades, it makes them spin around, turning the drive shaft (axle) they are mounted on. The drive shaft turns a gearbox and the gearbox is connected to the generator, which produces the electricity.

Turbine teamwork

The three main parts of a wind turbine are the tower it stands on, the spinning rotors, and the generating equipment itself, built into a nacelle (streamlined case). These parts work together to produce the maximum power. The nacelle rotates on the tower so that it faces into the wind. The blades can also change their pitch (angle) so that they capture wind energy as efficiently as possible.

Bracing struts give strength to the structure

Nacelle side panel

Rotor blade

Gearbox increases spinning speed to drive generator

Drive shaft carries power from rotor and gearbox to generator

Hub: blades can change pitch by swivelling on the hub, which enables the turbine to collect more energy

Hub cover protects the components inside the hub

Yaw motors turn turbine to face into the wind

Yaw bearing: turbine rotates on this to face into wind

Nose cone

Rotor blade

WIND POWER

What is wind?

The power we think of as wind energy actually comes from the Sun. Wind is made when the Sun heats different places by different amounts. Hot air rises over warmer places and cool air rushes in underneath. Differences in temperature and air pressure between different places cause winds to blow over huge distances. People can harness the power of the wind to fill sails and push yachts along (left).

Lost at sea

This satellite image shows winds over the surface of the Pacific Ocean. The dark red areas, in the stormy south, have gale force eight winds with speeds reaching 72kph (45mph).

Wind power is the world's fastest growing source of renewable energy. More than 10 times as much power is made with wind turbines today than a decade ago. In Europe, wind provides electricity for around 40 million people; in the USA, about two million get their power this way. Some people think wind could one day provide much of the world's energy, but currently just 1 per cent of electricity is made this way.

Offshore wind

It takes about 1,000 wind turbines to make as much electricity as one large coal or nuclear power station. Countries with a coastline, such as Denmark, have built offshore wind farms to take advantage of the windy conditions at sea.

Wind dangers

Some people think wind turbines should be banned because their spinning blades can kill birds, but very few studies have been done. German conservationists have estimated that 20 times as many birds and bats are killed each year by traffic and high-voltage power lines than by wind turbines. Ornithologists (people who study birds) believe that wind farms should be situated away from important bird habitats and migration routes.

Micro power

Small wind turbines can make enough electricity for a single building. This turbine (above) is on the roof of an environmental centre in the UK. It makes enough power for lights, computers, and a small workshop. By saving electricity, the turbine will pay back the cost of installing it in about 12 years.

Wind in the sails

Wind power is nothing new. Historians think windmills were invented in Persia (now Iran) about 1,400 years ago. It then took another 500 years for the idea to spread to Europe. In the past, windmills were primarily used for grinding grain into flour. These windmills (above) stand on the windy plateau of La Mancha in central Spain.

Windbreaks

Wind power can sometimes be a nuisance, particularly for farmers. In China's Gobi Desert (right), fierce winds blow sand into towering dunes that can suddenly wipe out fields and homes. In an attempt to stop this, farmers grow windbreaks of tall trees, both to hold back the sand and to stop the gales from devastating their crops.

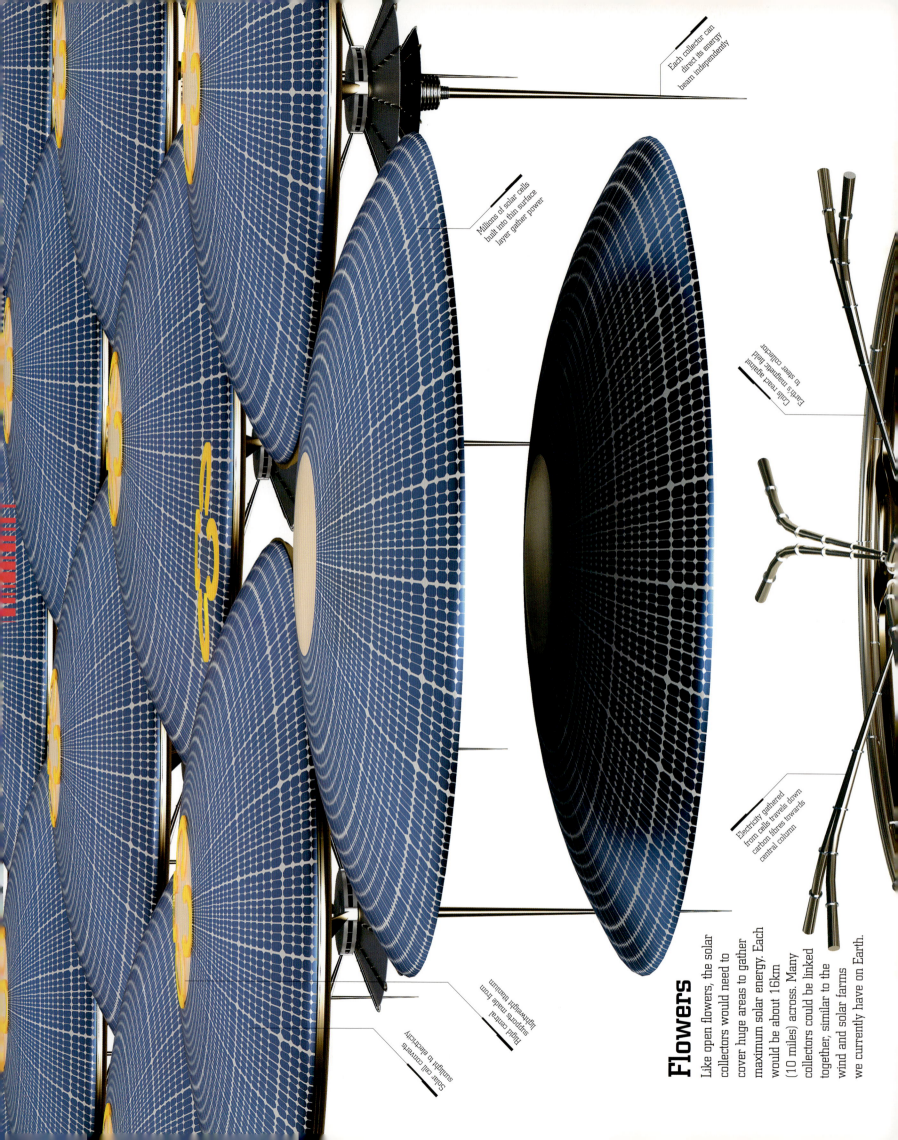

Each collector can direct its energy beam independently

Millions of solar cells built into thin surface layer gather power

Coils react against Earth's magnetic field to steer collector

Electricity gathered from cells travels down carbon fibres towards central column

Rigid central supports made from lightweight titanium

Solar cell converts sunlight to electricity

Flowers

Like open flowers, the solar collectors would need to cover huge areas to gather maximum solar energy. Each would be about 16km (10 miles) across. Many collectors could be linked together, similar to the wind and solar farms we currently have on Earth.

FUTURE POWER

With Earth's fuel supplies running low, we may soon need to look to the sky for power. Most of our energy already comes from the Sun, one way or another, but we could harvest this power more efficiently by building solar-electric power stations in space. Once the electricity had been generated, giant masers (microwave lasers) would beam it down to central collectors on Earth, from where it would flow to our homes as normal.

93

Going up

To build space power stations, we'd need to transport equipment into orbit about 36,000km (22,000 miles) above Earth's surface. Scientists have already suggested a possible solution: an elevator into space. The motorized lifting equipment would crawl up and down a strong cable, shuttling back and forth between Earth and space.

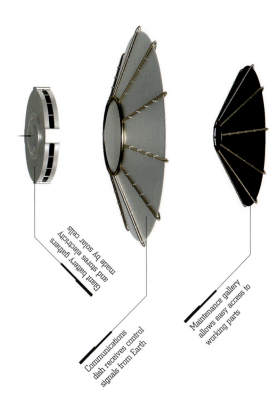

Capacitor stores electricity ready for conversion to microwaves

Maser (microwave laser) turns electricity into microwaves

Maser guide tube can direct power beam to any part of Earth

Communications dish receives control signals from Earth

Giant battery gathers and stores electricity made by solar cells

Maintenance gallery allows easy access to working parts

Inflatable outer structure allows section to be easily constructed and moved around

The race is on. Can you wash 36 plates, 12 cups and saucers, 12 glasses, and 60 pieces of cutlery in just 29 minutes? This dishwasher can. It works intelligently, using light-beams to measure how much washing-up is inside. Then it saves energy by using only as much water and detergent as it needs.

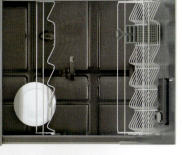

Stainless

Inside, a dishwasher is made of stainless steel: an alloy in which steel is combined with chromium to make it rustproof and stain-resistant. It can withstand years of hot water and powerful detergents.

Industrial strength

Some hotels and restaurants still employ people to wash dishes by hand, but most use industrial dishwashers. Many are like bigger versions of home machines, but the biggest models use conveyor belts to wash up to 5,000 plates per hour!

LOOKINSIDE

Top case

Weight

Holding brackets secure tub inside machine

Insulation stops heat escaping and makes machine more efficient

Back panel and heat exchanger

Side plate

Hose

Sump removes water from tub

Tub: rustproof, water-tight, stainless steel inner case

Exhaust duct helps dry dishes by removing hot, moist air after wash

Float mechanism controls amount of water in tub

High-temperature bottom rack for crockery

Drain hose

Filter catches food scraps and other debris

Water softener helps prevent limescale build-up

Seals

Base plate and drain

Water cycle

The heart of a dishwasher is a water-tight box called the tub. The pump at its base keeps the hot water circulating. It sucks water up from the bottom of the tub and squirts it out through spinning spray arms onto the dirty crockery.

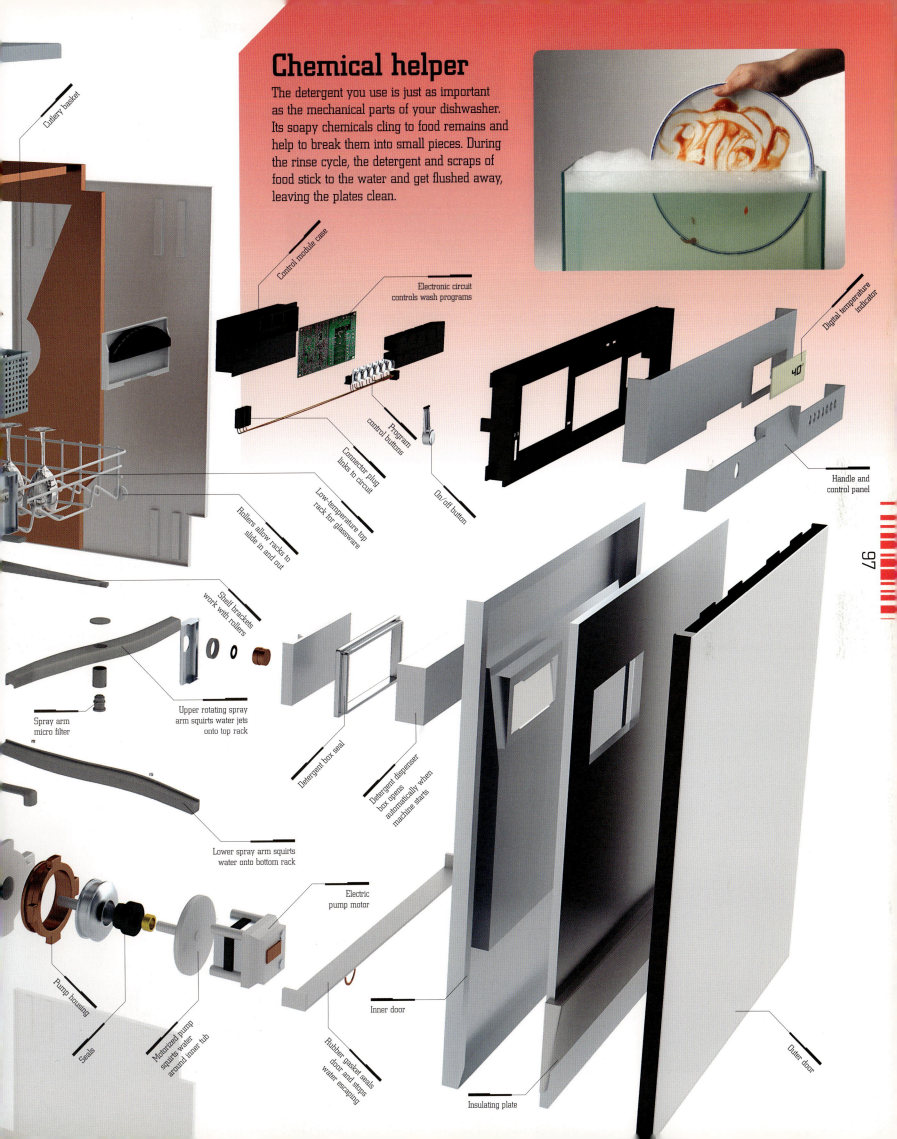

Chemical helper

The detergent you use is just as important as the mechanical parts of your dishwasher. Its soapy chemicals cling to food remains and help to break them into small pieces. During the rinse cycle, the detergent and scraps of food stick to the water and get flushed away, leaving the plates clean.

Cutlery basket

Control module case

Electronic circuit controls wash programs

Digital temperature indicator

Program control buttons

Connector plug links to circuit

Low-temperature top rack for glassware

On/off button

Handle and control panel

Rollers allow racks to slide in and out

Shelf brackets work with rollers

Spray arm micro filter

Upper rotating spray arm squirts water jets onto top rack

Detergent box seal

Detergent dispenser box opens automatically when machine starts

Lower spray arm squirts water onto bottom rack

Electric pump motor

Pump housing

Seals

Motorized pump squirts water around inner tub

Inner door

Rubber gasket seals door and stops water escaping

Insulating plate

Outer door

KEEP IT CLEAN

The average person will eat 82,125 meals in their lifetime – which means an awful lot of dirty dishes. If you spend just 20 minutes a day washing up, that's a year of your life spent slaving over the kitchen sink. It's hardly surprising that many of us choose to use dishwashers. They use hotter water and stronger detergents, so they kill more germs than washing by hand – and they will dry the dishes, too. Used properly, dishwashers can also be better for the environment.

Energy saver

You might think a dishwasher wastes water and electricity, but it uses up to four times less water than hand washing and can save energy too.

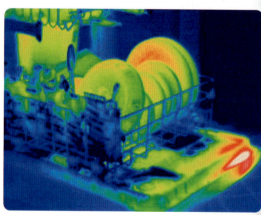

Hot stuff

Modern dishwashers work at temperatures of 60–65°C (140–150°F), about 20°C (35°F) hotter than hand washing. These machines remove almost 400 times more bacteria from dirty plates than hand washing.

Early dishwashers

The dishwasher was invented in 1886 by Josephine Cochrane (1839–1913), an American socialite. She was fed up with her servants chipping the china when they washed it by hand. In her machine, crockery was piled into baskets and squirted with water jets to clean it. This Thor machine from 1947 (left) could also wash clothes.

Dirty dishes

This photograph (below) was taken with an electron microscope. It shows the bacteria lurking on a kitchen scrubbing pad magnified about 10,000 times. After just one day's use, a typical washing-up sponge contains more than a billion bacteria!

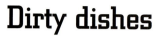
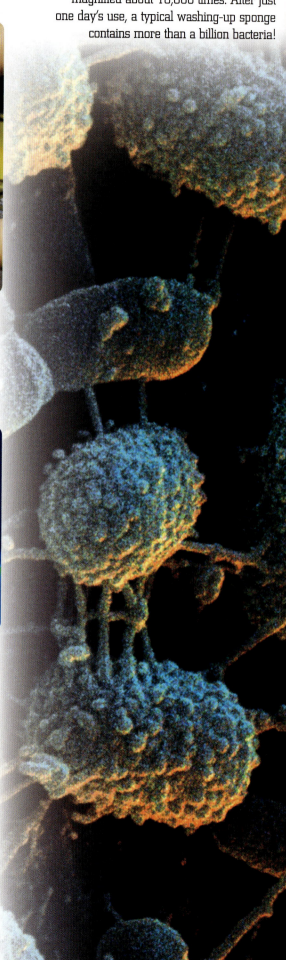

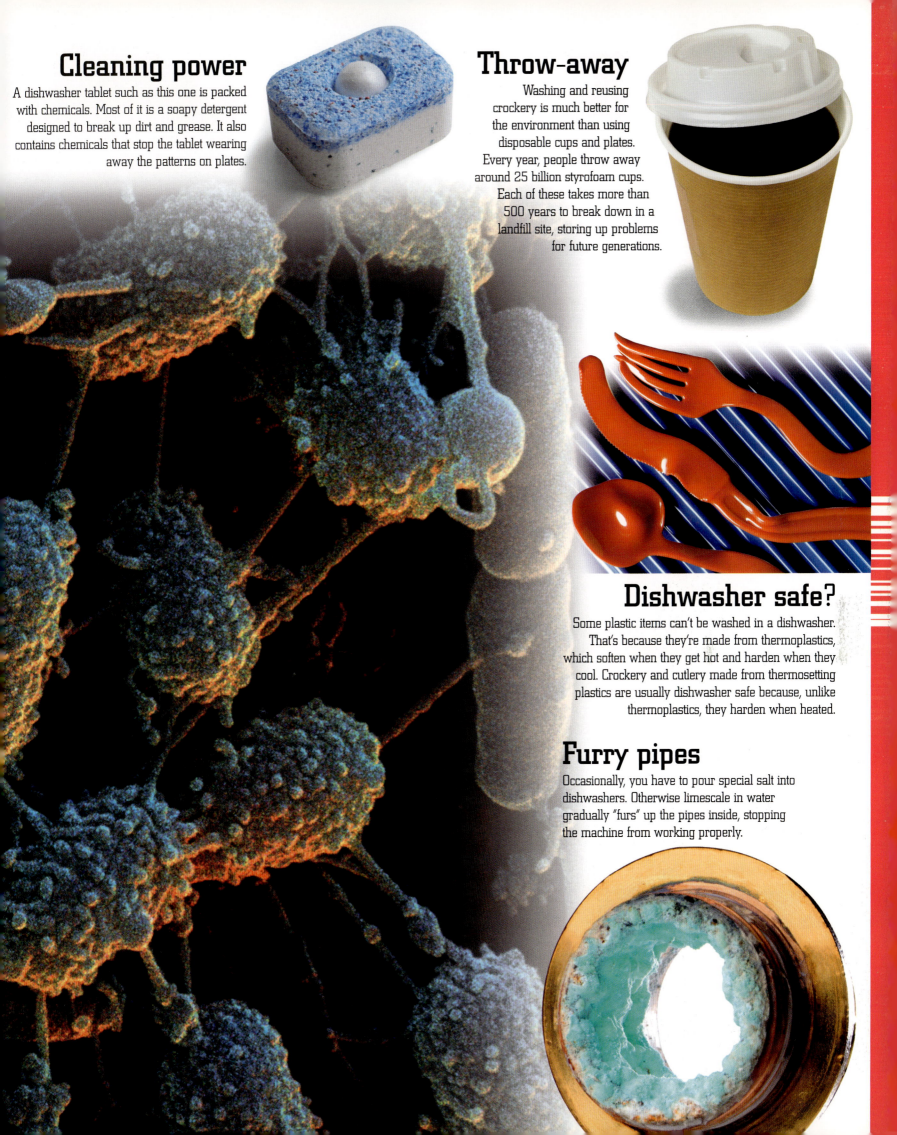

Cleaning power

A dishwasher tablet such as this one is packed with chemicals. Most of it is a soapy detergent designed to break up dirt and grease. It also contains chemicals that stop the tablet wearing away the patterns on plates.

Throw-away

Washing and reusing crockery is much better for the environment than using disposable cups and plates. Every year, people throw away around 25 billion styrofoam cups. Each of these takes more than 500 years to break down in a landfill site, storing up problems for future generations.

Dishwasher safe?

Some plastic items can't be washed in a dishwasher. That's because they're made from thermoplastics, which soften when they get hot and harden when they cool. Crockery and cutlery made from thermosetting plastics are usually dishwasher safe because, unlike thermoplastics, they harden when heated.

Furry pipes

Occasionally, you have to pour special salt into dishwashers. Otherwise limescale in water gradually "furs" up the pipes inside, stopping the machine from working properly.

WASHING MACHINE

FAST FACTS

Dimensions	84cm x 60cm x 59cm (33in x 23in x 23in)
Load capacity	7kg (15.4lb)
Final spin speed	1,400rpm
Water consumption	49 litres (11 gallons)
Number of programs	15

In many parts of the world, fresh water is so scarce that some people believe wars will be fought over it in future. Yet many of us still use up to 400 litres (90 gallons) worth each day. With many water-saving features, this intelligent washing machine could help to reduce this amount.

During a rinse, it uses invisible infrared beams to measure how much soap is left inside, and uses no more water to flush the soap away than absolutely necessary.

In a spin

Early machines left clothes sopping wet – modern ones spin at incredibly high speeds to remove most of the water. This machine has a top speed of 1,400rpm (revolutions per minute), which is equivalent to about 130kph (80mph)!

Easy to use

This washing machine has a helpful electronic display. It shows you what's happening using icons (picture symbols) and has a countdown timer so you know exactly when the wash is going to finish.

Fabric softener compartment

Soap dispenser drawer

Waterproof box protects electronic controller

Pipe trickles water through drawer to wash detergent into drum

Front-panel buttons operate circuit

Electronic controller

Sides of machine

Back of machine

Soap dispenser drawer handle

Buttons for selecting washing options

On/off switch

Program selector

Hinge bolt

Door hinge mount

Front of machine

Door catch mechanism

Hinge bolt

Pump mechanism

Inner door frame

Pipe for pumping water from drum

Toughened door glass

Door handle

Pump cover

102

LOOKINSIDE

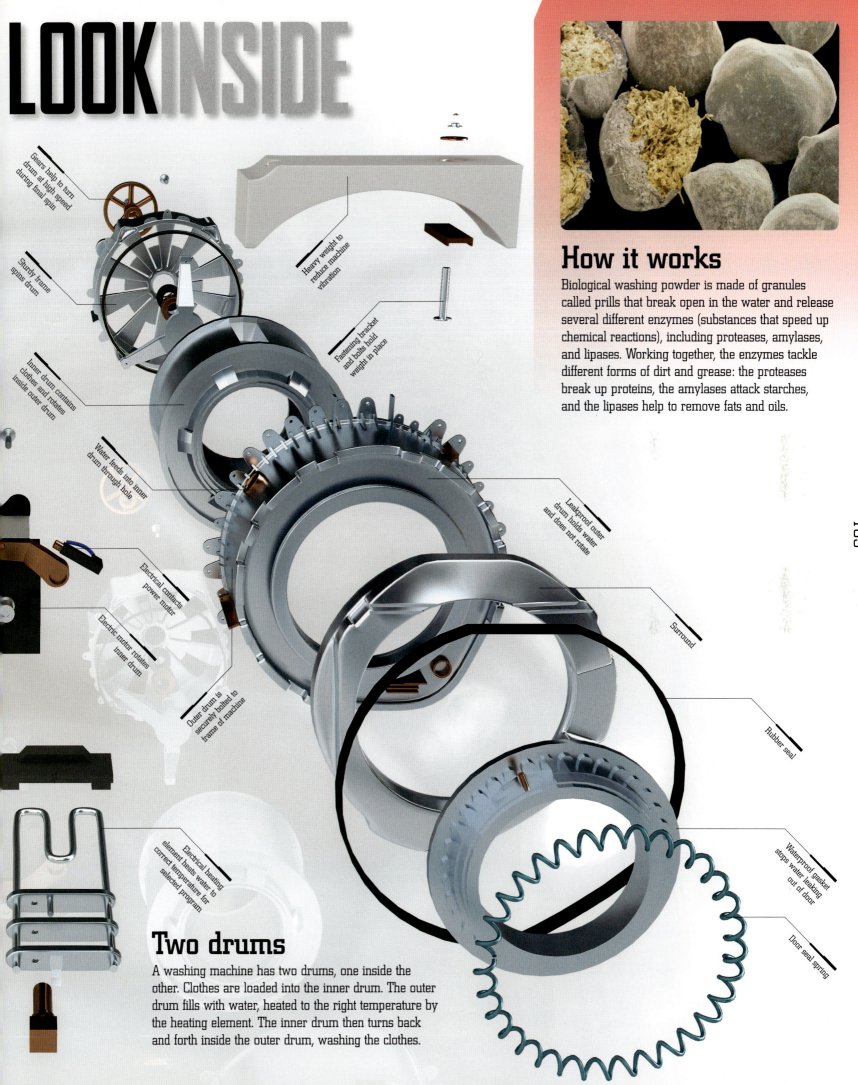

Gears help to turn drum at high speed during final spin

Sturdy frame spins drum

Inner drum contains clothes and rotates inside outer drum

Water feeds into inner drum through hole

Electrical contacts power motor

Electric motor rotates inner drum

Outer drum is securely bolted to frame of machine

Electrical heating element heats water to correct temperature for selected program

Heavy weight to reduce machine vibration

Fastening bracket and bolts hold weight in place

Leakproof outer drum holds water and does not rotate

Surround

Rubber seal

Waterproof gasket stops water leaking out of door

Door seal spring

How it works

Biological washing powder is made of granules called prills that break open in the water and release several different enzymes (substances that speed up chemical reactions), including proteases, amylases, and lipases. Working together, the enzymes tackle different forms of dirt and grease: the proteases break up proteins, the amylases attack starches, and the lipases help to remove fats and oils.

Two drums

A washing machine has two drums, one inside the other. Clothes are loaded into the inner drum. The outer drum fills with water, heated to the right temperature by the heating element. The inner drum then turns back and forth inside the outer drum, washing the clothes.

A CLEAN WORLD

Washing clothes can be a real chore – it's a problem that inventors have been trying to solve for more than 200 years. The first breakthrough, in 1797, was the invention of the scrubbing board: a ribbed piece of wood on which clothes were laid flat and brushed clean with soapy water. Technology has come a long way since then. The latest washing machines are microchip-controlled and eco-friendly: they wash at lower temperatures, but get your clothes cleaner and drier than ever.

Antique machine

By the 1920s, electric washing machines like the one pictured above had become popular. You placed your clothes in a metal drum, which swirled them through soapy water using a spinning paddle. Then you squeezed the clothes dry by feeding them through the "mangle" rollers on top.

Detergents

Powerful detergents get clothes clean – but they contain a chemical cocktail that harms the environment when they are flushed down the drain. Phosphates in detergents (which soften water) work like fertilizers when they reach our rivers and seas, causing huge growths of algae (water plants) that can suffocate fish. Perfumes in detergents and optical brighteners (which make our clothes gleam in sunlight) can also be toxic to fish and sea creatures. Some chemical companies now make eco-friendly detergents that do not contain these harmful ingredients.

Washing without...

We take clean water and electricity for granted – but billions of people across the world still have neither. In India, people wash their clothes in the River Yamuna (below), near the Taj Mahal, where pollution levels are 3,000 times higher than those considered safe.

Testing, testing

Water conducts electricity, so electric washing machines have to be carefully tested to make sure none of the electrics get wet. Each finished machine is sprayed with water from the outside to make sure it is leak-proof.

Toploader

Washing machines vary around the world. In Europe, people prefer front-loading machines that tumble clothes inside a rotating drum. In the United States and Asia, toploaders like this (above) are more common. Clothes are loaded from above, the drum stays still, and a big paddle wheel swishes the clothes around.

Launderette

People who live in cities can choose to take their clothes to a launderette (also called a laundromat). They can use the coin-operated machines themselves, or an attendant can wash their clothes for them. Launderettes are cheaper for occasional washing, but work out more expensive in the long term.

Waste not...

Most washing machines are sent to landfills when they wear out, but they can easily be recycled. Half a typical machine is made of valuable steel, and the rest contains useful materials such as aluminium, copper, and a mixture of plastics.

Control panel

Base keeps unit stable

Lid and outer case made of self-cleaning plastic

Plastic drum holds clothes

Retaining clip

Pipes blow clean air through drum to make clothes smell fresh

Ring holds inner drum in place

Ultrasonic loudspeakers blast high-frequency sound waves into drum

Everyone likes clean clothes, but washing and drying is a chore. In the future, washing machines could work a different way, using ultrasound and static electricity instead of soap and water. It'll take under a minute to turn dirty jeans back into clean ones – and because your clothes won't get wet, you'll be able to wear them straight away.

Sound asleep

Ultrasound (high-frequency sound) is best known as a way of monitoring unborn babies. High-frequency sound is beamed into the mother's womb from a probe on her abdomen. A computer uses the sound waves reflected back to build up 3-D images like this.

Dry clean

This future washer fires ultrasound waves into your clothes to shake the dirt loose, while electrostatic attractors outside the drum pull the loose dirt away. Gears spin the attractors round the drum to dislodge the dirt, which then collects in a trap at the bottom of the machine.

Electrostatic attractors use static electricity to pull loose dirt away

Ultraviolet light beams upward into clothes to kill germs

Filter collects dirt

Motorized carriage spins attractors around drum to release dirt

Cartridge stores dirt, compacted for easy removal

Non-magnetic support

MICROWAVE

A box that can cook food with a quick blast of energy waves seems like something out of science fiction – but you've probably got one standing in a corner of your kitchen right now. Every time you hear a microwave oven buzzing, it's pumping powerful radio waves into your dinner at the speed of light. A microwave can cook food around six times faster than a conventional oven.

Accidental invention

American engineer Percy Spencer (1894–1970) was experimenting with a radar (navigation) set one day. When stray waves of energy from his radar melted the chocolate bar in his pocket, Spencer realized he had found a new way of heating food.

Fast or slow

Microwaves cook liquid foods, such as soups, much faster than solid foods. That's because the entire liquid absorbs microwaves very quickly. But when you cook a large piece of solid food, the microwaves heat only the outer edge. The centre of the food cooks more slowly as the heat flows inwards. This takes much longer, so it is important to leave microwaved foods to stand after you take them out of the oven.

FAST FACTS

Typical dimensions	26cm x 49.5cm x 31.5cm (10.2in x 19.5in x 12.4in)
Power	800 watts
Materials	Wipe-clean, stainless steel interior
Number of programs	3 cooking and 3 re-heating

How it works

Microwaves are generated by a device called a magnetron and channelled into the cooking cavity. Inside the cavity, they bounce repeatedly off the metal walls and enter the food. When food absorbs microwaves, the water molecules it contains vibrate, and this causes a rise in temperature that cooks the food.

Cool cooker
This thermal photograph shows why microwaves are so efficient: most of the energy they use cooks the food and is not wasted heating the oven. The food bowl and its contents are hottest (shown red and white), while the cooking cavity is cooler (orange), and the outside is cold enough to touch (blue and green).

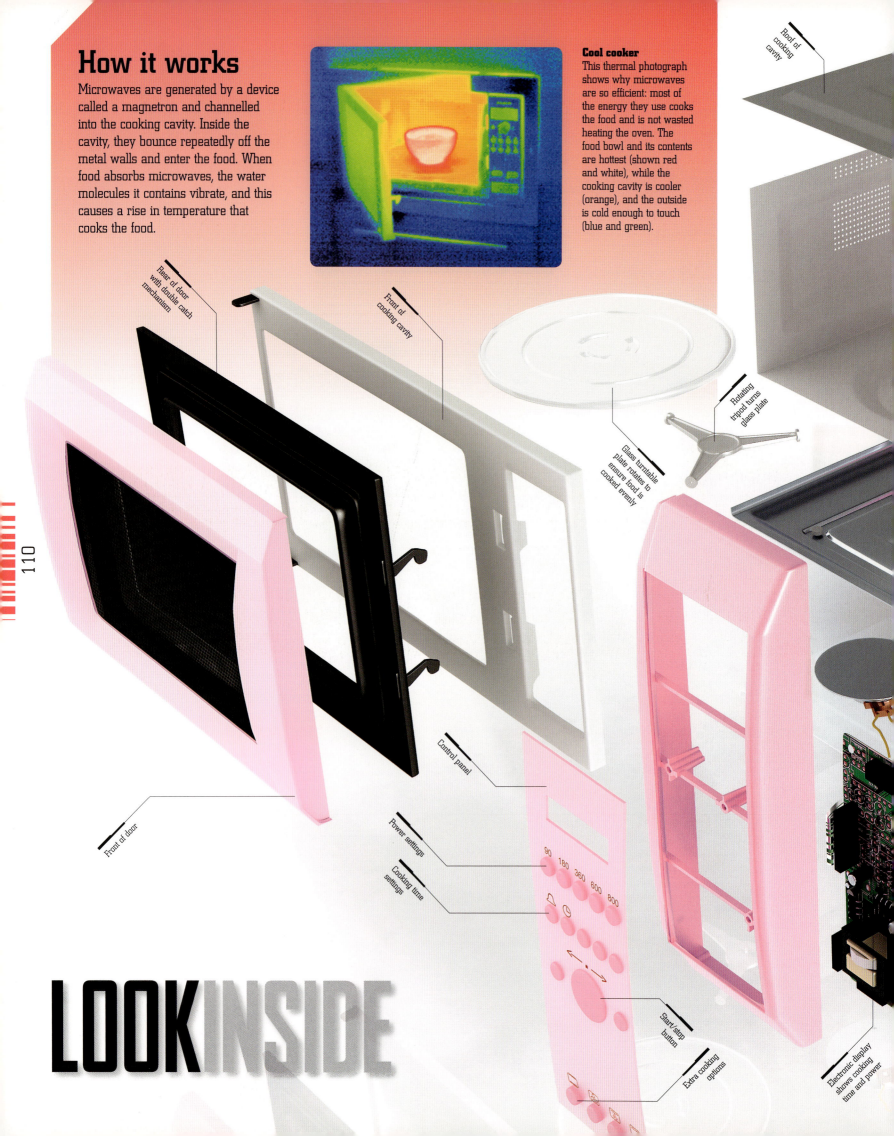

Roof of cooking cavity

Rear of door with double catch mechanism

Front of cooking cavity

Rotating tripod turns glass plate

Glass turntable plate rotates to ensure food is cooked evenly

Control panel

Power settings

Cooking time settings

90 180 360 600 800

Front of door

Start/stop button

Extra cooking options

Electronic display shows cooking time and power

LOOK**INSIDE**

Wipe-clean metal outer case

Radiation-proof back panel has ventilation holes to let steam escape

Cooking cavity has perforations to let steam (but not microwaves) escape

Power connector and fuse

Transformer produces high voltage to power magnetron

Bottom cover

Magnetron (microwave generator)

Magnetron cooling fins

Magnetron casing

High-voltage capacitor works with transformer to power magnetron

Electric motor powers cooling fan

Fan housing

111

Cooling fan

Electric turntable drive motor

Magnetron control circuit

Lamp holder and power supply

Mounting bracket

Lamp lights up cooking cavity

Door catch has electronic sensors to switch off oven if door is opened

Electronic circuit controls oven

Safe inside

Microwaves can be harmful to people, so a microwave oven has to be properly sealed to stop them from escaping. Inside the easy-to-clean case, there is a metal box called the cooking cavity. Holes in the cavity allow steam to escape, but microwaves cannot get through them. The door also has a gauze metal lining to keep microwaves inside.

ENERGY WAVES

We all think we know what the world looks like – it's right in front of us – but there's a whole other world that we can't see. All we can see is the light reflected off objects, but light is only one kind of electromagnetic energy buzzing around us. If our eyes could detect other kinds of energy too, we might see radio and TV programmes whizzing past our heads, phone calls soaring through the sky, and microwaves zapping about inside our ovens. We can't see these forms of energy, but we know they're there – and we can use them in all kinds of interesting ways.

Fast phones

The dishes on telephone towers like this (left) send and receive phone calls to and from similar towers in other cities using microwave beams. The towers have to be within each other's line of sight, which is why they're so tall.

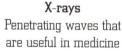

Missile spotting

These strange-looking "golf balls" (right) were built in the 1960s to house missile detectors at Fylingdales in Yorkshire, England. Working with similar bases in Greenland and Alaska, the detectors used microwave beams to scan the sky. The golf balls were 26m (84ft) across and could spot a missile from almost 5,000km (3,000 miles) away. They were dismantled in the early 1990s.

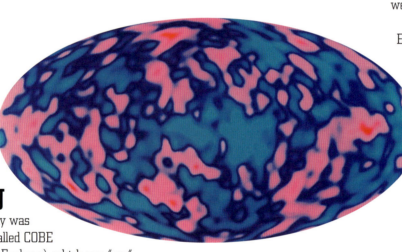

Big Bang

This picture of the sky was taken by a satellite called COBE (Cosmic Background Explorer), which can "see" microwaves. Different colours show areas of different temperatures (pink is hottest and blue coldest). Scientists have used this temperature map to help them understand how the Universe was formed about 14 billion years ago in a giant explosion called the Big Bang.

Electromagnetic spectrum

Light, X-rays, radio waves, and microwaves are all kinds of electromagnetic energy. All travel at the speed of light as undulating waves of electricity and magnetism, but the waves they contain are of different lengths and carry different amounts of energy. Gamma rays are shortest and radio waves longest.

Gamma rays
Short, high-energy waves made by radioactivity

X-rays
Penetrating waves that are useful in medicine

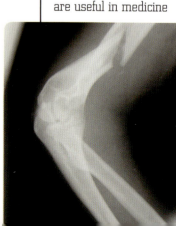

Microwave science

Scientists can study many things with microwaves. This satellite image shows how much water vapour (gas) there is in Earth's atmosphere. Areas with most water vapour are dark blue; areas with less are light blue. This kind of research helps scientists to understand Earth's water cycle.

Tornado chasing

Trucks like this (below) help weather forecasters predict when tornadoes will strike. The Doppler radar dish on the back fires a microwave beam into a storm. The reflected beam can be used to calculate the storm's speed and direction.

Curing cancer

Cancer is caused when runaway cells grow in people's bodies to make tumours. One way to kill tumours is to blast them with high-energy radiation, such as X-rays and microwaves.

Visible light

Ultraviolet rays
Present in sunlight

Infrared rays
Given off by hot objects

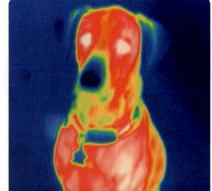

Microwaves
Short radio waves that can be used to cook food

Radio waves
Long waves that carry TV and radio signals

FAST FACTS

Capacity	Makes up to 6 cups
Time to make coffee	5–8 minutes
Materials	Stainless steel and plastic
Weight	4.5kg (9.9lb)
Cost	Approx. £40

Espresso yourself

In a coffee bar, espresso (a shot of hot, concentrated coffee) is the starting point for all coffee drinks. You can serve it as it is, add it to steamed milk (a latte), mix it with hot water (an Americano), or serve it with foamed milk and chocolate (a cappuccino).

Instant coffee may be convenient, but when it comes to flavour, there is no substitute for a velvety-rich espresso. An espresso machine extracts the maximum flavour by blasting high-pressure hot water through the coffee grains. A coffee maker like this uses water at 15 times the pressure of the air around us – roughly the same pressure a diver feels at 150m (450ft) under the sea!

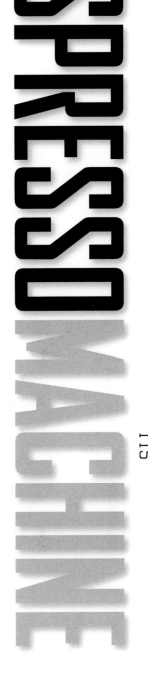

Home coffee shop

Coffee makers such as this one have two separate halves for making different drinks. On one side, strong espresso drips into the jug below, while on the other side, a hotplate heats milk that can be frothed up for a cappuccino or a latte.

LOOKINSIDE

Plastic top

Pressure cap

Two in one

The most important part of an espresso maker is the water heater and pressurizer unit on the left. Hot milk is prepared separately with the frother attachment on the right.

Frother on/off button

Electronic circuit board

Milk frother motor and blade

Heating element heats water in tank

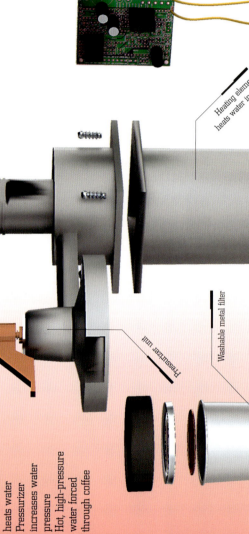

Washable metal filter

Filter holder

Pressurizer unit

How it works

There are many different types of coffee maker. Most of them extract the flavour from ground coffee (coffee beans crushed into a fine powder) by soaking it in near-boiling water for several minutes. An espresso machine makes coffee faster and stronger than other methods by forcing hot, high-pressure water through the ground coffee.

Strength selector

1 Water tank

2 Electric element heats water

3 Pressurizer increases water pressure

4 Hot, high-pressure water forced through coffee

❶

❷

❸

❹

Perfect espresso

The water is heated to just below boiling point (about 90°C or 195°F), and is then pressurized and forced through the coffee.

Milk frother cover

Milk frother hot
plate cover

Milk frother hot
plate

Milk frother
hot plate on / off
switch and
indicator
light

Air vents to cool
machine

Water tank

Underside of casing

Glass coffee jug

Drip tray metal plate

Drip tray

Base plate

Plastic trim

Coffee maker
on / off switch and
indicator light

DRINK UP

People drink two billion cups of coffee every single day, making it the world's favourite hot drink. Coffee has been popular for more than a thousand years. According to legend, it was discovered around 850CE when an Ethiopian goatherd named Kaldi noticed that his animals danced about after nibbling coffee beans. When Kaldi tried one himself, he felt much more alert. Coffee beans were soon being turned into stimulating drinks that gradually spread from Africa and the Middle East to Europe and America.

Cash crop

Coffee is one of the world's top 10 most important agricultural crops: the seven million tonnes of coffee produced each year is enough to fill a line of trucks 1,300km (800 miles) long. Around 50 countries (including Brazil, Colombia, and Indonesia) grow coffee that they export to the rest of the world.

Making coffee

Coffee is made from two main plant species named *Coffea arabica* and *Coffea canephora* (also called *Coffea robusta*). Arabica beans come mostly from Latin America, the Caribbean, and Indonesia, and make a stronger and more aromatic coffee than robusta beans, which come from Africa.

In an instant

Instant coffee powder (seen here under an electron microscope) is made by taking a very strong liquid coffee and removing its water. That can be done either by spray drying (using hot air) or freeze drying (cooling quickly). The grains formed this way are light and hollow and can be turned back into coffee by adding hot water.

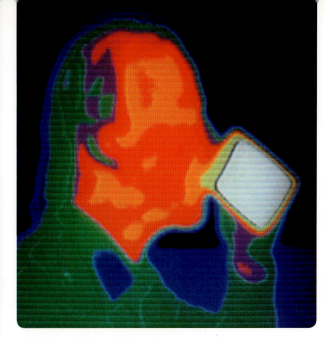

Feel the heat

This thermal photograph of a coffee drinker shows the hottest areas in white and red, and the cooler ones in blue and green. Hot drinks provide warmth to our bodies and can sometimes help to aid digestion.

Old school

Bedouins (Arab nomads) make coffee the traditional way. They roast the beans over an open fire to concentrate their flavour. The roasted beans are cooled, ground, and mixed with spices to make a delicious brew called *qahwah* or *gahwa*.

Hyperactive

Caffeine (the stimulating chemical in coffee) makes you more alert and active, but too much can make you restless and erratic. Scientists tested this by giving coffee to a spider. It became hyperactive and could build only this very chaotic web.

Coffee shopping

Coffee shops look similar the world over, but not all use espresso machines. In Turkey, coffee is more likely to be made by boiling ground coffee in a small metal pot. Filter coffee is popular in Vietnam. In Europe, many coffee shops serve cafetières (French presses), which use a metal gauze and plunger to remove coffee grounds.

Servants or slaves?

Before electric appliances were popular, wealthy people relied on servants, who were often little more than slaves. When appliances were first introduced, it was the servants who used them. Now most people have dispensed with servants and use appliances to do the chores themselves.

Women's liberation

The burden of housework used to fall on women, so advertisers sold appliances by making women feel guilty that their homes were not clean enough. As appliances became more affordable, housework became more automated. It's partly due to electric appliances that many more women now have challenging careers outside the home.

Culture clash

In 1959, two world leaders had a famous debate about electric homes. American Vice-President Richard Nixon (1913–1994) argued with Nikita Khrushchev (1894–1971), leader of the Soviet Union (nations led by Russia), about which country's appliances were best. Nixon said that capitalism (the American system) gave people better homes and lives, while Khrushchev insisted communism (the Russian system) was just as good.

ELECTRIC FRIENDS

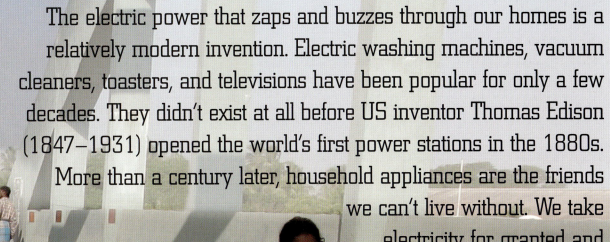

The electric power that zaps and buzzes through our homes is a relatively modern invention. Electric washing machines, vacuum cleaners, toasters, and televisions have been popular for only a few decades. They didn't exist at all before US inventor Thomas Edison (1847–1931) opened the world's first power stations in the 1880s. More than a century later, household appliances are the friends we can't live without. We take electricity for granted and notice it only in a power cut — when it disappears.

Material world

People in developing countries are much less likely to own household appliances. In India, 600 million people (half the population) are not connected to the electricity grid. Indian people who have electricity consume only about 7 per cent as much as people in western countries.

Has it helped?

People spend as much time on housework today as they did decades ago. The main reason is that we have higher standards now and appliances let us do more: we own and wash more clothes, get our homes cleaner, and cook more sophisticated meals. Although men help more, women still do the majority of household chores.

FACTOIDS

● The world will use 76 per cent more electricity in 2020 than it did in 1997. Industrialized countries will use 40 per cent more, but developing countries will use 164 per cent more. ● In industrialized countries, there are more than three times as many TV sets in use now as in 1980.

CORDLESS DRILL

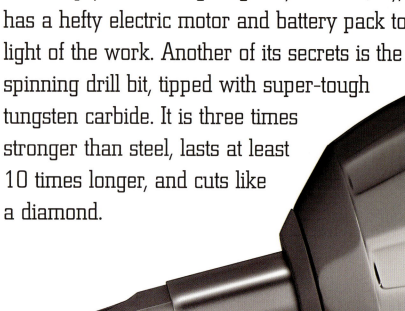

Squeeze the trigger of a cordless drill and you've got a good deal of power at your fingertips. It takes real effort to force a hole through brick, wood, or steel – materials that simply don't like giving way. Fortunately, this drill has a hefty electric motor and battery pack to make light of the work. Another of its secrets is the spinning drill bit, tipped with super-tough tungsten carbide. It is three times stronger than steel, lasts at least 10 times longer, and cuts like a diamond.

Drill science

Drilling won't work just by applying brute force. That force needs to be properly directed and concentrated in just the right areas. The drill bit is smaller than the chuck that grips it. As the chuck rotates, the surface of the drill bit moves a shorter distance, but with greater force. The bit is also smaller than the body of the drill. As you push from behind, it's like pressing on the flat head of a drawing pin: the force you apply to the drill case is concentrated into a smaller area on the drill bit, so that it pushes into the surface.

FAST FACTS

Speed	Up to 750rpm
Drill depth	Can drill 25mm (1in) of wood or 10mm (0.4in) of steel
Power settings	5
Cost	Approx. £35

Power pack

Cordless drills are easier and safer to use than drills with long electric cables that you could trip over. The black power pack on the base of this drill contains rechargeable batteries. They give around three hours of power before they need charging again.

LOOK INSIDE

Torque torque

At the heart of a cordless drill is an electric motor, which gets its power from the battery pack underneath. The motor drives the drill bit through the transmission gears in the middle. The transmission reduces the speed provided by the motor so the drill bit turns more slowly but with extra torque (turning force), and this makes drilling easier. Five different torque settings give five levels of power for drilling different materials.

Cross-head screwdriver bit

Chuck holds drill and screwdriver bits tightly

Selection of drill bits

Twist grip for tightening chuck

Twist grip adjusts level of torque

Connection between battery pack and base of drill

Batteries inside battery pack

Outer case of battery pack

How it works

An electric motor is a machine that uses electricity and magnetism to produce movement. If you pass electricity through a wire that is sitting between the poles of a magnet, the wire will jump up or down very briefly. If you bend the wire into a loop and connect it to a circuit, you can make it spin continuously. In an electric motor, thousands of loops of wire are bunched tightly together. Large curved magnets turn the motor in a drill with a great deal of force.

Wire loop

Electric current flows through wire loop

Magnet

Coil inside motor

Curved magnets wrapped around coil

Electric motor

Wire loop spins inside magnetic field

Battery

Motor axle rotates at high speed

Vents in plastic case let air in to cool electric motor

Toughened polycarbonate (plastic) case designed to survive knocks

Selection of screwdriver bits

Transmission gears provide five different power settings for different materials

Electric motor casing

Back panel

Copper contact feeds electric current to motor

Finger-operated trigger

Switch turns motor on when trigger is pressed

Electric cables take power from battery to motor

Pecking order

Woodpeckers are nature's best-known drillers. Their tough, sharp beaks can hammer into trees at 100 beats per minute in search of ants and other insects to eat. The birds blink before each peck to prevent wood chips damaging their eyes. Shock-absorbing structures in their heads prevent damage to their brains from the impact.

Early drills

People were drilling holes long before there was electricity. This prehistoric wooden drill has a bow string at the top. As you slide the bow back and forth, the string rotates the drill in the centre, grinding the bit into the material you want to drill.

Road works

This pneumatic (air-powered) drill (right) uses compressed (squeezed) air to punch a metal bit into the road at high speed. A typical drill bangs up and down 25 times per second.

Bad tooth day

Dentists can save your teeth by drilling out the rotten bits and replacing them with a hard substitute such as porcelain. The dentist's drill shown in this false-coloured photo (right) is coated with diamond fragments (shown in light orange) and spins at more than 100,000 times per minute.

DRILLING DOWN

People have been drilling holes since the Stone Age, but there's nothing prehistoric about modern drills. Big holes or small, there's a machine that can do the job for you. When railway engineers decided to link the UK and France with the 50km (31-mile) Channel Tunnel, it took 11 huge spinning drills seven years to finish the task. At the opposite end of the scale, scientists have recently found a way of drilling holes several times thinner than a human hair using tiny electrical sparks.

Drilling for oil

Oil rigs are very sophisticated drills. Instead of a short metal bit, they use a "string" of hollow metal pipes that can stretch 8km (5 miles) or more underground. The latest drills, known as "snakes", can be steered along curving paths to extract much more oil than conventional drills.

Going underground

This tunnel boring machine (TBM), or "mole", drills railways and roads. Its rotating cutter is about 9m (30ft) across and deposits rock onto rail trucks following behind. Machines like this can drill around 1km (0.67 miles) of tunnel per month.

Laser drills

Laser drills like this one are used to make precision parts for aircraft. They can drill microscopic holes about the size of a human hair.

Screaming as they go, these people are experiencing the terrifying delights of the Nemesis Inferno corkscrew ride at Thorpe Park, UK. In the final loop, riders experience forces 4.5 times stronger than gravity.

ENTERTAINMENT ANDLEISURE

A grand piano looks like a bizarre piece of wooden furniture – until someone lifts the lid and starts playing it. Even then, you'd never guess that the notes you're listening to are being made by an intricate machine, first designed in the 18th century, that has more than 12,000 separate parts. Other gadgets that entertain us have their secrets too. Many people love the challenge of computer games, especially ones that are fast and realistic. What makes today's game consoles so much better than yesterday's are incredibly powerful microchips that work like supercomputers. Technology makes play time more interesting and fun – and you'll find out why if you look inside it.

PLAYST

FREEPLAY RADIO

Radio brings the world closer: spin slowly through the dial and you'll hear voices and songs that have crossed continents to reach your home. If you live in a country where electricity is hard to come by, radio may have been out of reach – until now. This Freeplay radio is powered by winding a handle, so it can work anywhere on Earth. One minute of winding gives an hour of play. It even has a built-in torch!

See through

Manufacturers usually go to great lengths to hide an appliance's working parts neatly inside it, but Freeplay has built this radio into a clear plastic case. You can see its powerful electricity generator spinning as you crank the handle. You can also see the electronic parts that turn incoming radio signals into sounds.

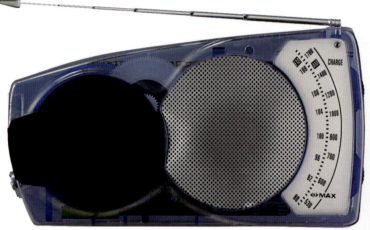

FAST FACTS

Power source	Wind-up generator, solar power, or mains
Torch	Uses long-lasting LED (light-emitting diode)
Battery life	One full charge gives 25 hours of play. Battery lasts more than 5,000 hours
Cost	Approx. £30

FM 108 AM CHARGE
1700
1400
106 1200
104 1000
100 800
96 700
92 600
MAX
88 530

Clockwork Universe

Before electric power became popular, many machines were driven by clockwork. This was a way of storing power in a machine by winding a handle. The handle tightened a stiff metal spring which, as it slowly unwound, turned gears that drove the machine. This orrery (model of the planets) is clockwork-driven.

LOOKINSIDE

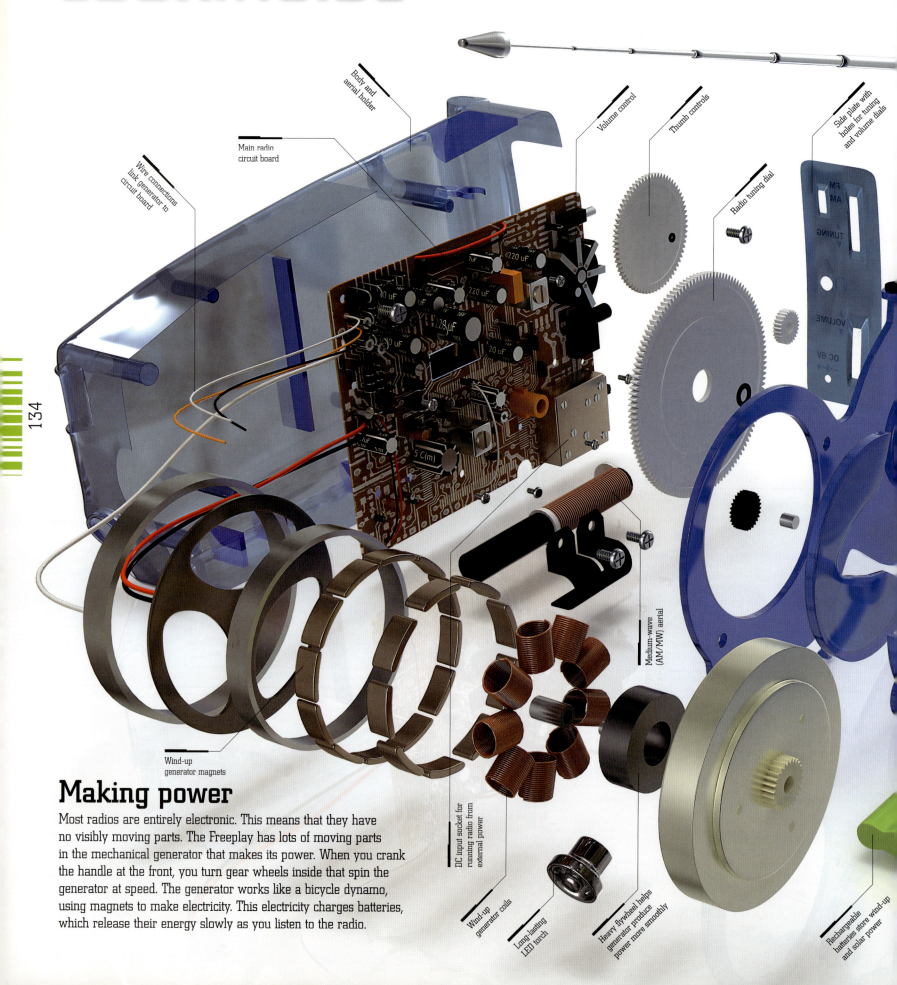

Body and aerial holder

Main radio circuit board

Wire connections link generator to circuit board

Volume control

Thumb controls

Radio tuning dial

Side plate with holes for tuning and volume dials

FM
AM
TUNING
VOLUME
DC 6V

Wind-up generator magnets

Medium-wave (AM/MW) aerial

DC input socket for running radio from external power

Wind-up generator coils

Long-lasting LED torch

Heavy flywheel helps generator produce power more smoothly

Rechargeable batteries store wind-up and solar power

Making power

Most radios are entirely electronic. This means that they have no visibly moving parts. The Freeplay has lots of moving parts in the mechanical generator that makes its power. When you crank the handle at the front, you turn gear wheels inside that spin the generator at speed. The generator works like a bicycle dynamo, using magnets to make electricity. This electricity charges batteries, which release their energy slowly as you listen to the radio.

How it works

Radio is a way of sending sounds, music, and other information between two places without using any wires. At a radio station, people's voices are captured using microphones and turned into electrical signals. These signals are encoded in radio waves and then beamed through the air, in all directions, using a powerful transmitter aerial. The radio set you have at home is a receiving device that captures the radio waves, decodes the signals they contain, and turns them back into sounds you can hear. A radio set looks complex, but the way it works can be broken down into a series of simple stages.

From signal to sound
Five of the electronic parts connected to a radio's circuit board are especially important. The aerial (1) captures incoming radio waves. The capacitor (2) tunes the radio by selecting a single frequency of radio wave. The diode (3) helps turn the radio waves back into sound. The transistor (4) boosts the sound so that it is powerful enough to drive a loudspeaker (5), which makes the sounds you can hear.

❶

❷

❸

❹

❺

Telescopic FM aerial

Solar panel

Station frequency indicator

Speaker grill

Wind-up generator gears

Front body with holes for generator handle, loudspeaker, and radio dial

Radio loudspeaker basket

Radio loudspeaker cone

Wind-up generator crank

Solar television

TV pictures are beamed by radio waves, so you can pick them up anywhere. But you still need electricity to power the set. These villagers in Niger, West Africa, are watching a battery-powered TV run from solar panels.

Solar panels

Solar panels, such as this one (above) in a remote part of Bolivia, convert the Sun's energy directly into electricity. A panel this size makes about 100 watts – enough to power a light bulb. The electricity can be used immediately or stored in batteries for later.

PEOPLEPOWER

More than a century since the first power stations were built, a quarter of the world's people still have no electricity. Until recently, there were two problems in bringing power to developing countries – one was constructing the power stations themselves, which cost as much as £2 billion and take years to build. The other problem was transmitting power to remote places, which means building expensive overhead power lines or underground cables. Poor countries have often seen electricity as a luxury that must come after clean water and basic health care. That's now changing thanks to technologies like solar power and rechargeable batteries, which allow people to make and store electricity whenever and wherever they need it.

Mobile phone

Landlines (ordinary wired telephone lines) are uncommon in most developing countries. In Africa, fewer than one person in a hundred has a phone of this kind. Mobile phones are much more common than landlines because they need no expensive wiring to a local exchange. Their batteries can be charged with small solar cells.

Solar water pump

More than 1.1 billion people (one-sixth of the world's population) still lack access to clean water. Solar-powered pumps such as this one in Namibia (below) could reduce that number. The solar panels drive an electric motor that sucks water up from under the ground. Some pumps also use the ultraviolet part of sunlight to disinfect the water they collect.

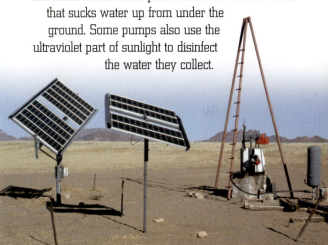

Solar cooking

People in some developing countries get up to 80 per cent of their energy by burning wood. It's usually the job of women and children to spend several hours a day walking to collect the fuel. An alternative is a solar cooker like this one (below). The huge dish-shaped mirror gathers the Sun's hot rays and reflects them onto the cooking pot in the middle.

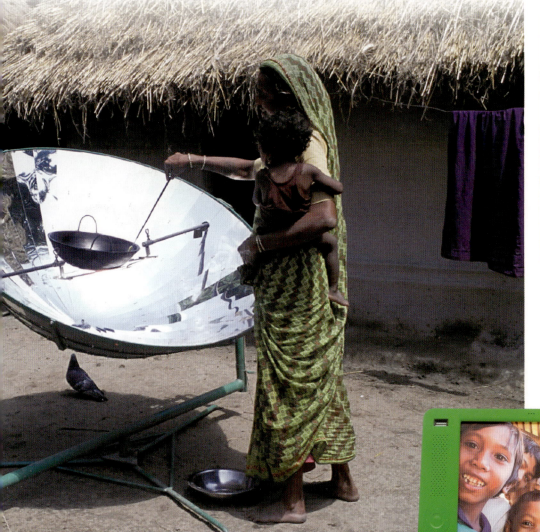

Solar lanterns

Solar lights can help people work or study at night in places with no electricity. During daytime, solar panels capture sunlight and store its power in batteries that power the light at night.

Wind-up laptop

With no electricity and few telephones or books, many children in developing countries struggle to get an education. This new, low-cost laptop could help. It's powered by a wind-up handle and has a wireless (Wi-Fi) link to the Internet.

KEF MUON SPEAKERS

Loudspeakers that sound fantastic usually come in ugly black boxes. These KEF Muons, which are among the world's most expensive speakers, are something else entirely. With curvy aluminium cases swimming in reflections, they look good enough to stand in an art gallery. Each unit contains nine separate speakers (seven in the front and two in the back) and can make as much noise as a jet aeroplane taking off. Launched in a limited edition, only 100 pairs of Muons will ever be produced.

CD ROM

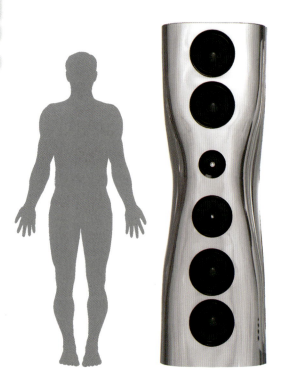

Sound sculptures

The prototype (test version) of the Muon speakers was sculpted by a computerized lathe (cutting machine) from an adult-sized block of solid aluminium. The final versions are made by a process called superforming, where giant sheets of aluminium are heated to high temperatures, bent using air pressure, and then trimmed to size.

Art of noise

The striking Muon speakers were developed by renowned British industrial designer Ross Lovegrove. Inspired by the twisting shapes he finds in nature, Lovegrove transforms humdrum products into works of art. His creations are exhibited in such places as New York's Museum of Modern Art.

FAST FACTS

Dimensions	200cm x 60cm x 38cm (79in x 24in x 16in)
Weight	115kg (253lb)
Material	Case made from 6mm-thick (0.2in) superformed aluminium
Cost	£70,000 per pair
Output	118dB

Thick, superformed aluminium back case

Ace module makes speaker sound like a much bigger and louder one

Foam pads

Internal bracing

250mm (9in) bass drivers (woofers) produce low bass notes

Two bass speaker units at rear bounce sound off walls and around listener

Connection jacks to hi-fi

Internal bracing reduces vibrations

Rolled foam and foam pads help to reduce unwanted vibrations

Thick, superformed aluminium front case

How it works

The working part of a speaker is called the driver. It has a tough paper cone with a wire coil attached to its narrow end. Behind the coil, there is a permanent magnet. When electrical signals from the hi-fi flow through the coil, they turn it into a temporary magnet. Its magnetism pushes and pulls against the magnetism of the permanent magnet, making the cone move in and out.

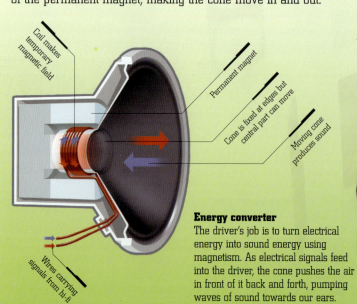

Coil makes temporary magnetic field

Permanent magnet

Cone is fixed at edges but central part can move

Moving cone produces sound

Wires carrying signals from hi-fi

Sound in motion

A speaker cone moves too fast to see – up to 20,000 times per second. If you balanced some light polystyrene balls on the cone, you would be able to see them jumping up and down as the cone moves in and out.

Energy converter

The driver's job is to turn electrical energy into sound energy using magnetism. As electrical signals feed into the driver, the cone pushes the air in front of it back and forth, pumping waves of sound towards our ears.

LOOK INSIDE

250mm (9in) bass driver (woofer)

Coil

Dust cap stops dust and fluff entering speaker system

250mm (9in) bass driver (woofer)

Coil made from copper-coated aluminium wire

165mm (6.5in) mid-range driver produces medium-range notes

Paper cone vibrates to produce sound

Sound-dispersing horn

Central driver is two drivers in one: a 165mm (6.5in) mid-range driver and a 25mm (0.9in) high-frequency driver (tweeter) that produces high treble notes

Outer ring seals speaker securely in case

Central chrome plug improves sound

250mm (9in) lower-mid-range driver produces voices and other low and medium notes

250mm (9in) bass driver (woofer)

250mm (9in) bass driver (woofer)

Magnet made from neodymium, a rare-earth metal

Cast aluminium basket holds speaker components together rigidly

Fabric suspension cushions cone when it moves back and forth

Rubber cone surround allows cone to move back and forth

Nine in one

Bigger drivers make lower notes than smaller ones. To produce the full range of notes (sound frequencies), the Muons have nine drivers of varying sizes. Seven large drivers called woofers produce deep bass notes. A lower-mid-range driver produces notes in the range the human voice makes. Finally, a single, tiny driver called a tweeter is built into the centre of another mid-range driver to make high treble notes.

SOUND WORLD

Birds chirping, friends laughing, sirens blaring, drums beating – our world is swimming with sounds that carry information. Animals interpret sounds to warn them of approaching dangers, but not all creatures hear things the same way. Snakes, for example, can hear through the muscles in their bellies, while crickets' "ears" are just below their knees! Human ears are sophisticated organs that allow us to hear sounds in stereo. They work like loudspeakers in reverse. Incoming sounds move our eardrums back and forth to make electrical signals, which our brains decode to give us the experience of hearing. Since the 19th century, we've developed sound equipment outside our bodies using science. With amazing loudspeakers and sound-recording machines, we can now make sounds and listen to them whenever and wherever we like.

Soundscape

Using a system with four or more loudspeakers, you can create a three-dimensional "sound landscape". Your brain is fooled into thinking you're outside in the real world, instead of sitting still in your living room. This effect, known as surround sound, is used to add realism and excitement to many adventure films.

Big noise

Rock bands have to make enough noise to fill stadiums packed with thousands of people. Their microphones and instruments feed sounds into electrical amplifiers, which boost the noise many times. These amplified signals then drive huge loudspeakers that recreate the original sounds many times louder.

Milestones

Phonograph cylinders

Although the great American inventor Thomas Edison (1847–1931) had hearing problems, he pioneered the idea of recording sounds so people could listen to things any time they wanted to. His mechanical phonograph, invented in 1877, recorded sounds onto a cylinder covered with tinfoil.

Gramophone

Gramophones replaced the phonograph cylinder in the 1910s. They played music by running a needle through a spiral-shaped groove in a circular plastic disc. The sounds were made louder by feeding them into a huge, trumpet-shaped horn.

Sound of silence

These noise-cancelling headphones (above) use a microphone and electronics to silence outside noises. The headphones play a reversed version of the noise into the pilot's ears, cancelling out unwanted sounds almost entirely.

Recording studios

Musicians can make complex music tracks by recording different instruments separately and then "mixing" the recordings together. In the studio, engineers use computerized desks to alter the sounds when they are played back through speakers or headphones.

Micro-speakers

A hearing aid has a microphone on the outside that picks up the sounds a deaf person cannot normally hear. The sounds are amplified and passed to a tiny loudspeaker, which plays them back much louder inside the person's ear canal.

Record players

Compact record players first appeared in the 1950s. Like gramophones, they used a needle to play back sound from flat plastic records. Instead of horns, they used small electric loudspeakers to amplify the sound.

Walkman

Sony invented the Walkman music player in 1979. People could now take their music anywhere. The walkman played back sound stored on magnetic tape through headphones.

MP3 player

The first MP3 player was made in 1998. MP3 players can store hundreds or thousands of music tracks in compressed (electronically squeezed) computer files. The tracks can be listened to using speakers or tiny earbud headphones.

Stop lever

Yoke

Hammer

Oscillating pinion

Minute counter jumper

Screw for minute counter jumper

Pallet fork

Chronograph wheel friction

Clutch

Winding crown

Barrel ratchet wheel

Hammer

Upper auto bridge

Precision gears

Chronograph bridge

Operating lever spring

Barrel and mainspring

Yoke

Pin

Hammer spring

Operating lever

Pusher

Pusher spring

Oscillating
weight

Crown gasket

Case middle

BREITLING

Screw for
ball bearing

Case back

BREITLINGWATCH

Time machine

The case of a Breitling is meticulously made. It's stamped from a single sheet of super-strong steel alloy or titanium by weights totalling 435 tonnes. It is then bathed and cleaned nine times and polished 15 times. The case alone consists of 59 separate parts.

Tick tock, tick tock – most watches speak the same language. If Breitling watches could talk, you sense they'd have more to say. Their movement (inner mechanism) contains more than 140 high-precision pieces. Even the simplest parts, the hands, are diamond-polished and machined by computer to an accuracy of less than one-thirtieth of a hair's breadth. It takes 41 painstaking processes to give a watch like this its "voice".

Crystal clear

The "glass" on a Breitling watch is actually a scratch-resistant sapphire crystal. Microscopically fine powder is grown into stalactite-shaped crystals that are sliced like salami, then ground and polished into shape. The slices are then coated on both sides to cut out 99 per cent of the glare from reflected light.

FAST FACTS

Materials	Steel case and bracelet
Diameter	44mm (1.7in)
Weight	120g (4.2oz)
Water resistant	300m (1,000ft)
Cost	£2,500–£21,000

It's automatic

This watch gets its power from the movement of your wrist. As you turn your hand, a heavy weight inside rotates back and forth, turning gears that store energy in a spring. This energy is slowly released to power the watch.

How it works

A watch like this stores power from the winding weight in its powerful mainspring. As the spring slowly unwinds, it drives a train of gears that powers a timekeeping mechanism called the escapement, built around a very fine hairspring. This expands and contracts, like a tiny beating heart, and drives precision gears that sweep the hands around the clock.

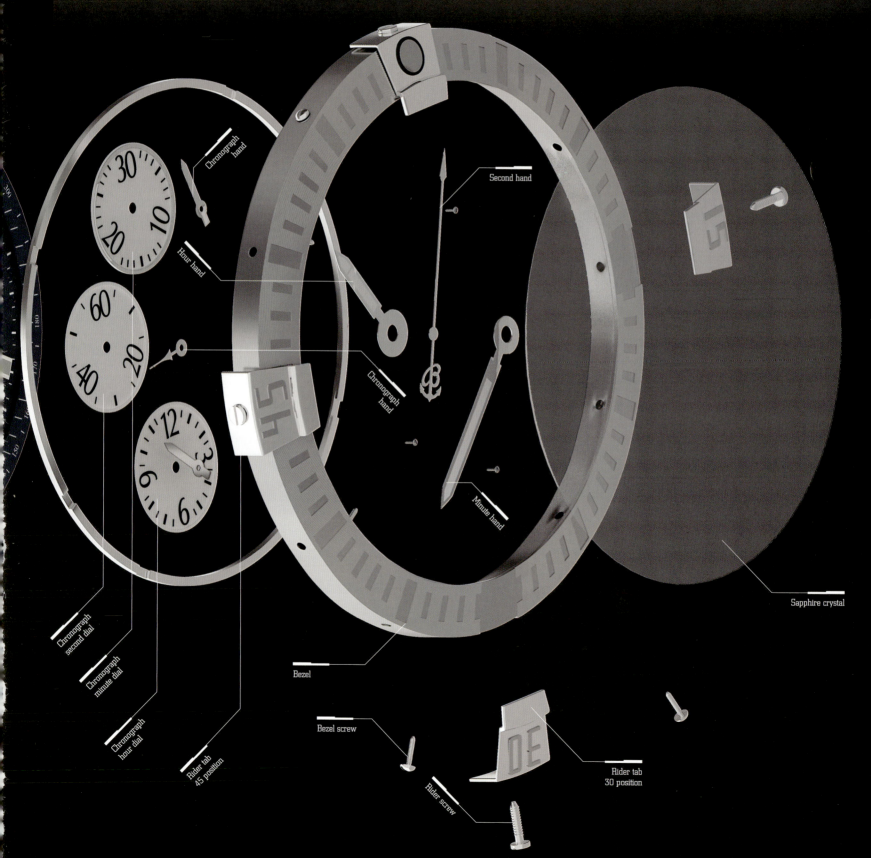

Chronograph hand

Second hand

Hour hand

Chronograph hand

Minute hand

Chronograph second dial

Chronograph minute dial

Chronograph hour dial

Rider tab 45 position

Bezel

Bezel screw

Rider screw

Rider tab 30 position

Sapphire crystal

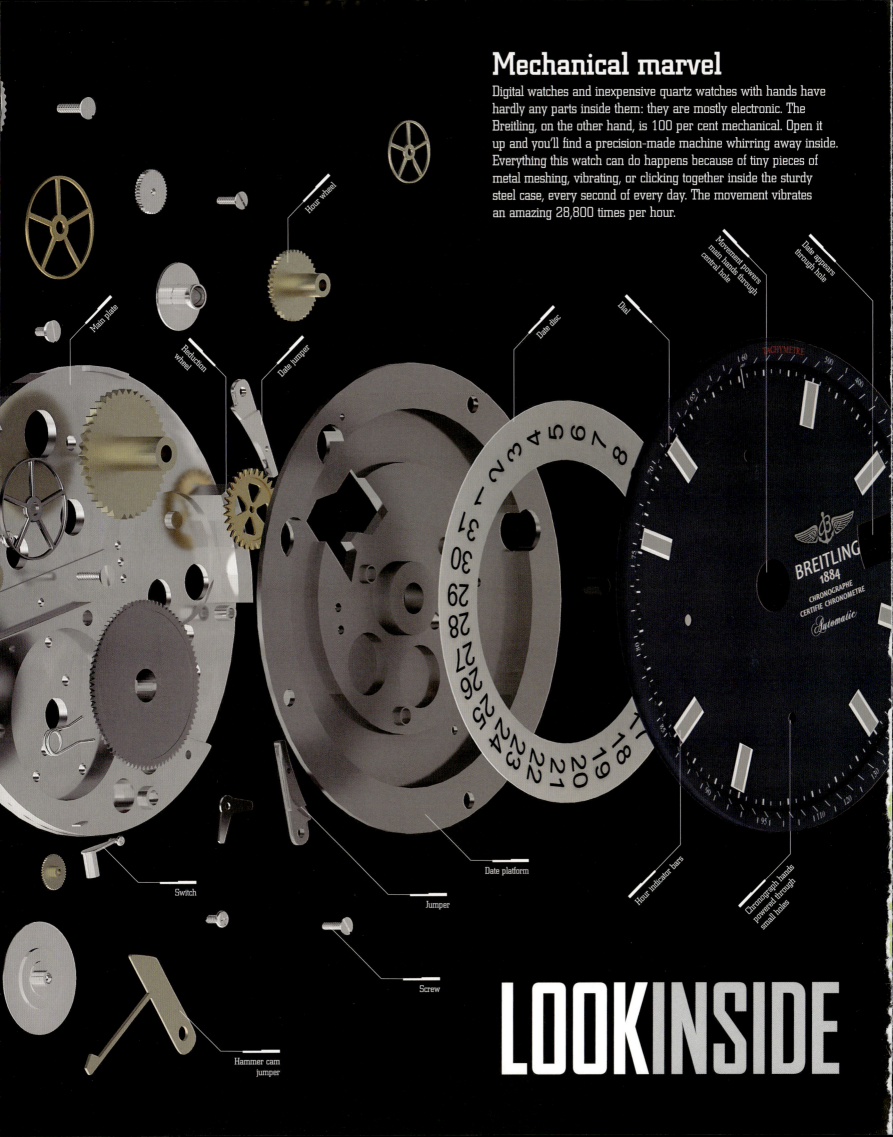

Mechanical marvel

Digital watches and inexpensive quartz watches with hands have hardly any parts inside them: they are mostly electronic. The Breitling, on the other hand, is 100 per cent mechanical. Open it up and you'll find a precision-made machine whirring away inside. Everything this watch can do happens because of tiny pieces of metal meshing, vibrating, or clicking together inside the sturdy steel case, every second of every day. The movement vibrates an amazing 28,800 times per hour.

Hour wheel

Main plate

Reduction wheel

Date jumper

Date disc

Dial

Movement powers main hands through central hole

Date appears through hole

Switch

Jumper

Date platform

Hour indicator bars

Chronograph hands powered through small holes

Screw

Hammer cam jumper

TACHYMETRE

BREITLING
1884
CHRONOGRAPHE
CERTIFIE CHRONOMETRE
Automatic

LOOKINSIDE

TAKING TIME

Thanks to long-distance travel and communication technologies such as the telegraph, telephone, and Internet, people have found themselves telling time in increasingly sophisticated ways. In ancient times, it was fine to measure hours vaguely with the creeping shadow of a sundial or a trickle of sand grains. In the modern world, we count seconds with quartz watches and nanoseconds using the super-accurate pulses of atomic clocks. Time moves no faster, but we're more aware of it passing than ever before.

Atomic clock

In an old-fashioned clock, the pendulum swings roughly once a second. In an atomic clock, atoms of the chemical element caesium "swing" back and forth more than 9 billion times each second. The best atomic clocks lose only one second in 20 million years!

Milestones of sound

Sundial
Thousands of years ago, people saw the heavens as one big clock and told time by watching the Sun, Moon, and stars. Ancient monuments such as Stonehenge may have been built as giant Sun clocks. This ornate sundial is typical of the "watches" sailors used to tell time in the 17th century.

Sand clock
Before accurate clocks appeared, hourglasses like this were used to measure short periods of time. Each glass drains sand in exactly 15 minutes, so the whole clock can keep time accurately for an hour. It was made in Italy from finely carved ebony and ivory.

Shipping time

To measure longitude (your east-west position) accurately, you need to know the time. This meant that navigating the seas was a risky business until Englishman John Harrison (1693–1776) developed the chronometer, a clock that could keep time on rough seas. Watches like the Breitling, which many pilots wear to help them navigate, are the modern-day equivalent.

Railway time

Originally, every place in the world kept its own time. In England, for instance, Bristol was 10 minutes behind London. When long-distance railways and telegraphs started linking cities in the 19th century, people had to agree on a shared time system and synchronize their watches.

Airport time

Thanks to jet aeroplanes, we can fly round the world so fast that we arrive before we started! This "time travel" is possible because everyone in the world tells time using an agreed system of "zones" centred on Greenwich in London.

Internet time

Time zones make no difference on the Internet – all that matters is whether you're online. Internet time divides the day into 1,000 units called ".beats" and is the same wherever you are. When it's 5pm in Tokyo, 8am in London, and 3am in New York, the Internet time is @375 .beats in all three cities.

Pendulum clock
A pendulum (swinging weight) of a certain length takes exactly the same time to move back and forth. Dutch physicist Christiaan Huygens (1629–1695) built the first pendulum clock in December 1656.

Spring-driven watch
Once people had learned to make miniature metal gears and springs, clocks shrunk into watches small enough to carry. This spring-driven watch dates from the 18th century.

Quartz electronic clock
Instead of telling time with a moving pendulum or gears, this watch counts the vibrations of a tiny quartz crystal when electricity passes through it.

ENTERTAINMENT SYSTEM

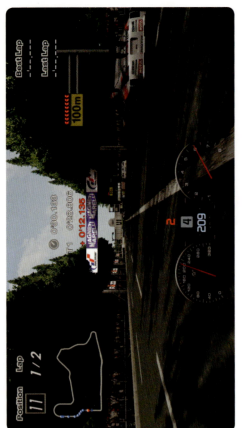

Lifelike

To produce realistic graphics, games programs need to contain a huge amount of information. To deal with all this data, the PlayStation uses a type of high-capacity DVD drive called Blu-ray. A Blu-ray disc can store 10 times more information than a normal DVD, which means game graphics can be much more detailed.

Serious games call for a serious games machine. Where an ordinary personal computer has a single microchip as its "brain", Sony's PlayStation 3 uses a more advanced chip called a cell broadband engine, split into nine parts, that can work much faster. It has roughly the same power as a supercomputer (massively powerful scientific computer) from the mid-1990s.

FAST FACTS

Memory	Hard drive: 20GB–80GB
Microprocessor	3.2GHz cell processor
Performance	218 GFLOPS
Disc media	CD, DVD, and Blu-ray
Connections	USB, Wi-Fi, and Bluetooth

PLAYSTATION 3 EVOLUTION

Power tower

The PlayStation 3 has a built-in Wi-Fi (wireless Internet) connection that lets you play games with up to 40 other people at a time, anywhere in the world. You can also download extra games, chat to your friends, and automatically update your system.

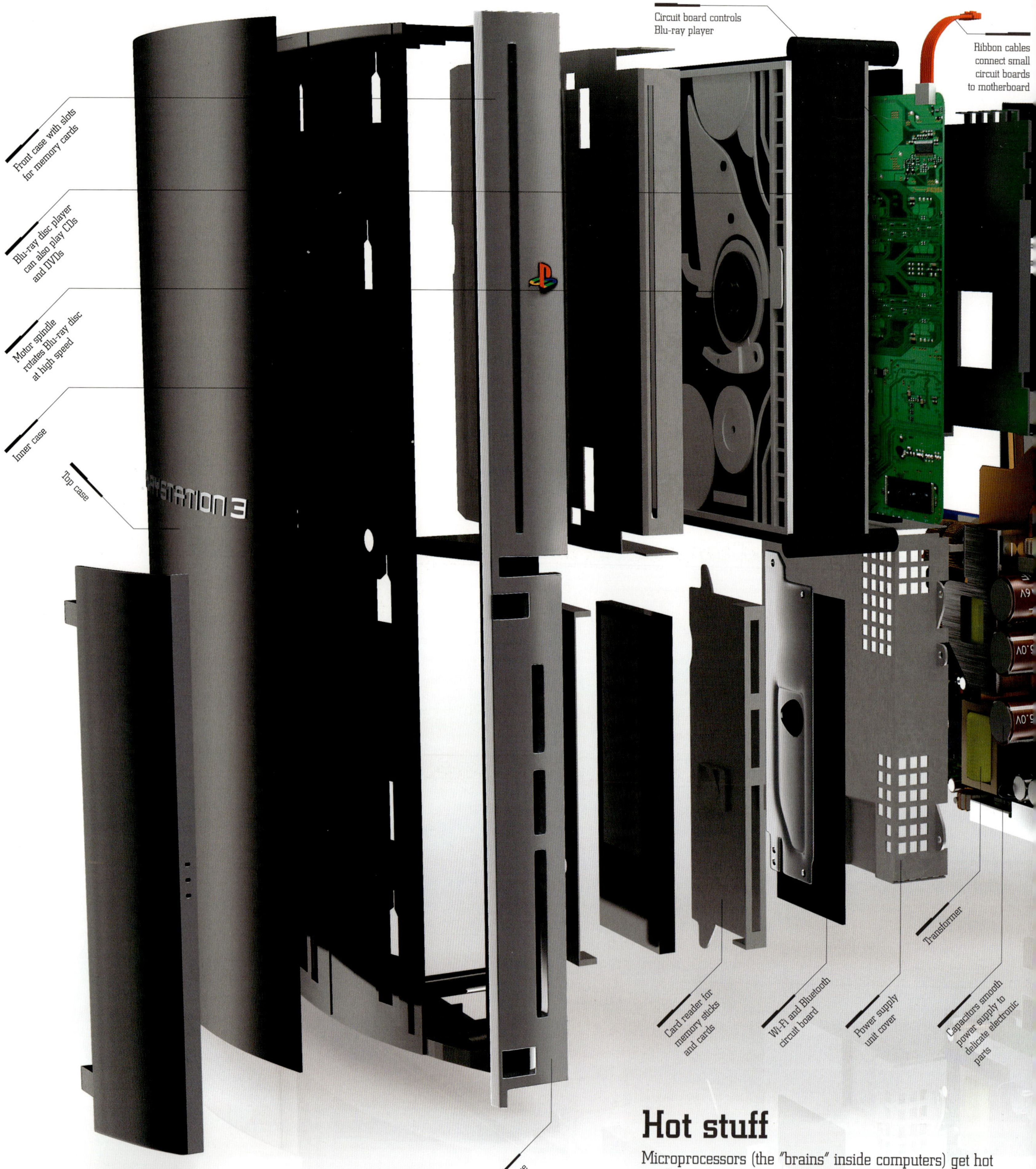

Circuit board controls
Blu-ray player

Ribbon cables
connect small
circuit boards
to motherboard

Front case with slots
for memory cards

Blu-ray disc player
can also play CDs
and DVDs

Motor spindle
rotates Blu-ray disc
at high speed

Inner case

Top case

PLAYSTATION 3

Card reader for
memory sticks
and cards

Wi-Fi and Bluetooth
circuit board

Power supply
unit cover

Transformer

Capacitors smooth
power supply to
delicate electronic
parts

Front case

LOOKINSIDE

Hot stuff

Microprocessors (the "brains" inside computers) get hot because massive amounts of electrical activity take place in a tiny space inside them. The PlayStation gets hotter than less powerful computers and needs a huge internal cooling system. The giant cooling fan at the back is several times bigger than the ones in laptop computers, and the huge copper cooling pipes also help to channel heat away.

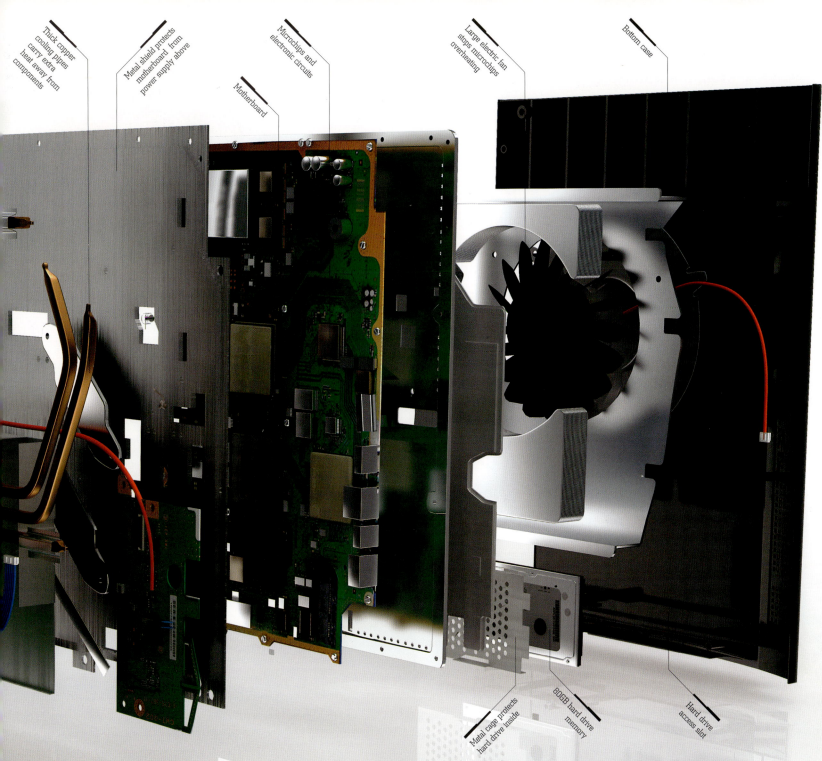

Thick copper cooling pipes carry extra heat away from components

Metal shield protects motherboard from power supply above

Motherboard

Microchips and electronic circuits

Large electric fan stops microchips overheating

Bottom case

Metal cage protects hard drive inside

80GB hard drive memory

Hard drive access slot

How it works

The most important part of the PlayStation is a powerful microprocessor chip, which consists of nine separate processors built into a single computer chip. Eight of these processors help the PlayStation to process information at blistering, supercomputer speeds. The ninth acts as a supervisor, controlling and overseeing the work of the other eight.

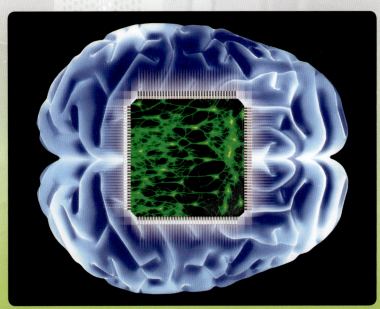

Brain power

An ordinary computer has to finish one job completely before it can start another. This is called serial processing and it's sometimes very slow. The eight processors in the PlayStation can work on several different jobs at once so they finish much faster. This is called parallel processing and it's how our brains work.

GAME ON

Playing computer games may be fun, but it's also a serious business – a leading entertainment industry worth billions to the world economy. Computer games used to be things you could play only by yourself. Now, thanks to the Internet, millions of us go online each day to play with people we've never met on the other side of the world. As more and more people discover the Internet, and games move from consoles to handheld devices such as mobile phones, computer games will become even more popular.

Go anywhere

Unlike a hefty PlayStation, this handheld Nintendo DS is light enough to take anywhere. It has a bright display, touchscreen input, and wireless Internet access. The battery lasts 19 hours – long enough to survive the most boring journey!

Cyber cafés

Cyber cafés are very popular in Asian countries, especially with young people who want to play games or access the Internet. In democratic countries such as South Korea and Japan, people can use the Internet freely, but in nations like China, Vietnam, and Burma, governments monitor access and block any websites they disapprove of.

Bad for you?

Some people argue that video games may cause problems, such as bad eyesight, if you play them too much. However, research has found that strategy games can improve children's thinking and reasoning, while online games boost social skills (dealing with other people).

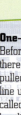

Milestones

One-armed bandit (1880s)
Before computer games were invented, there were mechanical slot machines. You pulled a metal lever on the side to try to line up coloured wheels and win a prize called the jackpot. Also known as one-armed bandits, machines like this are still popular in arcades today.

Pong (1970s)
Pong (computerized ping-pong) became the first widely popular computer game in 1972. Originally a coin-operated arcade game, it was later sold as a console that plugged into a home TV.

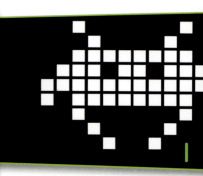

Serious play

Hardware (equipment) and software (programs) developed for playing games can be used to help the disabled and people with other special needs. Playing games can also help people recover strength and coordination after accidents and illnesses.

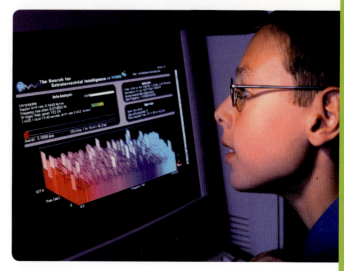

Aliens online

Is there life out in space? A project called SETI@home (Search for Extra-Terrestrial Intelligence at home) aims to find out. It uses spare time and processing power on people's home computers to search telescope data for alien signals.

Supercomputer

Computer games consoles are as powerful today as supercomputers used to be in the mid-1990s. You might have the power of this Cray supercomputer (above) in your home!

Space Invaders (1980s)
By the early 1980s, computers were fast, affordable, and had colour screens. *Space Invaders* was a popular 1980s game in which you had to fight off an attack from flying aliens. It was one of the first computer games to have sound effects.

Myst (1990s)
In the 1990s, games with stunning artwork came on compact discs. In one best-seller, *Myst*, the player had to solve mysteries on a fantasy island.

Virtual reality
Virtual reality (VR) uses headsets and other interactive devices such as gloves to fully immerse you in a computer-generated world. Although the technology is still in development, future games may use VR to create a more realistic experience than ever before.

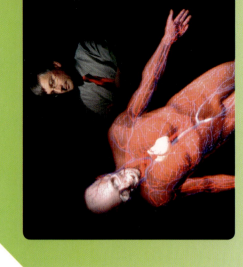

Body double

Holograms have many important practical uses. Doctors at the University of Calgary, Canada, are building detailed holographic models of the body to help them study diseases. They can even "walk around" inside computer reconstructions of cells, body tissues, and entire organs.

Graphics processing circuit board and memory chips

Casing to protect electronics

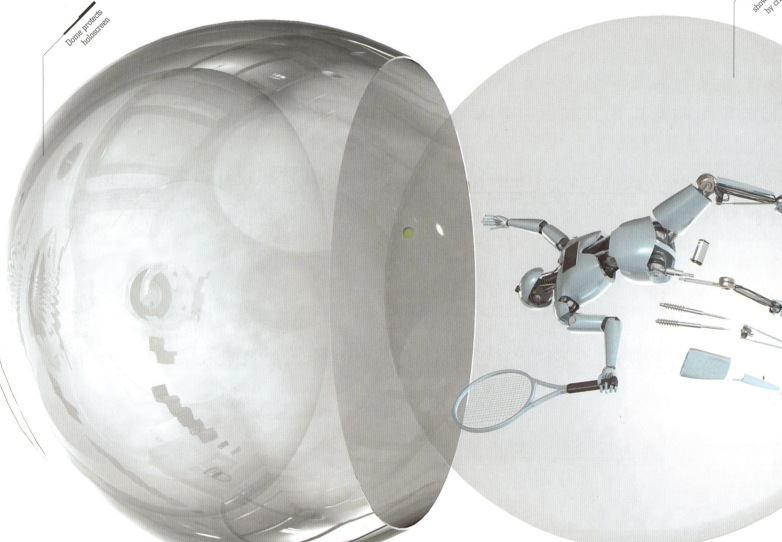

Dome protects holoscreen

Projection screen shows image made by criss-crossing laser beams

Holograms

Holograms, like the security pictures you may have seen on credit cards, are 3-D images that seem to be frozen inside plastic or glass. They are made by scanning laser beams over objects. Unlike a normal photograph, which is just a pattern of light and dark, a hologram stores all the details of the laser light waves reflected from objects. Realistic, 3-D images of those objects can be recreated by shining light onto the hologram. In this 3-D television, holograms are created moment by moment inside the glass viewing bubble when laser beams cross over in mid-air.

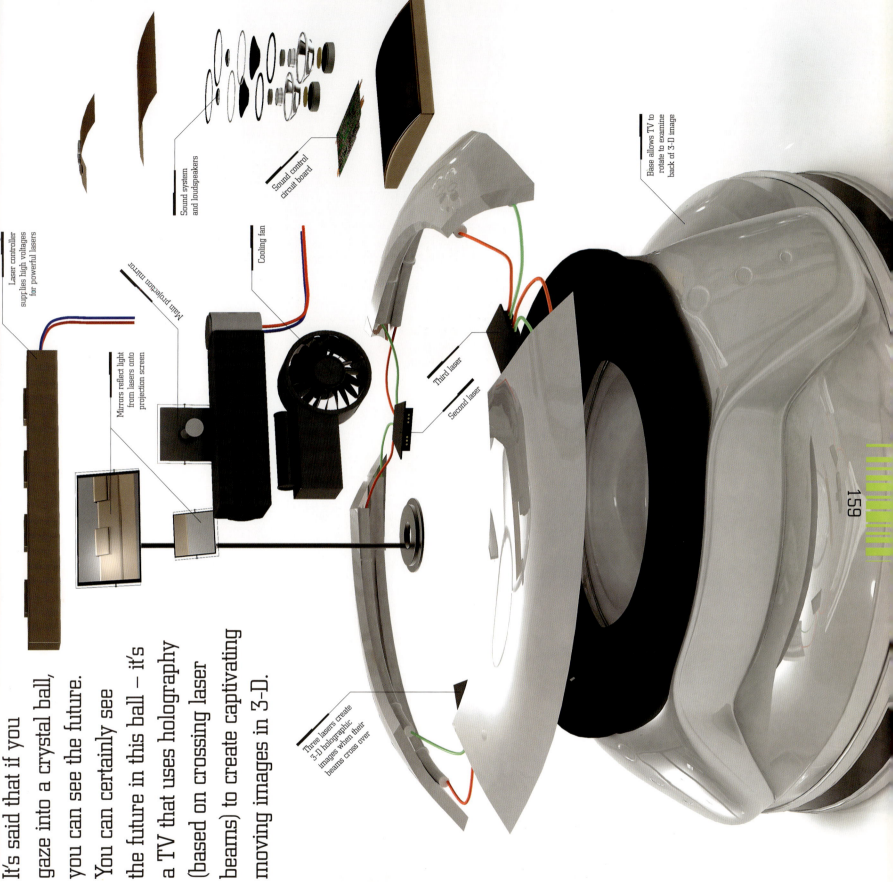

It's said that if you gaze into a crystal ball, you can see the future. You can certainly see the future in this ball – it's a TV that uses holography (based on crossing laser beams) to create captivating moving images in 3-D.

Laser controller supplies high voltages for powerful lasers

Main projection mirror

Mirrors reflect light from lasers onto projection screen

Cooling fan

Sound control circuit board

Sound system and loudspeakers

Third laser

Second laser

Three lasers create 3-D holographic images when their beams cross over

Base allows TV to rotate to examine back of 3-D image

FUTURE HOLOGRAPHIC TV

Pleasure centre

Experiments with animals are very controversial, but they can sometimes help us learn more about ourselves. In 1954, American scientists Peter Milner and James Olds tried an experiment where they allowed rats to give tiny electric shocks to their own brains by pressing a switch. Instead of hating the shocks, the rats loved them, and pressed the switches more than 2,000 times an hour. This is because the shocks triggered the rats' brains to release a pleasure-giving chemical called dopamine. Our brains release similar feel-good chemicals. This may explain why we like to do things we enjoy again and again.

Creative play

Everyone can be creative – it just means doing things in original, surprising, and fun new ways. This sculpture is a good example of all three. It was made out of pencils by South-African-born artist Jennifer Maestre.

Work or play

People enjoy their work when they do it in creative ways, making it feel more like play. That could mean something as simple as decorating your desk, or you may invent a new way to do your job that is unique to you. For example, scientists have found that chefs find their job more rewarding when they spend time arranging food attractively on the plate.

PLAY TIME

Watch a footballer shooting for goal, a dancer spinning across the stage, or a pianist pounding the keys, and you'll see people at the very peak of their powers. When we do things we love, even work feels like play. But why do we need to play and why is it so much fun? Children play to discover how the world works. Adults play too – and scientists have been studying them to work out why they enjoy it so much.

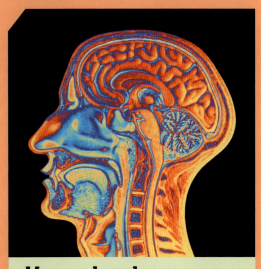

Happy heads

Images such as this one are produced by scanners to show which parts of people's brains are active when they are happy, angry, or sad. Scientists have found that these emotions are complex and can be produced by many different combinations of brain activity.

Endorphins

When we push our bodies to their limits, our brains release natural painkillers called endorphins into our bloodstream, which make us feel better. Scientists believe that people may choose to do frightening activities such as parachute jumping and rock climbing to produce a release of pleasure-giving endorphins.

Learning to play

Stress at work can cause serious health problems, but people often find it hard to relax and sometimes need encouragement to take time off work. Postcards and posters such as this one give us some ideas about how we might enjoy our leisure time.

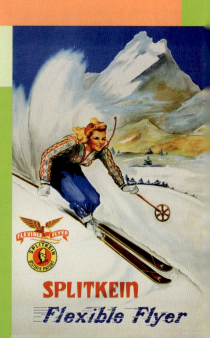

SPLITKEIN
Flexible Flyer

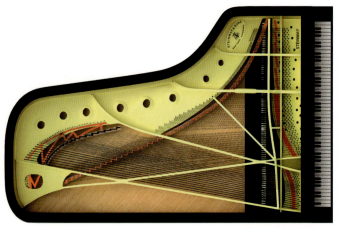

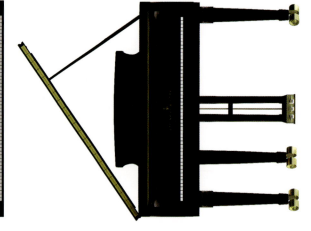

STEINWAY PIANO

Musicians are only as good as the instruments they play, so the finest pianists demand the finest pianos. A thousand tiny details make a Steinway grand piano the instrument of choice for 90 per cent of the world's professionals. The case, for example, comes in a choice of 11 different wood finishes. They include everything from rich, golden satinwood, patterned like a bee's wing, to the deep, dark shine of ebony veneer (shown here). All the veneer is carved from a single tree to ensure the case polishes up to perfection. Such careful craftsmanship pays dividends – Steinway grand pianos have gained more in value over time than vintage cars, fine wines, and even gold! Lovingly built by hand, an instrument like this takes a year to make – and will last for a lifetime.

Cast iron

One essential part of a piano is a heavy cast iron plate (the part with holes in). The 200 or so strings pull inwards with 20,581kg (45,373lb) of tension. This is a force equivalent to that of three elephants sitting on the case, and without the iron plate, the piano would implode.

In the bank

Steinway maintains a "bank" of 300 pianos across North America that pianists can borrow for performances. They simply choose one they like from the nearest dealer. Chinese pianist Lang Lang (1982–) is shown here testing a piano in the Steinway basement in New York City.

FAST FACTS

Length	274cm (8ft 11¾in)
Width	156cm (5ft 1¼in)
Weight	480kg (990lb)
Cost	£50,000–£75,000

LOOK INSIDE

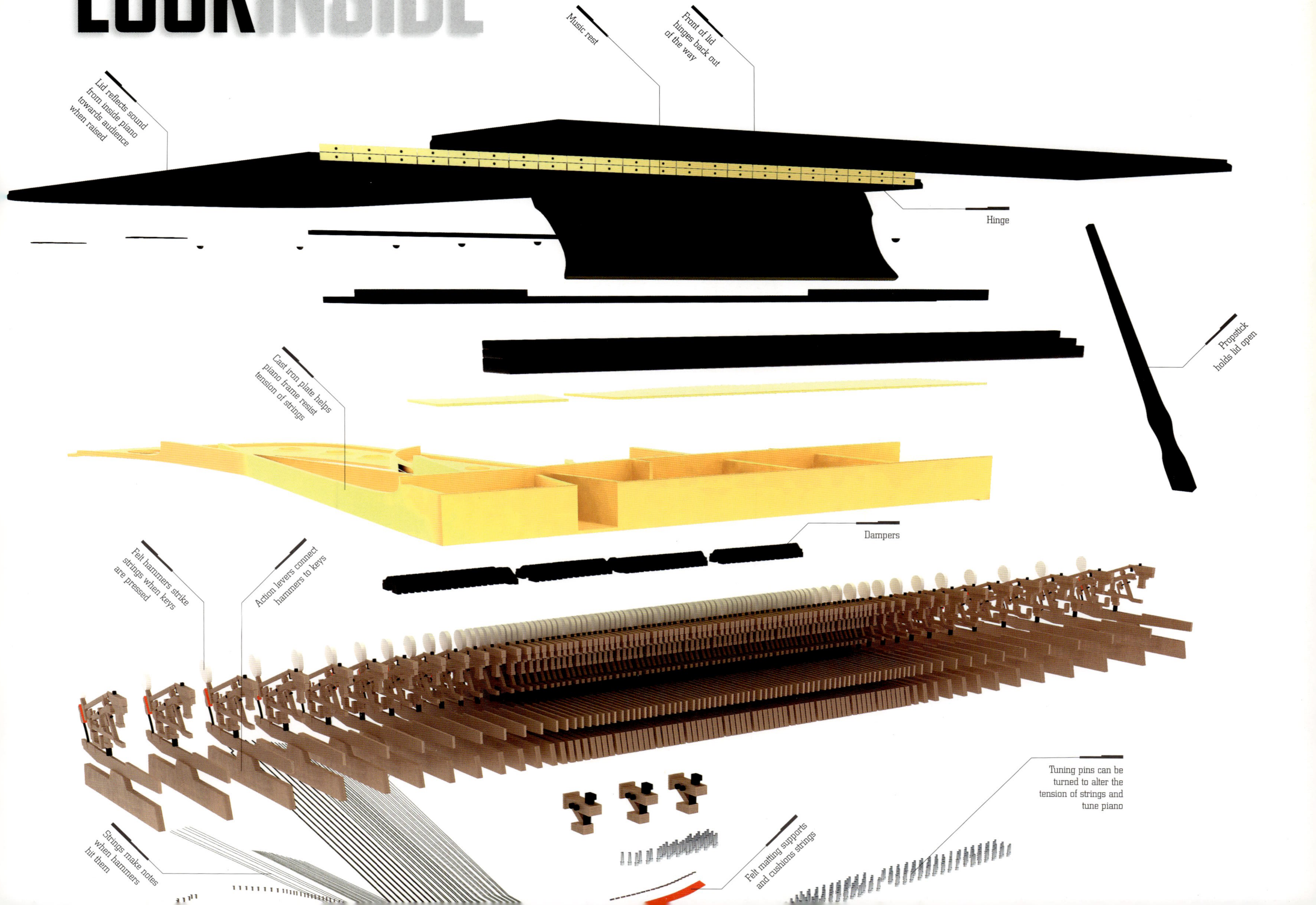

Propstick holds lid open

Hinge

Front of lid hinges back out of the way

Music rest

Lid reflects sound from inside piano towards audience when raised

Cast iron plate helps piano frame resist tension of strings

Dampers

Action levers connect hammers to keys

Felt hammers strike strings when keys are pressed

Strings make notes when hammers hit them

Tuning pins can be turned to alter the tension of strings and tune piano

Felt matting supports and cushions strings

Making notes

When you press a key, it pushes a lever. The middle of the lever flicks a hammer up, which vibrates the string and makes a note. The back of the lever pushes up a felt damper above the string. When the key is released, the damper falls back and stops the vibration to end the note.

Hammer

Key

Damper

Lever

How it works

A piano is a string instrument, because strings make the sounds you hear. But it's also a percussion instrument because the strings are hit by tiny hammers linked to the keys you press. Each key hits up to three strings when pressed, giving a richer sound.

Right sustain pedal makes all notes last longer by holding all the dampers up

Middle pedal makes pressed keys produce longer-lasting notes

Left, soft pedal

Pedal lyre rods operate soft and sustain mechanisms when you press pedals

Lyre block houses pedals

Lyre pillar supports pedals

Black keys play sharp and flat notes

White keys play notes A to G

Keyboard lid

Bridge holds strings above soundboard so they vibrate freely

Soundboard, made of spruce wood amplifies the sounds the strings make

Rear leg

Castors make it easy to move piano, which weighs as much as seven men

Rear leg block

Sturdy wooden case covered in polished veneer

Laminated rim made from layers of hard maple wood bent by hand

Under the lid

There are more than 12,000 parts in a Steinway piano, most of them hidden from view. Some parts help to generate the musical sounds. Others change the quality of those sounds. When you press the pedals, these parts can make the sound quieter or keep a note going after you stop pressing the key. You might think that the lid is simply there to keep the dust out, but it, too, has an important job to do: reflecting sound towards the audience.

PIANOPLAY

Many great composers, including Mozart and Beethoven, were also great pianists. But pianos are not just used to play classical music: you can find them everywhere from churches to schools and bars. One reason they're so popular is the sweeping scale of 88 keys – big enough for two hands to play two separate tunes, which is impossible on most instruments.

Pianola

Player pianos (or pianolas) were invented in the late 19th century for people who liked piano music but couldn't play. These intricate automated machines played themselves by reading patterns of holes punched in reels of paper.

Synthesizer

French musician Jean-Michel Jarre (1948–) (right) helped to popularize electronic music in the 1970s. The synthesizers he plays are electronic keyboards that can create any sound you can imagine and modify existing sounds in unusual ways. Electronic music dates back to the early 20th century, when inventors made the first electronic instruments from radio parts.

Milestones

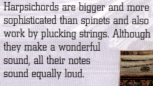

Spinet
Keyboard instruments such as the spinet made music by plucking strings. Using a simple mechanism, pressing each key caused a different string to be plucked. Spinets had about half as many keys as a modern piano and date from the early 17th century.

Harpischord
Harpsichords are bigger and more sophisticated than spinets and also work by plucking strings. Although they make a wonderful sound, all their notes sound equally loud.

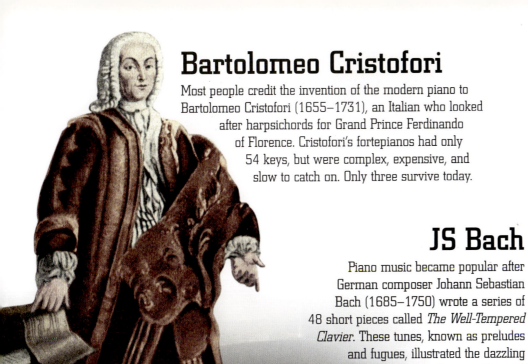

Bartolomeo Cristofori

Most people credit the invention of the modern piano to Bartolomeo Cristofori (1655–1731), an Italian who looked after harpsichords for Grand Prince Ferdinando of Florence. Cristofori's fortepianos had only 54 keys, but were complex, expensive, and slow to catch on. Only three survive today.

JS Bach

Piano music became popular after German composer Johann Sebastian Bach (1685–1750) wrote a series of 48 short pieces called *The Well-Tempered Clavier*. These tunes, known as preludes and fugues, illustrated the dazzling possibilities of what was then still a relatively new instrument.

John Cage

Musicians are still finding new ways to use pianos. In the 20th century, radical American composer John Cage (1912–1992) popularized the use of a "prepared piano". This involves changing the sound of a piano in striking ways by placing nuts, bolts, and other objects under the strings.

Fortepiano
Bartolomeo Cristofori developed the harpsichord into a more versatile instrument that could play both loud and soft notes, which he called a *gravicembalo col piano e forte* (harpsichord with soft and loud). Known as a fortepiano, it was smaller and quieter than a modern piano.

Upright piano
Before recorded music was invented, many bars employed pianists, who played upright pianos such as this. The mechanisms were built into compact, upright cases.

Modern electronic piano
Table-top keyboards such as this one make sounds using electronic circuits and small speakers. With almost no moving parts, they are much less expensive than pianos.

GIBSON ELECTRIC GUITAR

Six-string sound

Traditional acoustic guitars have hollow wooden bodies and make broadly the same sound however they are played. The notes they make last only as long as the guitar vibrates when you pluck the string. Electric guitars are very different. Their six steel strings can make a huge range of sounds, from thumping bass notes and staccato rhythms to high-pitched screams like a human voice. The notes can last as long as the guitar player wants because their sounds are produced electrically.

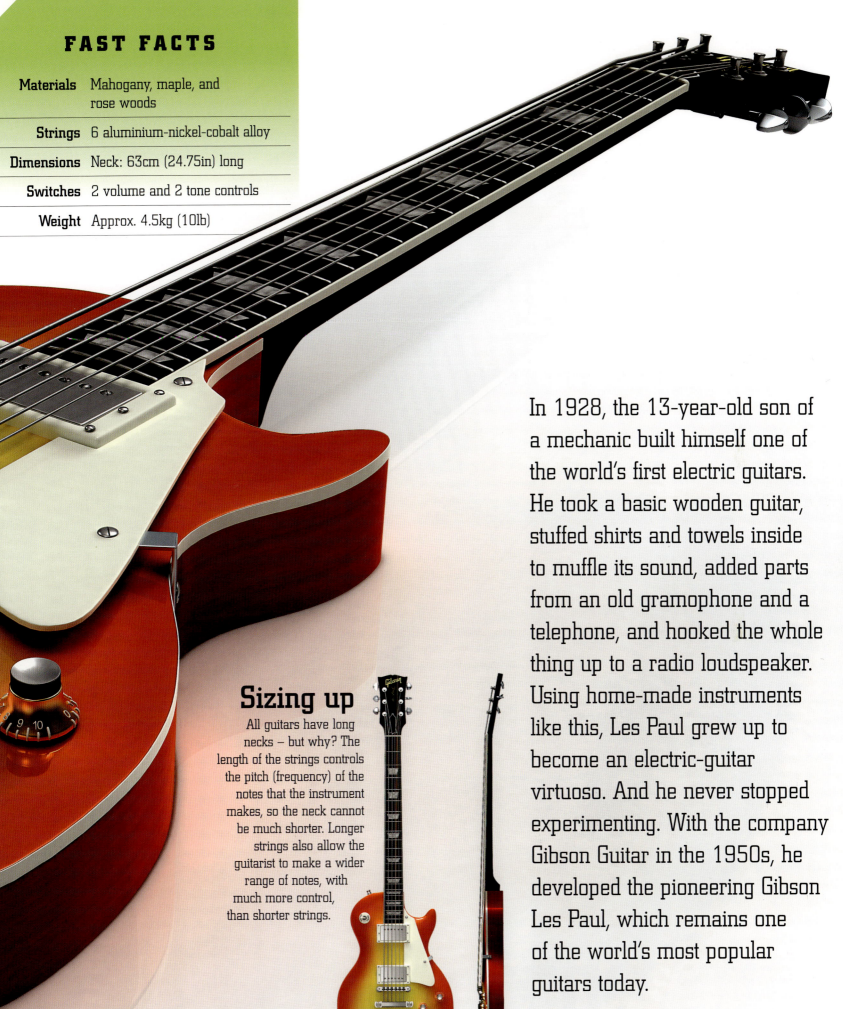

FAST FACTS

Materials	Mahogany, maple, and rose woods
Strings	6 aluminium-nickel-cobalt alloy
Dimensions	Neck: 63cm (24.75in) long
Switches	2 volume and 2 tone controls
Weight	Approx. 4.5kg (10lb)

Sizing up

All guitars have long necks – but why? The length of the strings controls the pitch (frequency) of the notes that the instrument makes, so the neck cannot be much shorter. Longer strings also allow the guitarist to make a wider range of notes, with much more control, than shorter strings.

In 1928, the 13-year-old son of a mechanic built himself one of the world's first electric guitars. He took a basic wooden guitar, stuffed shirts and towels inside to muffle its sound, added parts from an old gramophone and a telephone, and hooked the whole thing up to a radio loudspeaker. Using home-made instruments like this, Les Paul grew up to become an electric-guitar virtuoso. And he never stopped experimenting. With the company Gibson Guitar in the 1950s, he developed the pioneering Gibson Les Paul, which remains one of the world's most popular guitars today.

LOOK INSIDE

Pickup power

The magnets in the pickup generate a magnetic field (pattern of magnetism) that stretches up through the strings. When the guitar strings move, they cut through and change the magnetic field. The changing field makes a burst of electricity flow through a coil of wire wrapped around the pickup.

Magnet in pickup

Signals travel to amplifier.

Magnetic field

Magnetic field

Guitar string

Coil of wire

How it works

A typical electric guitar makes sounds using two electromagnetic devices called pickups. When you pluck one of the guitar strings, the pickups sense its vibrations and produce electrical signals. These feed out into the amplifier connected to the guitar, which boosts them in strength and makes a noise loud enough to hear.

Strings attached

An electric guitar has a sturdy wooden neck to keep the strings taut, while the large body is shaped so the instrument is easy to cradle and play. The pickups underneath the strings make the electric sound signals. These signals travel from the pickups to the amplifier through a simple electrical circuit hidden inside the guitar's body.

Nuts hold strings at top

Frets help with accurate note play

Strings

Headstock

Machine head (tuning peg) adjusts tension of string and tunes guitar.

Neck

Fretboard inlays made of pearl

Fretboard

Rear pickup

Front pickup

Pickup selector switch

RHYTHM TREBLE

Saddle screws can be loosened to adjust bridge position

Bridge supports strings so they vibrate freely

Pickguard

Volume control for rear pickup

Tone control for rear pickup

Output socket connects guitar to amplifier

Inner wiring and electronics

Pickup mount

Bridge mount

Tailpiece fastens strings to case

Volume control for front pickup

Front case

Tone control for front pickup

Strap connector

THE WORLD'S FAVOURITE

People have been making music since prehistoric times, using musical instruments made from the things around them. Horns made from conch shells have been used for millennia and, in the 1990s, historians discovered a flute made from a hollowed-out bear bone that was 45,000 years old. Stone-Age people were ingenious, but they had nothing to rival the electric guitar – a music machine powerful enough to shake a stadium. Loud and angry or soft and sweet, guitars can be used to play all kinds of music, from rock and soul to jazz and folk. And a guitar is small enough to carry around. No wonder it's the world's favourite instrument.

Les Paul

Now in his nineties, Les Paul remains one of the world's best-loved guitarists. With painful arthritis in his hands, he can no longer play chords the way he used to. Even so, he still won two Grammy awards in 2006 for his latest album – aged 91!

Ancient ancestors

Electric guitars were invented in the 20th century, based on six-string acoustic guitars developed a century or so before. These, in turn, evolved from string instruments such as the mandolin and lute (right). Popular in Renaissance Europe, the lute can be traced back to ancient Egyptian times.

Cheap and cheerful

Many people learn to play acoustic (classical) guitars like these (above) before moving on to electric guitars. Acoustic guitars are quieter than electric ones, but they are cheaper and easier to carry around as they don't need an electric amplifier.

Guitar heroes

Electric guitars make music – but they also make a statement. Rowdy and rebellious, guitar-driven rock has been the soundtrack to young people's lives since the 1950s. No two players sound exactly the same. The best electric guitarists, such as Keith Richards, shown here with his band The Rolling Stones, have instantly recognizable styles.

Spanish guitar
Acoustic guitars such as this are also known as Spanish or classical guitars. They have wooden bodies and six strings made from nylon or metal.

Guitar synthesizer
This unusual Roland G-707 (below) dates from the 1980s. It was played like a guitar but had a similar sound to a synthesizer.

12-string Rickenbacker
Twelve-string guitars produce a much richer tone than six-string ones. Guitars like this one (left) were popularized by The Beatles.

Otwin 4/6
This unusual instrument (right) is two guitars in one. The top part is a four-string bass, while the bottom part is a six-string rhythm guitar.

Making a guitar

Most electric guitars are moulded from solid plastic, but prestigious makes like the Gibson and acoustic guitars are still built by hand (left). The wooden sides of an acoustic guitar are bent into curves by rolling them over a hot pipe.

Variety

Electric guitars come in every shape and size. Guitars that play the melody (main tune) of a song typically have six or 12 strings, while bass guitars have four strings and play low, deep notes. Some make a mixture of electric and acoustic sounds.

LEGO ROBOT

Can you build a robot that walks like a human? It's one of the hardest problems that robot scientists have to grapple with. You can have a go too with a construction kit called LEGO Mindstorms. It comes with a programmable computer brain and 519 plastic body parts. That's still not quite as sophisticated as the human body with its 206 bones and 700 muscles, but it's a step in the right direction.

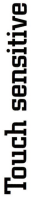

Touch sensitive

This factory-style robot arm can tell the difference between a red ball and a blue one. When its claw closes over a ball, a light sensor measures the colour. If the ball is red, the robot keeps its claw closed and carries the ball away. If the ball is blue, the robot opens its claw and drops the ball.

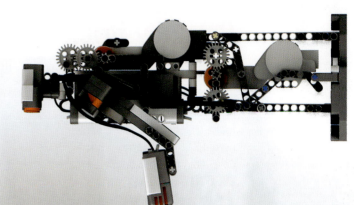

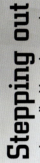

Stepping out

This LEGO robot walks like a human but works like a machine. For muscles, it has servo motors: electric motors that can move very smoothly and with great precision. Instead of a brain, it has a powerful computer in its chest called an NXT. You can connect this to an outside computer to program the robot with its instructions.

FAST FACTS

Sensors Touch, sound, light, and ultrasonic

Processor NXT computer can connect to 3 motors and 4 sensors

Power 6 AA batteries

Computer Connects to a PC with USB link or wireless Bluetooth link

Brick by brick

You can put six basic LEGO bricks together in 915 million different ways, so imagine how many different robots you can make with just the pieces shown here! LEGO Mindstorms was developed in 1998, and became LEGO NXT in 2006.

Gear wheel transmits force from servo motor

Angled bricks form shoulders

Straight bricks form upper arms

Axle allows parts to rotate

Cog to move legs

Pin fixes different parts together

Touch sensor on end of robot's arm

Servo motors control arms and legs

Servo motors control arms and legs

How it works

Robots work in broadly the same way as computers because they have computers as their "brains". To kick a ball, a robot has to follow three stages called input, processing, and output. Humans do things in a similar way, but for us, the stages are called perception, cognition, and action.

Input (perception)
First, the robot has to see the approaching object as a ball. Colour, shape, and movement help the robot to tell the difference between the ball and other nearby objects.

Processing (cognition)
Now the ball has been recognized, the robot has to decide what to do with it. It does this by following a series of instructions in its computer program.

Output (action)
The program tells the robot to move its foot forward so that it makes contact with the ball. The robot's servo motors allow it to kick the ball accurately.

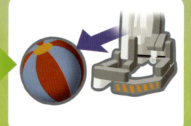

Ultrasonic sensors
work as robot's eyes

Gear wheel

Interactive servo
motor turns head

Holes allow bricks to
be fastened together

177

Microchips inside
NXT computer
controller

Cables connect
sensors and motors
to NXT controller

Control switches

Sound sensor lets
robot react to noises

Outer casing of NXT
computer controller

ROBOCULTURE

Robots seem like visitors from the future, but they're just as much a part of the past. The ancient Greeks had automata (steam-powered automatic machines) more than 2,000 years ago. Since the word "robot" was coined in 1938, scary metal monsters have appeared in many books and films. Even now, when most people think of robots, they imagine clanking contraptions taking over the world. The reality is different: robots are more likely to help us weld cars, run factories, and care for the sick. They're very much our friends, not our foes.

Magic Mike

Toy robots like this Magic Mike became hugely popular in the 1950s and 1960s, when robots started to appear in science-fiction films and TV series. Mike talks, makes space sounds, trundles along, flashes his eyes, and opens and closes his hands.

Metropolis

A German film called *Metropolis*, made in 1926, was one of the first to feature robots. Set in a bleak futuristic city in 2026, it features a robot who encourages workers in an underground city to stage a revolution.

Transformers

Transformers, a film made by Steven Spielberg in 2007, features robots who can disguise themselves as cars, trucks, and other real-world machines. Like many robot characters, the ones in *Transformers* have human-like emotions and machine-like powers.

Driving force

Robots have been helping people make cars since 1961, when the first robot was used at a General Motors factory in New Jersey, United States. Factory robots don't need bodies: they can manage with a single, computer-controlled arm.

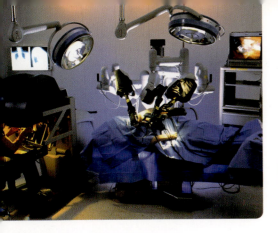

Robot surgery

Difficult medical operations call for the world's best surgeons, but what if they're in another country from the patients who need their help? Robot surgery may be the answer. The surgeon sits at a console, like a video game, controlling a robot that might be on the other side of the world. As the surgeon steers the controls, the robot carries out its instructions with utmost precision.

ASIMO

This Japanese robot is so lifelike, you might think there was a person hiding inside. About the size of a 10-year-old, ASIMO walks, runs, climbs stairs, waves, and dances with incredibly realistic movements. It's powered by a rechargeable battery that gives it an hour of life between charges.

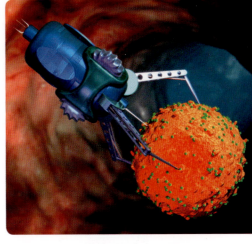

Nanorobots

Some scientists think robots will eventually be small enough to inject into our bodies. Known as nanorobots (or nanobots), they could hunt down viruses or cure illnesses that are too complex for doctors to treat from outside.

FUTURE ROBOT

If you're aiming for a gold medal, you need the world's best coach. In the future, when sportsmen and women are reaching the limits of what humans can do, robots like this could help them go further. It's a fully computerized sports coach who trains with you, videos what you do, and analyzes your performance.

Perfect partner

Robo-coach helps you practise any sport, from archery to swimming. Standing more than 2.1m (7ft) tall, it's 10 times stronger than most humans and can play non-stop sport for 36 hours until its batteries run flat. The video camera records your performance, and you can watch the playback later on the TV in the chest. Robo-coach even gives you a massage when you're tired!

Hands are strong enough to crush steel

Camera in forehead records your performance

Supercomputer brain

Robot "abdominal" muscles

3-D flatscreen display plays back performance

Electric motors operate body joints 1,000 times faster than human muscle

Body shell has matt finish so it doesn't dazzle in sunlight

Fingers can move in ways human fingers can't

Gripping stuff

It's difficult for robot designers to copy the amazing dexterity of our hands. Each human hand has 27 bones and more than 30 muscles. Our index fingers alone have seven muscles. Constant two-way communication between our hands and brains enables us to handle objects in thousands of different ways.

High-speed motors in legs give running speeds of about 60kph (40mph)

Joints are coated with friction-free nanoparticles so they never need oiling

Hydraulics and springs in leg muscles

Body shell made of titanium and aluminium alloy reduces robot to one-third human weight

Multi-axis motors give full knee movement

Kangaroo-scale feet let robot jump more than 3m (10ft) in the air

LONDON EYE

CD ROM

Spinning slowly on the South Bank of the River Thames, the London Eye has a diameter more than 150 times that of a bicycle wheel. Up to 800 people at a time can fly in the London Eye's 32 sleek glass capsules. From the top, they are treated to fantastic views right across London.

Balancing act

When you sit on a bicycle, your weight pushes down on the frame. The frame in turn balances on the wheels, supported by the spokes. The London Eye is more like a bike resting upside-down on its saddle. The wheel and capsules, which together weigh more than 300 elephants, are supported by the spokes and hub, which hang from a frame resting on the ground.

Millennium Wheel

Built to celebrate the Millennium, the London Eye was officially opened on 31 December 1999 with a spectacular firework display. A line of 2,000 precisely synchronized fireworks fired up from floating barges in sequence, making it appear as if a sheet of flames was moving up the river. This was followed by a giant display that the organizers hoped would be visible from space.

FAST FACTS

Height to top	135m (443ft)
Capsule weight	10 tonnes each
Total weight	2,100 tonnes
Rotation speed	0.9kph (0.6mph)
Time to rotate	Approx. 30 minutes

184

Steel frame

Building the Eye

Parts of the London Eye were built in six European countries before being shipped to London. They were put together a bit like flatpack furniture, using a floating crane, on a temporary "island" on the River Thames. The engineers then made the bold decision to lift the finished structure into place in a single day.

Testing, testing
Before the London Eye could be lifted, the crane's strength had to be tested. The wheel was firmly bolted to the river island and the crane pulled upwards with immense force to prove that none of the cables would break.

Going up
The London Eye was then heaved up by hydraulic jacks, which pulled on cables as they

Panels made from laminated glass

Space capsule

The London Eye is much more glamorous than an old-fashioned Ferris wheel. Each of the spacious glass capsules is fully enclosed and climate-controlled, with a mechanism underneath that keeps it perfectly level. The working parts are all under the floor, so you get an uninterrupted 360° view stretching up to 40km (25 miles) in each direction.

Two sets of batteries for emergencies

Capsule drive motor

Self-levelling stability system

LOOKINSIDE

RIDE TIME

There's nothing we like more than being scared out of our wits. Many people will pay to be flung through the air or spun around at top speed. Rides work in many different ways. We see the world from high up so it looks strange and surprising. We feel weird sensations as our bodies twist and turn. We can get all the thrills of doing something dangerous on rides designed to keep us safe.

Ferris wheel

The first Ferris wheel had an iron frame and wooden cars, and was half the size of the London Eye wheel that now stands by the River Thames. It was built in Chicago in 1893 by American bridge-builder George Ferris (1859–1896). It cost $400,000 (about £5 million today).

Icy roller coaster

On the first roller coasters, built in 15th-century Russia, you clambered up about 100 rickety stairs and whizzed back down on a sledge made of ice and straw at around 80kph (50mph).

Modern rides

This roller coaster (right) is one of many that were built in the United States in the first half of the 20th century by John A. Miller (1874–1941), the pioneer of modern roller coasters. His cars had safety brakes to stop them rolling backward and extra wheels underneath the track to stop them coming off on tight bends.

Wooden roller coaster

Wooden coasters, such as the Roar in California, United States, (left), deliberately shake and rattle to provide a truly terrifying ride. It takes just two minutes to get from one end to the other, but in that time you race down 1km (0.6 miles) of twisty track at 80kph (50mph), while feeling 3.5 times the force of gravity.

Metal rollers

Roller coasters made from super-strong steel can have more steeply twisting track and overhead corkscrew turns than wooden ones. Powered by the force of gravity, the cars can reach speeds of more than 160kph (100mph).

Zorbing

Zorbing is like a roller coaster without the track. Instead of sitting in a car, you're strapped inside a gigantic bouncy ball and pushed down a hill. You tumble head over heels till you reach the bottom.

Kingda Ka

The world's highest and fastest ride is Kingda Ka in New Jersey, United States. The cars can reach a staggering 200kph (128mph) after plunging down a vertical track three times taller than the Statue of Liberty.

Spinning stars

Roller coasters and Ferris wheels are only two of many kinds of ride. Star Flyers (above) spin 24 people at a time from a huge central tower more than 90m (300ft) off the ground.

This electron microscope view shows the complicated surface of a microchip. The coloured tracks connect the working parts of the chip together.

DIGITAL TECHNOLOGY

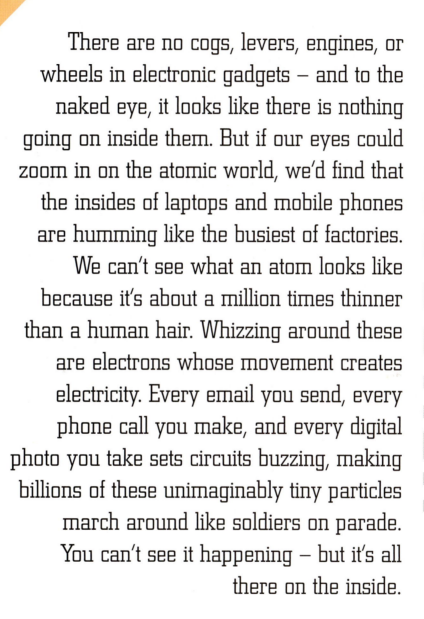

There are no cogs, levers, engines, or wheels in electronic gadgets – and to the naked eye, it looks like there is nothing going on inside them. But if our eyes could zoom in on the atomic world, we'd find that the insides of laptops and mobile phones are humming like the busiest of factories. We can't see what an atom looks like because it's about a million times thinner than a human hair. Whizzing around these are electrons whose movement creates electricity. Every email you send, every phone call you make, and every digital photo you take sets circuits buzzing, making billions of these unimaginably tiny particles march around like soldiers on parade. You can't see it happening – but it's all there on the inside.

Think thin

Phones are packed with more and more features, but they seem to get thinner and lighter every year. In 1983, a mobile phone was as big as a brick and weighed 800g (28oz). Made from strong but lightweight plastic, a modern touchscreen phone is six times lighter and slips easily into your pocket.

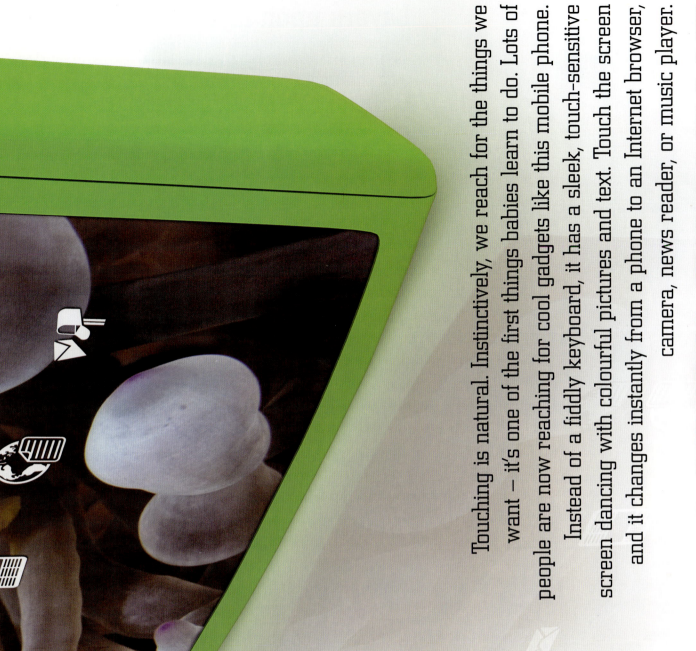

MOBILE PHONE

Touching is natural. Instinctively, we reach for the things we want – it's one of the first things babies learn to do. Lots of people are now reaching for cool gadgets like this mobile phone.

Instead of a fiddly keyboard, it has a sleek, touch-sensitive screen dancing with colourful pictures and text. Touch the screen and it changes instantly from a phone to an Internet browser, camera, news reader, or music player.

FAST FACTS

Dimensions	115mm x 61mm x 12mm (4.5in x 2.4in x 0.5in)
Weight	130g (4.6oz)
Display	9cm (3.5in) colour multi-touch
Camera	3 megapixels
Battery	Lithium-ion with 8 hours of talk time

Pocket computer

The gadgets we carry may be mobiles, but they're no longer just phones. With touchscreen technology, a mobile phone becomes as powerful and flexible as a portable computer. It can link to the Internet through the radio-wave connection that normally carries your calls, so you can send emails, browse websites, or download music and videos.

Layers upon layers

The touchscreen of a mobile phone is made up of lots of different layers. At the base, the LCD creates images and words by lighting up patterns of pixels (tiny coloured squares). The touch-sensitive transparent layer sits above it. The various other layers include shims (spacing and filling layers) to protect the LCD and touchscreen from knocks, scratches, moisture, and dirt.

Plastic frame holds display layers in place

Outer casing made of strong, durable plastic

Top layer of screen made from clear perspex

Plastic shim (filler) frames the display

Glass top cover is 0.5mm (0.02in) thick

Vertical sensor grid: protective glass 2mm (0.08in) thick with touch-sensor lines printed on top

Colour LCD screen with horizontal sensor grid on top

Metal shield protects electrical components

Foam shim cushions LCD display and sensitive components beneath

Plastic frame holds internal components in place

Scratch-resistant screen protector made from very thin plastic

Wireless – inside and out

Mobile phones are wireless: unlike landlines (non-mobile telephones), they make calls using radio waves instead of being plugged into the wall. They are also mostly wireless inside. Many parts are soldered (electrically connected) to a circuit board (a piece of plastic covered in metal connections). Other components, such as the LCD screen, plug directly into the circuit board or have very short wires.

How it works

Early touchscreens could detect only one finger press at a time, but the latest multi-touch models can detect any number. When you press the screen, it doesn't squash down under your finger like a keyboard. Instead, your finger changes the electric field on a grid of sensors printed on one of the inner layers. The electronics detect this change and use it to recognize what you pressed.

Touch screen
Your fingers can press the plastic in several places at once.

Grid detects
Your fingers change the electric field on the sensor grid.

Circuit converts
The phone's electronic circuits recognize the points you pressed.

Electronic components control touchscreen

Digital camera

Loudspeaker in earpiece

Lithium-ion battery provides eight hours of talk time

SIM card holder

Plastic back of case and battery holder

Compact aerial built into circuit board

Microchips on main circuit board

Metal screening separates circuit from battery

Microphone

Battery charging connector

SIM card stores personal account details and phone numbers

IN TOUCH

There are more than six billion people in the world, and more than three billion mobile phones. Every minute, 1,000 more people buy a phone for the first time and join in with the most versatile medium of communication ever invented. The growth in mobile phones has been spectacular. It took 20 years for the first billion people to get connected, but the most recent billion have bought their phones in the last two years alone. In some parts of the world, including Europe, many people own more than one phone – and there are more mobile phones in these places than people!

Early mobiles

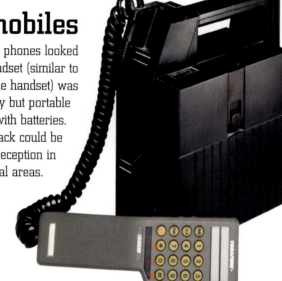

This is what mobile phones looked like in 1985. The handset (similar to an ordinary telephone handset) was connected to a heavy but portable case filled mostly with batteries. The aerial on the back could be extended for better reception in rural areas.

Mast in disguise

Phone masts relay calls between mobile phones and the phone networks they use. To work properly, masts have to be mounted on hilltops or tall buildings. Many people find ordinary metal masts (which look like giant TV aerials) unattractive. This one has been disguised with fake plastic branches to look like a tree.

Waste of phones

Most people replace their mobile phone every 18 months or so, but only 4 per cent of mobiles are properly recycled. Many end up in landfills. Their plastic cases take up to 500 years to break down, while their batteries and electronic components can release toxic metals such as cadmium, mercury, and lead into the environment.

World favourite

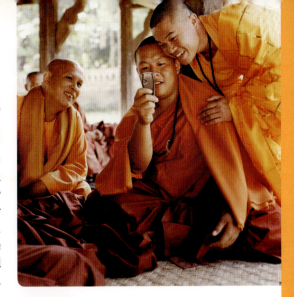

Phone keyboards tend to have symbols on the function buttons instead of letters or words, so people in every country can understand them. The most popular mobile phone system, GSM, is used in more than 200 countries.

Health risk?

Scientists have not proved that mobile phones are safe – or unsafe. Some have found that phone users have more risk of brain tumours, while others say there's no effect at all. These images show how people's brain activity changes when they use phones.

Big in Japan

Mobiles are more than just portable phones – they also work as cameras and music players. In Japan, people use a system called i-mode to send emails, play games, and browse the Web. Some phones even work as wallets, paying for your shopping when you swipe them over the checkout (right).

Distractions

Drivers are four times more likely to have an accident if they use a mobile phone, so driving with a phone is now illegal or restricted in at least 30 countries. Some research has shown that talking to a passenger is just as distracting, however.

FUTURE FLEXIPHONE

Bone phone

Handheld phones could become obsolete if we find a way of beaming sound signals directly into a person's head. One possibility is to give people tooth implants containing microchip radio receivers and vibration devices. The chips would vibrate in response to incoming phone calls, passing the sound to your inner ear through your jawbone. Nobody would even know you were on the phone!

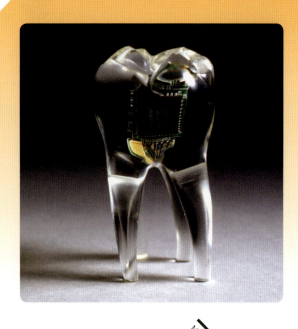

Magnets hold phone strap closed when it wraps around your wrist

Case can flex and twist in any direction

Electronic components on ultra-thin circuit board

Ultra-thin and lightweight plastic battery charged by solar cells

The 19th century gave us the telephone. The 20th century brought us the mobile phone. In the 21st century, phones will develop into flexiphones – personal communicators that are flexible in more ways than one. Today, people carry mobile phones and music players, paper diaries and address books. In the future, our phones will help us do just about anything we want, from sending emails and ordering shopping online to having live video chats with friends anywhere in the world.

Lightweight

All the phone's electronic components, including the screen, are printed onto thin layers of flexible plastic. Power comes from ultra-thin solar cells in the outer case, so only a small battery is needed. With a more compact screen and battery, the phone weighs as little as a pencil. Magnets in the case strap it onto your wrist like a watch.

Display layers as thin as cellophane can produce pin-sharp video pictures

Solar cells built into plastic case charge battery

Multiple flexible layers are built up to give phone its unique properties

SIM card stores phone numbers and account details

DIGITAL PEN

The old saying "The pen is mightier than the sword" highlights the power of well-chosen words. Combine a pen with a computer, and you have something even more impressive. A digital pen doesn't simply write on paper: its built-in camera automatically detects the marks you make, so the words you write can be beamed to your computer and edited as easily as if you'd typed them in.

Well connected

A digital pen is electrically powered. Every so often, you have to put it back in its docking station to recharge the battery inside. The docking station also links to a computer with a USB cable. When the pen is docked, all the things you've written with it are uploaded automatically to your computer.

Hard copy

When computers first became popular, people spoke of a "paperless society" with all communication in electronic form. Two-thirds of people now use email at work, but there's 50 per cent more paper in our offices than there was in the 1960s. It seems that people still prefer the convenience of a hard copy that they can write their comments on.

FAST FACTS

Memory	100 A5 pages of text
Weight	908g (32oz) in box
Dimensions	157mm x 24mm x 21mm (0.6in x 0.9in x 0.8in)
Operating time	Up to 3 hours
Standby time	Up to 20 hours
Data transfer	Wireless Bluetooth or USB connection to computer

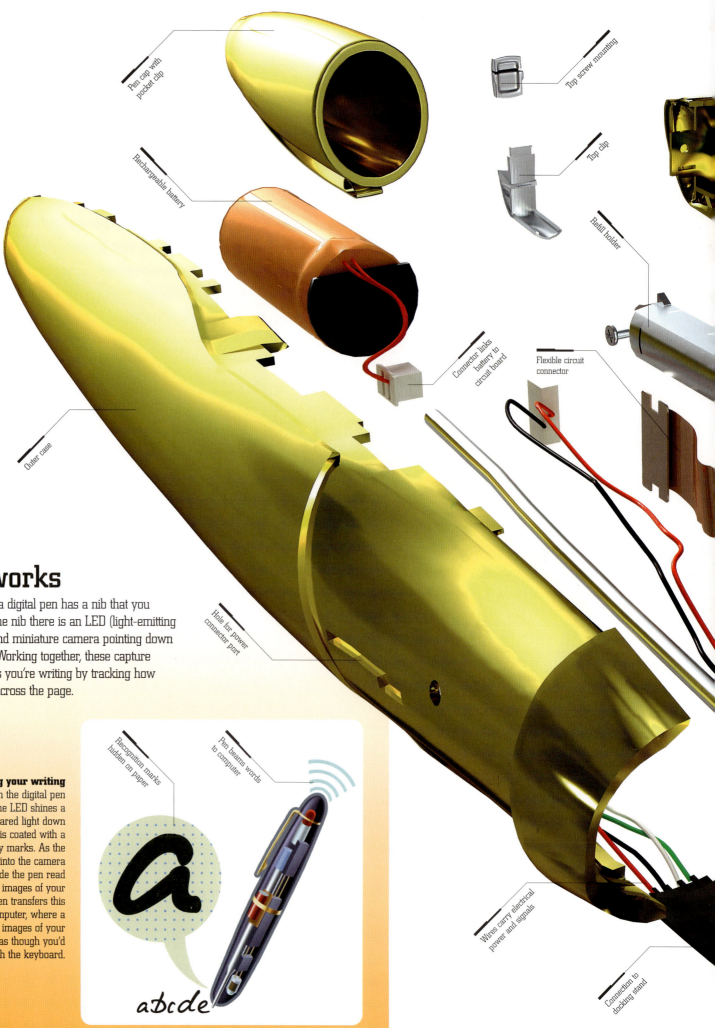

Pen cap with pocket clip

Rechargeable battery

Outer case

Top screw mounting

Top clip

Refill holder

Connector links battery to circuit board

Flexible circuit connector

Hole for power connector port

Wires carry electrical power and signals

Connection to docking stand

How it works

Like a normal pen, a digital pen has a nib that you write with. Next to the nib there is an LED (light-emitting diode) transmitter and miniature camera pointing down towards the paper. Working together, these capture images of the words you're writing by tracking how you move the pen across the page.

Reading your writing

When you write with the digital pen on special paper, the LED shines a beam of invisible infrared light down onto the paper, which is coated with a grid of extremely tiny marks. As the light reflects back up into the camera lens, microchips inside the pen read the marks and store images of your handwriting. The pen transfers this information to your computer, where a program converts the images of your writing into text, just as though you'd typed it with the keyboard.

Recognition marks hidden on paper

Pen beams words to computer

a

abcde

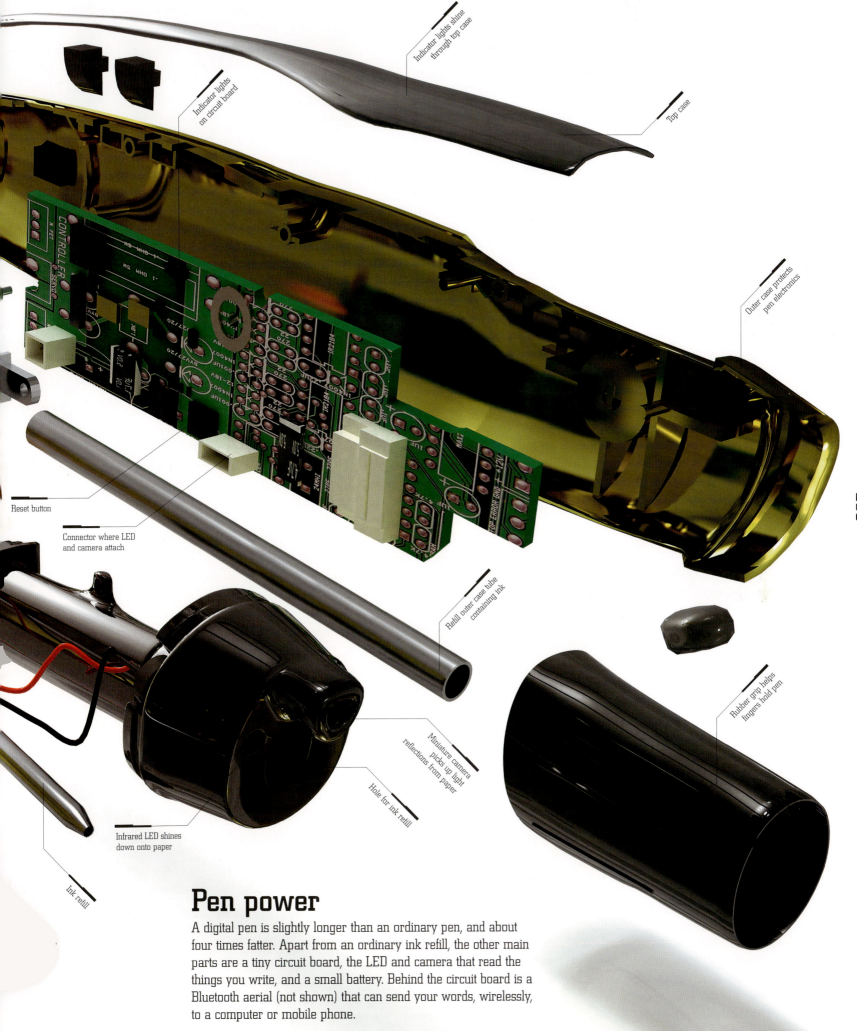

Indicator lights shine
through top case

Top case

Indicator lights
on circuit board

Outer case protects
pen electronics

CONTROLLER

Reset button

Connector where LED
and camera attach

Refill outer case tube
containing ink

Rubber grip helps
fingers hold pen

Miniature camera
picks up light
reflections from paper

Hole for ink refill

Infrared LED shines
down onto paper

Ink refill

Pen power

A digital pen is slightly longer than an ordinary pen, and about
four times fatter. Apart from an ordinary ink refill, the other main
parts are a tiny circuit board, the LED and camera that read the
things you write, and a small battery. Behind the circuit board is a
Bluetooth aerial (not shown) that can send your words, wirelessly,
to a computer or mobile phone.

SAVING DATA

Humans have invented some ingenious ways to store information, which means that we can draw on the knowledge of the generations that came before us. Even after we have died, others can build on our achievements, and this is how civilization has advanced. Ancient inventions such as paper and writing marked the beginning of the age of recorded history. In our age, very recent inventions such as computers and the World Wide Web will carry the history we make today far into the future.

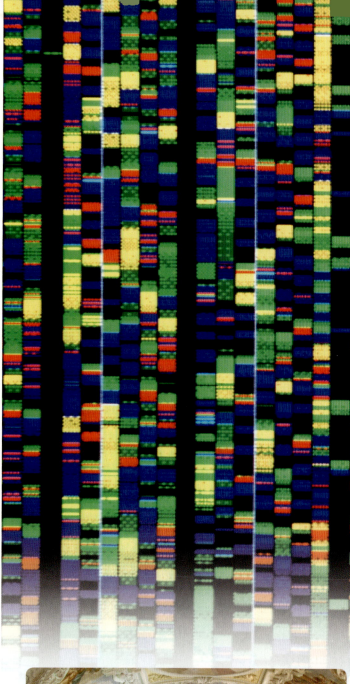

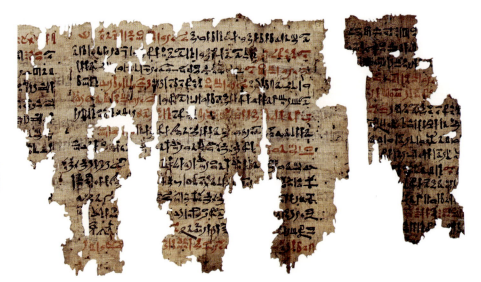

Papyrus

Paper was invented about 5,000 years ago by the ancient Egyptians, who made it from the stem of a plant called papyrus. The 3,700-year-old Edwin Smith Papyrus, above, is the world's oldest medical book. It describes how the body works and lists some medical cures that are still used today.

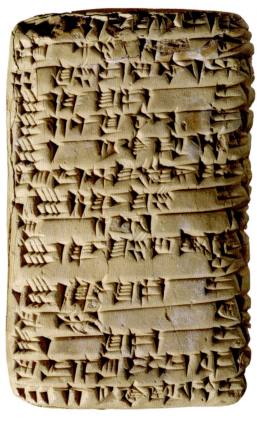

Cuneiform

Writing materials are useless without an agreed system to record your ideas. The first ever written language, called cuneiform, involved making line marks in clay with a piece of wood called a stylus. Cuneiform was invented in Mesopotamia (now part of Iraq) about 5,500 years ago.

Information is power

If knowledge is power, the owners of libraries are very powerful indeed. Here, the accumulated knowledge of whole civilizations is stored. Ornate libraries such as this one in the Strahov Monastery, Prague, Czech Republic, celebrate the power of books and words.

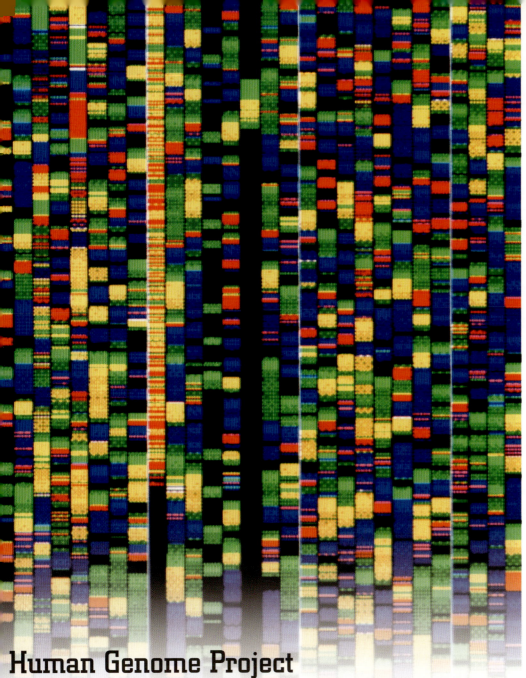

Human Genome Project

Thanks to computers, information is easier to store and share than ever before. The Human Genome Project is a huge computer database of genetic information (shown here as coloured bands) that scientists can access using the Internet to develop cures for illnesses such as cancer.

Easy access

Blind people find it hard to access information in books, but computers can help. Instead of using screens, screen readers speak words aloud. Some blind people use Braille displays like this one (left). It converts documents into raised dots that blind people read with their fingers.

Semantic Web

Tim Berners-Lee (right, 1955–) invented the World Wide Web so that scientists could share their work. His next project, the Semantic Web, will let machines share information too. In the Semantic Web, all Web content will be written in a language that computers can understand as well as in human languages such as English.

Digital libraries

The British Library shares some of its rare and valuable books on a website called Turning the Pages. You read digital books by dragging the pages with your mouse. These detailed plant pictures are from *A Curious Herbal* by Elizabeth Blackwell, dating from 1737.

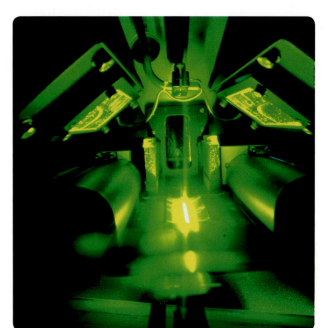

Recognizing writing

People can read computer printouts, but most computers can't yet read human writing. This mail sorting machine (above) uses a laser to read postal codes written on envelopes. It prints the codes on the paper as a pattern of fluorescent dots that other sorting machines can read.

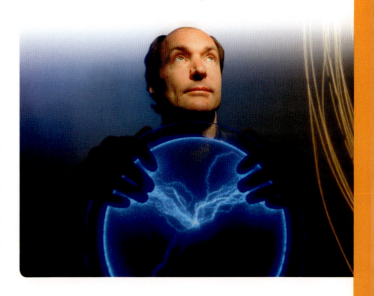

CAMCORDER

CD ROM

If you watch a film lasting two hours, more than 170,000 photographs dance briefly before your eyes. Your brain doesn't see them as separate images but blends them into a continuous moving picture. Until recently, making movies was something only professional film-makers could do. But modern electronics have made cameras smaller, simpler, and more affordable, and anyone can now make a film with a camcorder. Pictures are stored on tape or in digital memory, so if you don't like your film, you can record over it.

FAST FACTS

Dimensions	118mm x 92mm x 64mm (4.7in x 3.6in x 2.5in)
LCD screen size	6.9cm (2.7in)
Optical zoom	34 times
Weight	350g (12.4oz)
Recording system	MiniDV tape

Instant playback

Until video was invented, movie cameras worked like old-fashioned film cameras: the pictures you recorded had to be slowly and laboriously developed. With a modern camcorder, you can instantly play back what you have filmed. Pictures are stored in digital form, so you can easily upload them onto websites and share them with your friends.

Handheld film crew

Hollywood films have expensive budgets, giant sets, and dozens of people in the film crew. If you're filming with a camcorder, you have everything you need in the palm of your hand. Weighing only a fifth as much as professional video cameras, camcorders are light and portable enough to film almost anywhere.

Plastic side case

Microchip

Read/write head uses a spinning magnet to write information to tape and read it back

Electronic circuit board controls optics, digital video, and LCD screen

Plastic top case

Tape mechanism

Front strap attachment

Tape eject button

Tape spool winds tape back and forth

Metal cassette holds tape in place

Protective plastic lens cap

Objective lens captures image

Microphone holes for recording sound

Zooming in

The most important part of a camcorder is the imaging system – the lenses that capture an image. In this model, the imaging system consists of lenses and a motorized mechanism. The motor moves the lenses in and out, so they are closer to or more distant from one another. This allows the camera to zoom in to up to 34 times magnification.

From image to tape

Camcorders store pictures on tape in four stages. First, the lens at the front captures an image of the object. Then a light-sensitive microchip called a CCD (charge-coupled device) turns the image into a long string of numbers. An electronic circuit in the camera uses mathematics to compress (squeeze) the numbers so they need less room to store. Finally, the numbers are recorded in sequence onto a compact magnetic MiniDV tape.

❶

❸

❹

1 Lens
2 CCD
3 Circuit
4 Tape

How it works

Early movie cameras took 24 photographs ("frames") each second and stored them on a reel of film (light-sensitive plastic). Modern digital camcorders work differently. They convert each frame into digital format (a long string of numbers) and store this on tape instead. When you play back the tape, the process runs in reverse: the numbers are turned back into pictures that you can watch on the LCD display.

Viewfinder lets you see what you're filming

Rechargeable battery pack

CCD captures image

Circuit board

Tape control buttons

Motorized mechanism for moving zoom lenses

Button-cell battery

Connecting tracks on circuit board link electronic parts together

Loudspeaker in side of case plays back recorded sound

Zoom lenses

LCD display

Hinge allows LCD display to fold in and out

Microphone

Fold-out plastic LCD display surround

Push-button controls for playback

Slots house playback buttons

LOOKINSIDE

ONSCREEN

When a huge steam locomotive came charging towards a crowd in Paris, France in 1896, people screamed, panicked, and dived out of the way to save themselves. In fact, the train was just an enormous filmed image projected onto a screen, but it seemed frighteningly real at the time. The people who watched it were the audience in the world's first cinema, and they had never seen a film before. More than a century later, films haven't lost the power to move us, but some things have changed. We're more likely to watch a film at home on the television than in an auditorium with other people, and we've learned to use the technology of capturing moving pictures in other interesting ways.

Electronic news-gathering

It can take several years to make a feature film, but sometimes we need pictures more quickly. TV news cameras instantly capture pictures with digital video. Then they transmit them immediately back to a studio, anywhere in the world, using satellite trucks like this one.

Big screen

In many western countries, cinemas reached the peak of their popularity in the 1940s. Audiences have fallen by more than 90 per cent since then, largely because of television and home video. That's not the case in India, which has the world's biggest film business. Indian film-makers produce more than 1,000 films a year, shown in more than 13,000 cinemas. Most Indian people still prefer to watch films in cinemas and only 8 per cent of films in India are watched on videos at home.

Milestones

Zoetrope (1860s)
This zoetrope shows the scientific idea behind films, called persistence of vision. This is when you see a series of pictures so fast that your brain merges them together. If you peer through a slit on the spinning zoetrope, you don't see lots of still pictures – you see a single moving image. The Zoetrope was invented by Austrian scientist Simon Stampfer (1792–1864).

Cinématographe (1895)
The French brothers Auguste and Louis Lumière invented the first practical film camera and projector in 1895. The following year, they opened the world's first cinema in the Grand Café in Paris.

CAMERA

Moments vanish in the blink of an eye, but you can capture them forever with a camera like this. The pictures digital cameras take are like mosaics of tiny squares called pixels. The Canon EOS-5D takes pictures made up of an impressive 13 megapixels (one megapixel is a million pixels). Our eyes have 10 times more light-detecting cells in their retinas, but no way of storing the images they see or showing them to others.

Under control

Until microchips became popular in the 1980s, cameras were heavy and entirely mechanical. Virtually everything on the Canon is electronically controlled by buttons on the top, back, and sides. That makes it lighter, more reliable, and easier to use.

FAST FACTS

Weight	810g (28oz) without lens
Materials	Case made from polycarbonate (plastic) and magnesium alloy
Image quality	4,368 x 2,912 pixels
Shutter speed	1/8,000s to 30s
Monitor	6.4cm (2.5in) LCD screen
Cost	£1,800 (with lens)

Playback

The most exciting part of taking photographs is seeing the results. The Canon EOS-5D has a large colour LCD (liquid crystal display) screen that can show your pictures one at a time or play them back one after another in a slideshow. Vertical (portrait) shots can be rotated automatically so they display properly. You can also set the camera to show the settings used alongside each image.

Eye cup

Viewfinder

Multi-controller button
similar to a touchpad

"Set" button confirms
camera settings

Quick control dial
selects menu options

Flash contacts power
flash gun from camera

"Hot shoe" bracket
holds flash gun in
place

Manual/automatic
control and mode
selector dial

Direct print button
prints photos when
printer is connected

Buttons control photo
playback on LCD
screen

LCD monitor
displays picture

Image-processing
microchips

Electronic circuit
board

AF (auto-focus)
selection

AE (auto-exposure)
lock button

LCD information
panel shows current
camera settings

MENU

INFO.

JUMP

Tough plastic case

Computer and video
equipment plugs
into side

Depth of field
preview button

Lens release
button allows
lens to be
removed

Lens locks into place
through pinholes

SLR mirror reflects
image from lens into
viewfinder

CCD sensor captures
images electronically

LCD panel
illumination

Auto focus and
white balance

Drive mode and
speed

Self-timer lamp

Strap attaches here

Metering mode,
flash, and exposure

Main dial controls
shooting settings

Shutter switch
takes photograph
when pressed

Memory
card slot

Battery
compartment

Battery compartment
cover and hand grip

Canon

Scientific study

Film-making technology lets us study the world at a safe distance. This vulcanologist (volcano scientist) is filming the lava flowing down Mount Etna, the largest active volcano in Europe. Films have important scientific value because they can be stored and compared over time.

Big Brother

Most of us appear in films every day without knowing it because security cameras like these watch our every move. Cameras have helped to solve some high-profile crimes, but it is uncertain whether they reduce crime more generally.

Piracy

Video and DVD recorders make it easier than ever for people to make illegal copies. According to the film industry, piracy costs the major film studios about £12 billion a year in lost earnings. Most happens in China, Russia, and Thailand.

Video cassettes (1970s)
Video recorders were invented in the 1950s, but were too expensive for most people. They became popular in the 1970s when Sony released this affordable machine called the Betamax, which could record from a video camera or direct from a home television.

DVD players (1990s)
Video recorders were unreliable, and their tapes often broke or wore out. Many people have now switched to DVD recorders, which are more reliable and easier to use.

Internet video (2000s)
In the future, even things like DVDs may become obsolete. Already, people use webcams to record videos and send them directly over the Internet. Soon, we may download all our films instead of buying them from shops.

TAKING PICTURES

Photographs freeze a moment in time forever. By taking a photo, we can show other people things that are far away in both distance and time. For some people, photography is a serious, creative art form; for others, it's a convenient way to remember happy events. But photographs have more serious uses too. There are limits to what our eyes can see and our brains can remember. Photographs help us overcome our limits and record the world in ways that can be crucial to our daily lives.

Nature close-ups

Stunning photography brings nature to life. Words would struggle to capture the intricate details on the face of this fly, and no artist could make it sit still long enough to sketch the myriad colours of its eyes. Macro (close-up) photographs like this reveal minute features we could never see with the naked eye.

Milestones

Camera Obscura
Around 2,500 years ago, the Chinese discovered that images could be projected through a small hole onto a surface in a darkened room. Europeans called this "camera obscura" (Latin for dark chamber). This is where the word camera comes from.

First photographs
Englishman William Henry Fox Talbot (1800–1877) helped to invent modern photography. His method involved using silver chemicals to make pictures from "negatives" (reversed versions) of what his cameras saw.

Tough plastic outer casing protects delicate lenses inside

Focus settings marked on dials for manual focus

Focusing rings are ribbed for easy grip

Image stabilizer removes camera wobble

Image stabilizer lenses

Lenses work together to focus and zoom image

Focus mode switch to move between manual and auto-focus

Battery compartment cover

Removable lithium-ion rechargeable battery

IMAGE STABILIZER

SLR camera

Most inexpensive digital cameras don't take exactly the shot you see through the viewfinder, because the viewfinder does not look directly through the main camera lens. Professional cameras use a better system called single lens reflex (SLR). Inside, there is a hinged mirror that works like a periscope. When you look through the viewfinder, the mirror shows you what the camera sees through its main lens. The mirror flips up out of the way when you press the shutter to take a photo.

LOOK INSIDE

Image stabilizer contains lenses that stop the picture blurring if you shake the camera

Larger or smaller lenses can be screwed on for taking photos of close-up or distant objects

Objective lens collects light from scene

CANON LENS MADE IN JAPAN

24 35 50 70 105

24-150mm

Object to image

When you point your camera at an object (1), the lens captures light coming from the object. The light passes through the lens and hits the CCD inside (2). The CCD is a grid of light-sensitive cells that converts the pattern of light into a string of binary numbers (zeros and ones) that are stored in the camera's memory card (3). In digital form (4), a photograph is easy to copy onto a computer or send to a friend over the Internet.

How it works

If you take a photograph with an old-fashioned film camera, the camera stores the image directly onto a piece of plastic film. When the film is developed, you can still see a small version of the image on the film. Digital cameras are completely different. They use a CCD (charge-coupled device) that converts the image you see through the camera lens into a pattern of numbers. Instead of recording the image on film, the camera stores the numbers on a digital memory card.

Zooming in

Unlike a compact camera, you can change the lens on a professional camera to get different effects. The Canon can use lenses from 14mm (wide-angle lenses for taking close-ups of nearby objects) to 800mm (telephoto lenses that zoom in on distant objects like a telescope).

Solving crime

Photographic evidence can help the police bring criminals to justice. This forensic scientist is using a camera mounted on a tripod to photograph a footprint left at a crime scene. The torch in his left hand shows up the print more clearly when it's captured on film. Photographs have to be taken with great precision because they may be needed as evidence in court.

Journalism

Photographs record history as it happens. The moments just before President John F. Kennedy was assassinated in his car in November 1963 have been captured forever in photographs such as this.

Scientific research

Scientists find photographs extremely useful. Our eyes can't see what happens when atoms smash apart into smaller particles, but this photograph shows us. It was taken using a piece of apparatus called a bubble chamber. As fragments from smahed atoms move through the chamber, they leave tracks behind, a bit like the vapour trails aeroplanes make in the sky. Photos like this reveal the deep secrets of matter.

Film cameras
Photography was messy and time-consuming until American George Eastman (1854–1932) developed convenient plastic film. With cameras like the Brownie, his Kodak company turned photography into a popular hobby in the 1890s.

Instant cameras
Many people like to see photos as soon as they are taken. In 1947 American inventor Edwin Land (1909–1991) developed the Polaroid camera, which made instant pictures on chemically treated paper.

Photo sharing
Anyone can make instant photographs using a camera phone like this. Because the photos are made as digital files, you can email them to your family and friends or instantly upload them onto the Web.

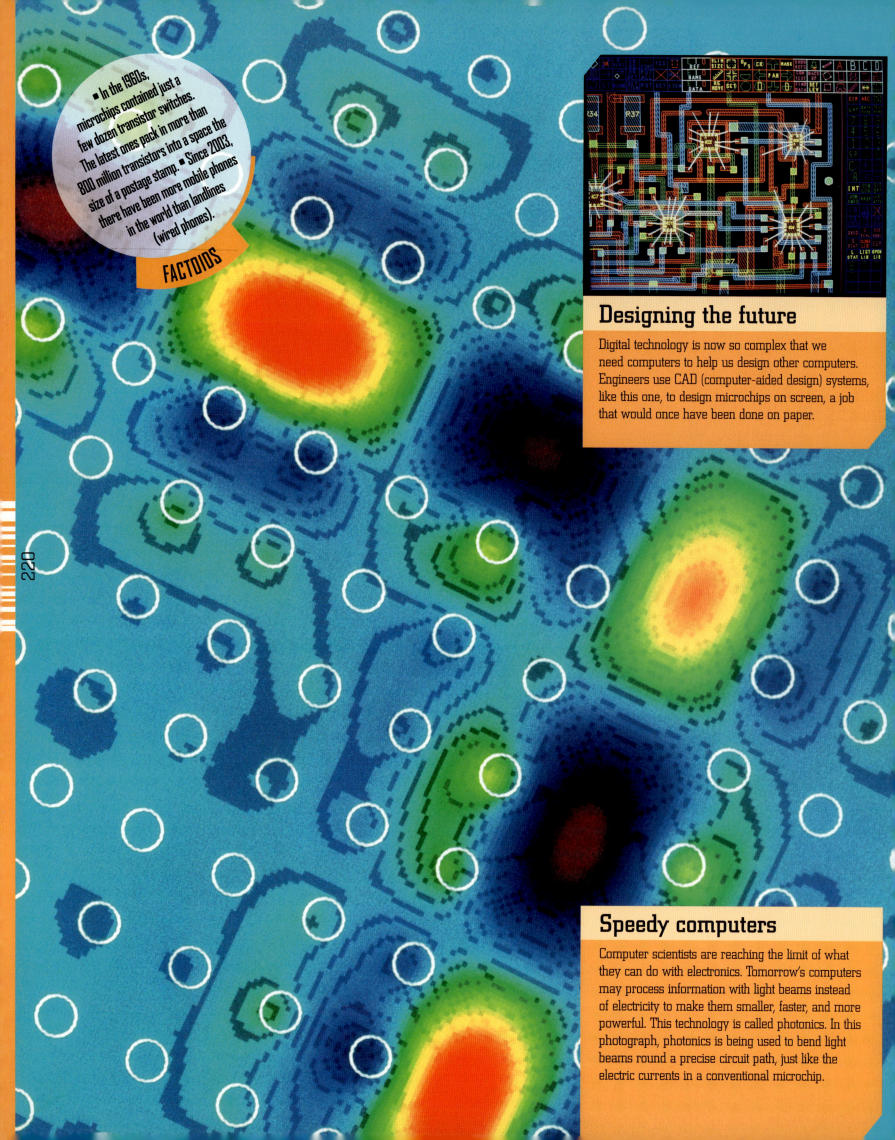

Designing the future

Digital technology is now so complex that we need computers to help us design other computers. Engineers use CAD (computer-aided design) systems, like this one, to design microchips on screen, a job that would once have been done on paper.

Speedy computers

Computer scientists are reaching the limit of what they can do with electronics. Tomorrow's computers may process information with light beams instead of electricity to make them smaller, faster, and more powerful. This technology is called photonics. In this photograph, photonics is being used to bend light beams round a precise circuit path, just like the electric currents in a conventional microchip.

Convergence

It is easy to share digital information between different gadgets. That's why mobile phones can play videos, and music players can store photographs. Soon we may not need separate phones, music players, cameras, and computers – one device will do everything. This idea is called convergence: it means our gadgets are gradually merging together.

Gone tomorrow?

Museums have scraps of written information several thousand years old, but no-one has the first email or mobile phone call, even though they are just a few decades old. Information stored on Web pages can seem to vanish as quickly as it appears. Organizations such as the Internet Archive maintain online libraries of Web pages to ensure that they are not lost.

LIVING BY NUMBERS

Sometimes it seems like the whole world is turning into numbers. Digital photographs, music tracks, Web pages, and TV programmes are at their heart long strings of zeros and ones. That's because electronic gadgets ultimately store and process all these things in number form. It's much easier to handle information this way but it's risky too, because digital information is less private, and easier to steal.

Space race

One of the best things about digital technology is that you can pack vast amounts of information into tiny volumes of space. You could fit 10,000 copies of the complete works of Shakespeare onto a single DVD, so all the books shown here would fit on just a few discs.

Prying eyes

When people shop online, the websites they visit use encryption (mathematical scrambling) to keep their personal details secure. Information sent in light beams down fibre-optic cables can now be protected using quantum encryption machines. If a criminal tries to unscramble the information locked in a light beam, the beam changes subtly, and it becomes obvious that someone has tried to break in.

Flat pack

A laptop computer has smaller and thinner components inside than a desktop. The case is usually made of a sturdy plastic such as polycarbonate. More expensive models use strong, light metals such as titanium.

FAST FACTS

Screen	38cm (15in) widescreen
Memory	2GB RAM and 250GB hard drive
Processor	Dual core
Battery life	4 hours
Network	Wi-Fi wireless Internet
Weight	2kg (4.4lb)

LAPTOP COMPUTER

In 1949, an issue of the hobby magazine *Popular Mechanics* daringly suggested: "Computers in the future may weigh no more than 1.5 tonnes." Back then, the idea of a laptop computer would have seemed utterly absurd. But thanks to incredible advances in miniaturized electronics, modern laptops are about 1,000 times lighter than *Popular Mechanics* predicted (weighing in at only 1–2kg or 2–4lb), and compact enough to carry almost anywhere.

Class of '77

Hardly any offices or schools had computers until the mid-1980s. A few lucky ones had chunky computers such as this 1977 Commodore PET. It had a tiny keyboard and screen, and a cassette tape recorder instead of a hard drive.

LOOK INSIDE

How it works

A computer is an "information processing" machine: you feed it data (such as words or images), it works on the data, and then it displays the results. Feeding in data is input, changing data is processing, and showing the results is output. Input comes mostly from the keyboard, mouse, memory, or disc drives, processing happens in the microchips, and output is usually displayed on an LCD screen.

Tablet screens

Liquid crystal display (LCD) screens became popular in the 1990s. Some are touch-sensitive, and can be used as flat drawing tablets. Screens like this work as both input and output at the same time, recognizing your penstrokes, and displaying them too.

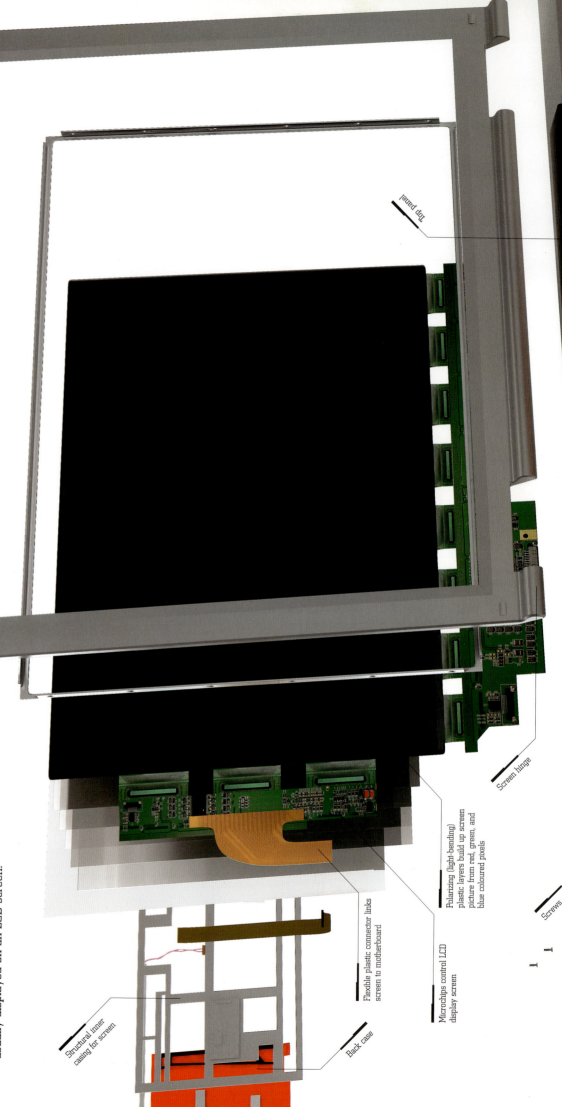

Plastic screen surround seals screen into case

Top panel

Screen hinge

Screws

Polarizing (light-bending) plastic layers build up screen picture from red, green, and blue coloured pixels

Flexible plastic connector links screen to motherboard

Microchips control LCD display screen

Structural inner casing for screen

Back case

Top of CD/ DVD drive

DVD drive (top of CD/ DVD drive)

Fan and heat sink (radiator) help to cool processor circuits

Trackpad buttons

Top of CD/ DVD drive

Keyboard

Monitor port (output connector) can drive full-sized screen

Printer port (output connector)

Socket screws help to hold connectors in place

Bottom casing has holes for connections and components

Hard drive arm

Hard drive actuator moves hard drive arm

Sound card (circuit board) provides stereo sound input and output

Hard drive stores data (information)

CD/DVD drive in sliding drawer

USB connectors to printers, webcams, and other peripherals

Circuit controls CD/DVD drive

Moving laser reads information

Motorized hub spins discs at up to 1,500rpm

Motherboard (main circuit board)

Central processor chip

Socket for expansion cards, such as extra memory or wireless modem

Rechargeable battery provides several hours of power

Hard drive hub spins drive disc at up to 7,200rpm

MICROCHIPS

In 1943, Thomas Watson, founder of the IBM computer company, guessed that there would be a market for "about five computers". How wrong he was. It's now estimated that there are two billion computers in the world. No-one knows exactly, because many modern computers are actually microprocessors (tiny computer chips) built into mobile phones, music players, and other gadgets. Watson's prediction was wrong because he never imagined computers would develop as they have. In the 1940s, a state-of-the-art computer cost about £2.5 million. Today, a microprocessor works a million times faster and costs 25,000 times less.

Portable power

Laptops became practical when the parts inside computers could be made smaller and lighter. One big difficulty was making powerful batteries that were small enough to carry. Fortunately, modern batteries are much smaller than this voltaic pile, the world's first ever battery, invented in 1800 by Italian physicist Alessandro Volta (1745–1827).

Always online

People originally found computers useful because they could process information quickly. Now it's just as important that computers can access and share information over the Internet. With wireless networking, you can go online almost anywhere – even up a

Remote computing

You can find computers in some unexpected places. Wrist computers give scuba divers precise information about their dives, including how long they can stay safely underwater and how quickly they can resurface.

Milestones

Abacus
The abacus, a frame with beads that slide along wires, was the world's first "portable computer". Invented in its most primitive form more than 4,500 years ago, it is still used in many countries today.

Babbage engines
In the 19th century, English mathematician Charles Babbage (1791–1871) tried to build complex calculators using thousands of moving parts. He ran out of money and the machines were never completed.

Little wonder

This millipede is holding a microprocessor: a complete computer, built onto a single tiny chip of silicon, that you might find working away inside a laptop computer or MP3 music player. A modern microprocessor contains 400–800 million tiny switches called transistors. That may sound powerful, but by contrast, the human brain contains about 100 billion switching cells (neurons).

Chip and pin

Most credit cards now have built-in computers. A "chip and pin" card has a microchip in one corner that stores your security number. When you pay for something, you have to enter the same number on a keypad to prove you really own the card.

Laptop for all

These laptops cost only $100 (£50), so schools in developing countries can afford them, and are ruggedly built to survive in hot and humid places. Their screens are designed to be visible in direct sunlight, because many children in these countries have classes outdoors.

227

Superpowered

In May 1997, an IBM supercomputer called Deep Blue beat Russian chess champion Garry Kasparov (1963–). The newest microprocessors used in PCs (personal computers) and laptops are already several times faster than those found in Deep Blue.

IBM mainframe
IBM dominated the computer industry in the 20th century. Its revolutionary System/360 was announced in 1964 and came with 150 different peripherals (add-on devices). It was very popular with businesses because it could easily be expanded into a more powerful machine as their needs changed.

Osborne 1
Launched in 1981, the Osborne 1 was the world's first real portable computer. It had a tiny 12.5cm (5in) screen and weighed 12kg (26lb) – six times as much as a modern laptop.

BlackBerry
These popular handhelds are like mobile phones crossed with computers. You can use them to send emails or messages, make phone calls, or browse the Web.

FUTURE SMART GLASSES

Our eyes are our windows on the world, but sometimes the world isn't the only thing you want to see. If you're walking in a strange place, you need to see a map. If you're expecting an urgent email, you might want to see a computer screen. In the future, smart glasses will help us with things like this. They'll also be able to zoom in and out like binoculars and even help us see at night.

First screen layer shows normal view seen by cameras

Cameras with zoom lenses and infrared night vision

Fourth screen layer provides night vision or Internet browsing

Third screen layer uses satellite navigation and maps to show you where to go

Second screen layer shows zoomed-in details of first layer

Plastic nose piece makes screens more readable by stopping sunlight from leaking in underneath frames

Bionic eyes?

At the University of Washington, United States, researchers have produced a contact lens with a flexible, see-through display built into it. It's designed to display information superimposed on whatever you are looking at, without any kind of screen. Although the technology is still in development, it could revolutionize the way we use computers in the future. Instead of staring at a screen, you would simply look ahead – web pages, emails, maps, TV programmes, or videos would simply float before your eyes!

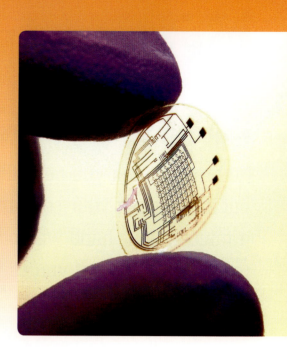

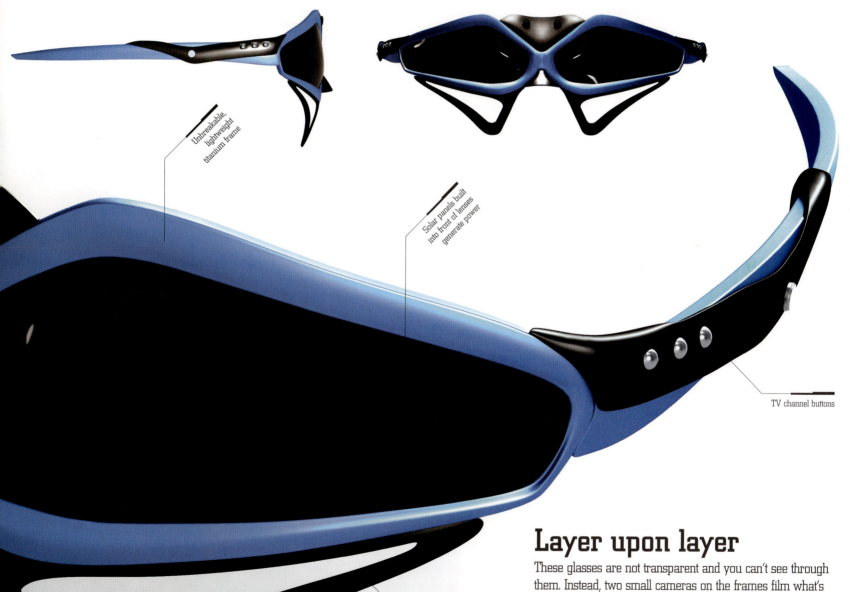

Unbreakable, lightweight titanium frame

Solar panels built into front of lenses generate power

TV channel buttons

Frames work like mouse switches: you click on items on screen by screwing up your left or right cheek

Layer upon layer

These glasses are not transparent and you can't see through them. Instead, two small cameras on the frames film what's in front of you and then display it on the back of the "lenses", which are actually small screens facing your eyes. Each screen can show multiple layers, superimposing extra information on top of what you normally see. As you walk along, you can have a computer-drawn map overlaid in front of you, or you can read emails and search the web.

COMPUTER MOUSE

You might think you get little exercise sitting at a desk, but if you push your computer mouse just 10 times a minute, your hand will move something like 80km (50 miles) a year. If you click the buttons a few times a minute as well, that's about a million clicks each year on top. All this can punish the muscles in your wrist and forearm, so mice have to be well designed to reduce the risk of injury and long-term damage.

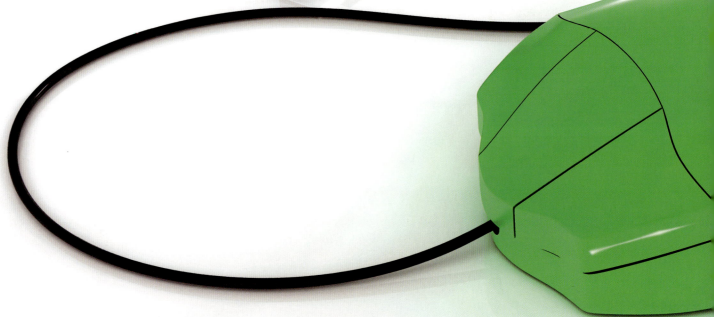

FAST FACTS

Weight	100g (3.5oz)
Connection	USB/wireless
Dimensions	110mm x 60mm x 35 mm (4.3in x 2.4in x 1.4in)

Cordless mice

Some computer mice still send signals to computers through cables, but newer ones tend to be cordless (wireless) and use invisible radio waves instead. Older computers can be converted to use newer, cordless mice with plug-in radio-transmitter sticks like the one shown here (far right).

Shining down

Optical mice recognize where they are by reflecting a light off your desk. You don't need a mouse mat, and slightly rough surfaces are better than very smooth, polished ones. This is because the grooves and bumps work like tiny landmarks, helping the mouse to work out where it is.

LOOK INSIDE

Mechanical mouse

A mechanical mouse has a large rubber ball inside. As you move the mouse, the ball moves as well, turning two plastic wheels. The wheels have little spokes around their edges that interrupt a pair of light beams as they turn. The electronic circuit works out where you are moving the mouse to by counting the number of times the light beams are broken.

USB stick enables computer to receive radio-wave signals from mouse

Top case made of light, rigid ABS plastic

Top case made of light, rigid ABS plastic.

USB cable attaches to computer

Small switches detect mouse button clicks

Processor chip

Optical detectors measure movements by shining infrared light through holes in tracking wheels

Processor chip with built-in light detector underneath

Scroll wheel for reading pages quickly

Scroll wheel holder

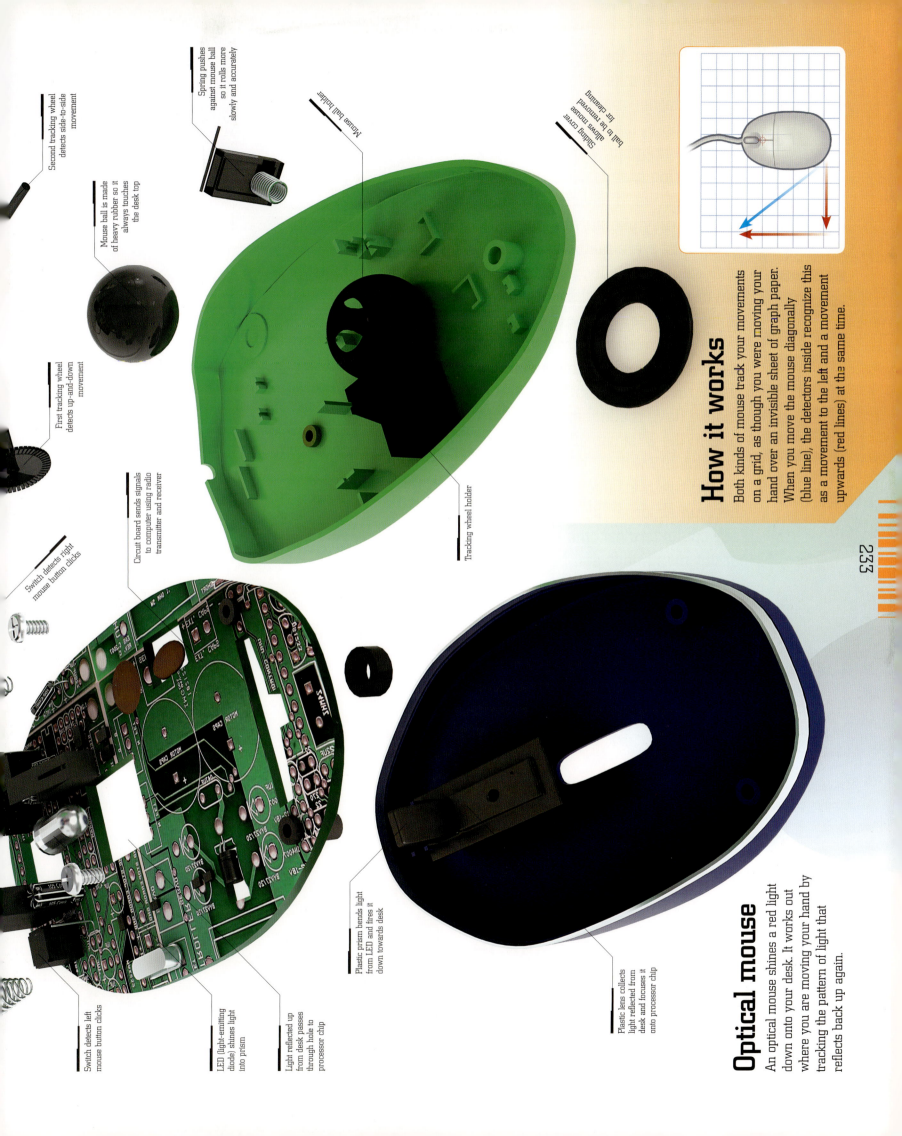

Second tracking wheel detects side-to-side movement

Spring pushes against mouse ball so it rolls more slowly and accurately

Mouse ball holder

Sliding cover allows mouse ball to be removed for cleaning

Mouse ball is made of heavy rubber so it always touches the desk top

First tracking wheel detects up-and-down movement

Circuit board sends signals to computer using radio transmitter and receiver

Switch detects right mouse button clicks

Tracking wheel holder

How it works

Both kinds of mouse track your movements on a grid, as though you were moving your hand over an invisible sheet of graph paper. When you move the mouse diagonally (blue line), the detectors inside recognize this as a movement to the left and a movement upwards (red lines) at the same time.

233

Switch detects left mouse button clicks

LED (light-emitting diode) shines light into prism

Light reflected up from desk passes through hole to processor chip

Plastic prism bends light from LED and fires it down towards desk

Plastic lens collects light reflected from desk and focuses it onto processor chip

Optical mouse

An optical mouse shines a red light down onto your desk. It works out where you are moving your hand by tracking the pattern of light that reflects back up again.

VIRTUAL WORLD

Computers put the world at our fingertips. Thanks to the invention of the Internet, many things we used to do in the "real world" – such as shopping, visiting a library, and making friends – we now do in the virtual world, online. Fifty years ago, the only people who used computers were mathematicians and scientists. Today, people have computers on their desks, in their homes, and even in their pockets. Tiny electronics have made computers much smaller and, crucially, devices like the mouse have made them easier to use. In the 21st century, we cannot imagine life without computers. As we reach for the mouse and become absorbed by the screen, our computers become extensions of our own minds and bodies.

ENIAC

Modern computers look friendly, but they used to be like this (above). Built in 1946, the enormous ENIAC (Electronic Numerical Integrator and Calculator) was 24m (80ft) long, weighed around 30 tonnes, and contained more than 100,000 electronic parts. It was so unreliable, it never went more than five days without breaking down.

The first mouse

Modern mice are made of plastic, but the first one was built out of wood. It was invented in 1963–1964 by American computer scientist Douglas Engelbart (1925–), who called it an "X-Y position indicator". Someone thought the curly cable looked like a mouse's tail, and the name "mouse" has been used ever since.

Second life

Millions of people use their computers to live out their fantasies. On the popular *Second Life* website (right), you can create a graphical version of yourself called an avatar and move it around an imaginary world. Real-world laws don't apply: you can create anything you can imagine – you can even fly!

The Apple Lisa

Launched in 1983, the Lisa was the first mass-produced computer with a mouse and picture-based screen. It was a flop, because it cost $9,995 – several times more than its rivals. But it led to the hugely popular Apple Macintosh, launched a year later.

Ergonomic mouse

Using a mouse or keyboard for too long can cause a painful condition called repetitive strain injury (RSI). This mouse has a ball on the side to minimize wrist movements and reduce the risk of RSI. Designing products people can use more easily is called ergonomics.

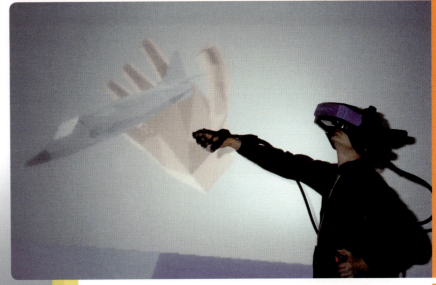

Virtual reality

Virtual reality takes the mouse a step further. You wear a wraparound headset and sensor gloves. As you move, the computer detects what you do and changes the picture you see, so you feel yourself floating through its imaginary world.

Humans obsolete?

From forecasting climate change to curing disease, computers are our partners in solving humanity's biggest problems. In the future, computers will become even more "intelligent" and helpful. There will never be a time when we don't need computers – but could there come a time when computers don't need us?

Precision printing

If you enjoy painting, you'll know you need a fine brush to do detailed work. Imagine the precision of using a paintbrush with a single hair and you'll have some idea of how detailed an inkjet printer can make its pictures. Canon's PIXMA can print 4,800 dots across and 1,200 dots down in an area slightly bigger than a postage stamp. Our eyes can't see dots that small, so pictures printed with this resolution (amount of detail) look as clear as photographs.

FAST FACTS

Dimensions	43.7cm x 14.7cm x 30cm (17.2in x 5.8in x 11.8in)
Number of ink nozzles	1,600
Speed	25 pages per minute (ppm) for black and white or 10.8ppm for colour
Ink	Separate tanks for black, cyan, magenta, and yellow
Cost	£44

INKJET PRINTER

Printing is one of the most important technologies of all time, but machines that can print on paper are quite a recent invention. Before the 15th century everything had to be copied out by hand, mostly by educated monks and nuns who took two to three hours to write a single page. Compare that to today's inkjet printers, which can run off a page in just 2.4 seconds – about 3,000 times faster!

Personal print shop

High-quality printing takes longer because more ink needs to be sprayed on the page. The printer also has to move the paper more slowly so that it has time to dry. The type of paper makes a big difference. Ordinary office paper soaks up ink like tissue. Photo-quality paper is coated with plastics or clays that stop the ink soaking and spreading, which makes the printing more precise.

How it works

Inside the printer, the print head glides repeatedly from side to side, squirting ink onto a sheet of paper that moves from the hopper at the back to the tray at the front. By combining different amounts of four separate inks (black plus the three colours cyan, magenta, and yellow), the printer can make any colour. The print head's 1,600 nozzles allow it to print at near-photographic quality.

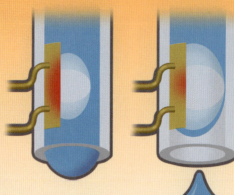

Ink drops
As the bubble grows, it squirts an ink drop out onto the paper. More ink is sucked in from the tank on top.

Heating up
Electricity flows through a heating element on the side of the ink reservoir.

Bubble forms
The heat vapourizes some of the ink and makes a bubble form in the reservoir.

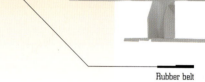

Rubber belt moves print head from side to side

LOOK INSIDE

Gears and belts drive rollers that move paper

Paper feed

Black ink cartridge

Cyan, magenta, and yellow ink cartridges

Print head squirts ink from cartridges down onto page

Rollers and spiked wheels pull paper forward through printer

Plastic base

Front folds out to make a tray for newly printed sheets

Left side case

Servo motor moves gears, belts, and paper rollers

Metal chassis inside printer holds parts securely

Back case

Paper goes in top

Flexible ribbon cable connects moving print head to circuit

Top folds up to form hopper for 80 sheets of paper

Motor moves print head from side to side

Paper feed mechanism loads paper into print mechanism one sheet at a time

Circuit board contains control electronics and power supply

Carriage moves print head from side to side

USB input from computer

On/off button and light

Paper feed button

Right side case

Paper maker

Paper was developed in 105CE by Ts'ai Lun, who worked for the Emperor of China. Made from hemp fibre, it was smoother and easier to write on than previous writing materials such as papyrus. From China, paper technology spread to Korea, Japan, and the rest of the world.

Type cast

Gutenberg didn't invent printing, but he greatly improved it. He developed thick, sticky ink, a new printing table based on a wine press, and metal type (blocks with raised letters on them that could be rearranged to print any page).

PRINTEDPAGES

The printed book you're reading now would have seemed like something from another world 550 years ago, when a German named Johannes Gutenberg (c.1400–1468) invented the modern printing process. Few books existed, hardly anyone could read, and there was no easy way to spread ideas. Printing changed all this. It became possible to copy books in huge numbers, which allowed civilization to advance more rapidly. Much of the information we share these days is in electronic form, in emails or on Web pages. But we still talk about "type" and "printing" – ideas that survive from Gutenberg's time.

Illuminated manuscripts

This is what books looked liked before Gutenberg developed the printing press. Each page is a work of art, laboriously hand-painted and lettered with gold. Books like this were called illuminated manuscripts. This one is part of a collection of 200,000 priceless volumes kept at the monastery of San Lazzaro degli Armeni in Venice, Italy.

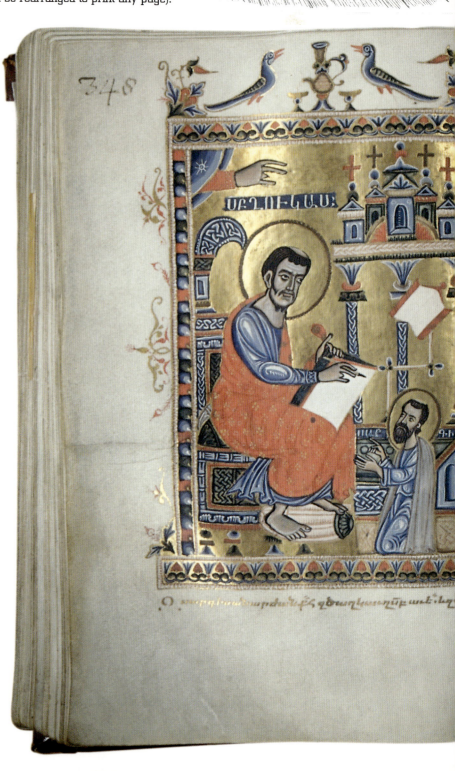

Making news

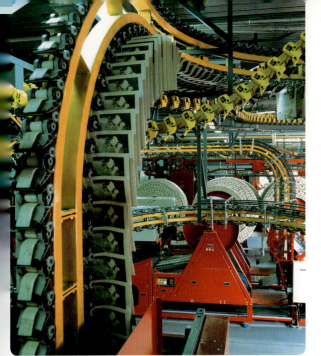

Newspapers were invented in ancient Rome. As the Romans had no printers, news was written on sheets that were then pinned up on walls. Printed newspapers first appeared in the 17th century. Modern newspapers and magazines are printed with rotary presses (high-speed spinning drums), such as this one (left), controlled by computers.

Carlson's copier

Chester Carlson (1906–1968) was determined to make his fortune from a great invention. But when he first showed big companies his idea for an "electrophotography" machine, none of them wanted to know. Later renamed the xerography machine (photocopier), it became the most important printing invention since the Gutenberg press.

Printing without paper?

Many of us now read books and newspapers online, but the words and pictures are still typically arranged like a printed page. Our eyes find it easy to scan and digest information laid out in this convenient way.

FUTURE 3-D PRINTER

Wouldn't it be good if you could make a copy of any object? Future printers will be able to make 3-D copies by building up billions of atoms. Three atomic blasters will fire the atoms, making a perfect copy in less than five minutes. Instead of expensive ink, the machine will use nothing but tap water – it will simply extract hydrogen and oxygen atoms from the water and transform them into any other atoms it needs.

Vacuum compartment is sealed during copying to keep air and dirt from contaminating the process

Third atom blaster

Water tank and atom creation unit

3-D today

3-D printers already exist. The one shown here (below) makes 3-D models from detailed designs drawn on a computer. The machine builds models from the bottom up by printing one thin layer of powder or resin on top of another – a bit like building a house up from layers of bricks. The whole process takes about four hours.

Carriage holds laser
onto guide rail

Guide rail allows atom
blaster to scan precisely
from left to right

Atom blaster
fires atoms into
compartment

Each blaster uses
three beams to hold
atoms in place and
position them precisely

Magnetic lens
concentrates and
focuses atom beams

3-D copy appears
in centre

Second atom blaster

Tray holds
completed 3-D item

Vent for air exhaust,
pumped out by vacuum

Magic box?

A 3-D object (such as a pair of intelligent glasses) appears in front of your eyes inside the 3-D printer – but that's science, not magic. The three atom blasters fire atoms together in three different dimensions. The blasters move on guide rails, much like the print head in an ordinary inkjet printer.

GLOSSARY

A

AC
Alternating current. A type of electric current that reverses direction every so often in a circuit.

acoustic
A type of guitar that makes sound from a hollow wooden body, without electric amplification.

additive
A chemical added to a material to change its properties.

aerodynamic
The curved or angled shape something has to make it move more smoothly through the air.

aerofoil
The shape of an aeroplane wing, with a curved upper surface and a straight lower surface. An aerofoil is designed to produce an upward force called lift as air flows over it.

air intake
An opening in a vehicle that allows oxygen to enter the engine to help burn fuel.

air pressure
The force that acts on things in the world around us, caused by invisible air molecules crashing into them.

air resistance
The force that slows down a moving vehicle caused by air flowing around it.

alloy
A metal mixed with smaller amounts of other metals (or sometimes nonmetals) to make it stronger, harder, or improve it in some other way.

aluminium
A strong and lightweight metal widely used to make aeroplane and spacecraft parts.

amplifier
A device that increases size or strength. The amplifier in an electric guitar makes sound louder. A transistor amplifier in a radio makes weak incoming radio signals stronger.

analogue
A way of representing an amount of something without using numbers – for example, with a pointer on a dial. An analogue watch has hands, while an analogue speedometer shows a car's speed with a moving pointer. See also digital.

appliance
A piece of electrical equipment used to perform jobs around the home, such as a washing machine, iron, or drill.

atom
The smallest amount of a chemical element that can exist.

avatar
A cartoon-like character that people use to represent themselves in computer games and Internet chat rooms.

axle
The strong rod on a moving vehicle around which the wheels turn.

B

bacteria
A single-celled microorganism. Some bacteria can be harmful because they carry disease; others can be helpful, such as those that aid digestion in our bodies.

battery
A portable power supply that generates electricity when chemical reactions happen inside it.

binary
A code for representing information using only the numbers zero and one. Binary code is used in computers and other forms of electronic equipment.

Bluetooth
A way of linking together electronic equipment over short distances without using wires. Many mobile phones use Bluetooth to connect to wireless headsets and personal computers.

bogie
A small truck carrying a set of wheels underneath a train or plane.

bulkhead
A strong partition separating one internal part of a vehicle (such as a ship or rocket) from another.

C

capacitor
A component in a circuit that stores electrical charge.

carbon dioxide
An invisible gas produced when things made of carbon burn in the oxygen that air contains. When carbon dioxide collects in the atmosphere, it contributes to the problems of global warming and climate change.

catalytic converter
A device that fits inside a car's exhaust and uses chemical reactions to turn pollution into harmless gases.

CCD
Charge-coupled device. A rectangular grid of light detectors used to generate a digital picture in a digital camera.

CD
Compact disc. A thin plastic disc, coated with reflective metal, used to store music or other information in digital form.

ceramic
A nonmetallic solid material, typically made from clay or porcelain. Ceramics can withstand high temperatures so they are widely used in situations where other materials might melt.

circuit
The closed path around which electricity flows.

circuit board
A flat piece of plastic covered with metal tracks that connect electrical components into a circuit.

climate change
The gradual transformation of Earth's weather that is being caused by global warming.

combustion
The chemical reaction in which a fuel burns with oxygen, usually from the air, to release energy. Carbon dioxide, water, and pollution gases are made as byproducts.

component
A small electronic part on a circuit board. Diodes, transistors, and capacitors are examples of electronic components.

composite
A material made by combining two or more others to produce an entirely new material with better properties.

computer
An electronic device that stores and processes information by following a series of instructions called a program.

crank
The handle on a machine such as a generator.

current
The flow of electricity through a material. Compare AC (alternating current) and DC (direct current).

cylinder
A strong metal can in a car engine where fuel is burned to produce energy. Power is produced when pistons move up and down inside the car's cylinders.

D data
The information that computers (and other types of digital technology) store, process, and share.

DC
Direct current. A type of electric current that always moves in the same direction around a circuit.

derailleur
A part of a bicycle gear that keeps the chain taut as it moves between sprockets (gear wheels) of different sizes.

detergent
A soap-like substance that makes washing more effective. A detergent breaks up and removes dirt and grease with the help of water.

diesel engine
A type of internal combustion engine that makes power by compressing fuel much more than an ordinary petrol engine.

digital
A way of representing information using only numbers. A digital watch represents the time using only a series of numbers. See also analogue.

diode
A component in a circuit that allows electricity to flow in one direction only. A diode is also called a rectifier.

disc brake
A brake that stops a vehicle by pressing rubber pads against a disc of metal positioned just inside the main wheel and tyre.

download
The process of copying files from the Internet onto your own computer.

drag
The force of air resistance that slows down moving objects.

DVD
Digital video/versatile disc. A thin plastic disc, coated with reflective metal, used to store information in digital form. A DVD is similar to a CD but can store around seven times more information.

E efficiency
The amount of energy that a machine uses effectively. If a machine is 60 per cent efficient, it uses 60 per cent of the energy supplied to do useful work and wastes the other 40 per cent.

electrical
A process that uses electricity to produce energy.

electricity
A flow of energy caused by electrons moving in a circuit.

electromagnetism
A combination of electricity and magnetism. An electric motor is electromagnetic because it uses both electricity and magnetism to make something move.

electron
A tiny particle inside an atom that carries a small negative electrical charge.

electronic
A type of appliance in which large electric currents are controlled precisely by smaller, more precise ones.

electron microscope
A type of microscope that makes much more detailed images than a conventional one by using beams of electrons instead of beams of light.

element
A chemical substance that cannot be broken down into anything simpler using only chemical reactions.

emission
A gas produced during a chemical reaction. Carbon dioxide emissions made by engines are one cause of global warming.

encryption
A way of making information secure by scrambling it using a mathematical process. For example, websites use encryption to protect people's credit card information when they shop online.

energy
A source of power or an ability to do something (such as climb stairs or move an object). In science, when something has energy it can work against a force.

engine
A machine that produces energy by burning fuel, such as a rocket or internal combustion engine.

exhaust
A pipe used to remove waste gases from an engine.

F **fibre optics**
A way of sending digital information down flexible glass or plastic pipes (known as fibre-optic cables) using precisely controlled beams of light.

force
A pushing or pulling action that alters the way an object moves or changes its shape.

four-wheel drive
A type of vehicle in which the engine powers all four wheels.

friction
The rubbing force between two objects that are in contact.

fuel
A carbon-rich substance, such as oil or coal, that releases energy when it burns in oxygen from the air.

fuel cell
A device similar to a battery that produces electrical energy from a chemical reaction, usually involving the gases hydrogen and oxygen. Unlike a battery, a fuel cell is supplied by a tank and keeps running as long as it has fuel.

fuselage
The main body of an aeroplane, not including the wings, containing the passenger seats and cargo hold.

G **gasket**
A seal that stops water from escaping from a joint between two parts inside a machine.

gear
A pair of wheels with teeth that mesh together. Gears can be used to change the power, speed, or direction of movement inside a machine.

generator
A machine that uses magnets and tightly wrapped coils of metal to turn movement into electricity. The generator in a wind turbine converts the movement of the turbine's rotor blades into electric power. See also motor.

global warming
The gradual increase in Earth's surface temperature caused by (among other things) a buildup of the gas carbon dioxide in the atmosphere. Global warming is causing Earth's climate to change.

gravity
The pulling force (force of attraction) between any two objects (masses) in the Universe. On Earth, we experience gravity as a strong pulling force toward the centre of the planet.

H **hard drive**
A magnetic disc, rotating at high speed, that stores data inside a computer even when the power is switched off.

hardware
The various electrical, electronic, and mechanical components that make up a computer system. See also software.

hub
The strong, central part of a wheel.

hydraulic
A mechanical system of fluid-filled pipes in a machine such as a digger or crane. Hydraulics help to increase the pushing, pulling, or lifting force a machine can exert. See also pneumatic.

hydrogen
A gas made from simple atoms that is lighter than air and can be used as a fuel.

I **immersive**
A type of virtual reality computer system in which all the things people can see, hear, and touch are created by a computer. In immersive virtual reality, people feel they are entirely within a computer-generated world.

infrared
A type of electromagnetic radiation produced by hot objects. Infrared radiation is similar to light, but the waves that carry it are longer.

input
The process of getting information into a computer. Typing things into a computer using a keyboard is a form of input.

internal combustion engine
A machine that produces heat energy by burning fuel with oxygen inside closed metal containers called cylinders.

Internet
A global network of computers that are informally connected by telephone and other telecommunications links.

Kevlar
A very strong fabric made from tightly woven carbon fibres. Kevlar is used to make bulletproof vests and other protective materials.

kinetic energy
The energy something has because it is moving.

landline
An ordinary telephone line, connected directly to the main phone network. Unlike a mobile phone, a landline cannot roam from place to place.

laser
A powerful and precise beam of light in which the waves all travel in step.

LCD
Liquid crystal display. A display on a piece of electronic equipment in which the numbers and other characters are produced by passing electric currents through crystals.

loudspeaker
A device that turns electricity into sound using a magnet and coil of wire to push a paper cone back and forth.

machine
A device usually powered by electricity or fuel that uses wheels, levers, gears, and other moving parts to do a job.

mechanical
A process carried out by a machine with moving parts.

memory
An electronic device that can store information.

microchip
An informal name for a microprocessor.

microprocessor
A computer built into a tiny piece of silicon about the size of a fingernail.

microwave
A type of electromagnetic radiation produced by a device called a magnetron and used in microwave ovens, radar, and telecommunications. Microwaves are similar to light, but invisible, and the waves that carry them are much longer.

mineral
A useful, nonliving solid substance mined from the ground. Coal, sand, and gold are examples of minerals.

molecule
The smallest amount of a chemical compound that can exist. A molecule consists of two or more atoms joined together.

motherboard
The main electronic circuit board in a computer or electronic device.

motor
A machine that uses magnets and tightly wrapped coils of metal to turn electricity into movement. See also generator.

MP3
Moving Picture Experts Group (MPEG) Audio Layer 3. A type of computer file that stores music in a very compressed (squeezed) form. This makes it easy to store the file in a smaller space or send it more quickly over the Internet.

nacelle
The housing (outer case) of a machine, such as a jet engine or wind turbine, that contains the main components.

nanotechnology
A technology through which people are attempting to create useful new materials by manipulating individual atoms and molecules.

NASA
National Aeronautics and Space Administration. An American government agency that carries out space research and runs missions into space (such as the Apollo moon landings and the Space Shuttle missions).

optical
A device that carries or detects light, such as a camera or camcorder lens.

parallel processing
A way of designing a computer so it solves a problem more quickly by working on more than one piece of it at once.

piston
A tight-fitting metal plunger that moves up and down inside the cylinder in an engine to convert heat energy into movement (mechanical energy).

pixel
A small coloured square that makes up part of the picture in a digital camera image or a computer or television screen. A typical digital photograph is made up of millions of pixels.

plastic
A material usually made from petroleum-based chemicals that is flexible when first created and easy to mould into different shapes.

pneumatic
A machine powered by compressed air flowing through pipes, such as a pneumatic road drill. See also hydraulic.

polarized
A type of light that has been passed through a filter so its waves move in only one direction.

pollution
A waste substance that is harmful to people or the environment.

polycarbonate
A tough, durable, and virtually shatterproof form of plastic.

port
The left side of a ship or aeroplane.

pressure
The force acting on a certain area of an object's surface. If the same force acts over half the area, it produces twice as much pressure.

processor
The central "brain" inside a computer where most information processing happens. The processor is usually built onto a single microchip.

pump
A mechanical device that moves a liquid or gas from one place to another. A pump typically has a piston that moves back and forth (as in a bicycle pump) or a rotating mechanism called an impeller (as in a dishwasher).

R **Radar**
A device that uses beams of invisible microwaves to detect approaching ships, aeroplanes, or other objects. Radar stands for radio detection and ranging.

radiation
A type of energy given off by a physical process. Hot objects give off invisible waves of heat, which consist of infrared radiation.

radiator
A device that gives off heat to the air around it when a hot liquid or gas flows through it. The radiators in homes give off heat when hot water flows through them. The radiator in a car cools the engine by giving off waste heat.

radio
A way of sending sound or other information between two places using beams of radio waves instead of wires.

receiver
An electrical device that picks up radio waves sent through the air by a transmitter.

rechargeable
A type of battery that can be recharged with energy hundreds of times by connecting it to a mains power supply. An ordinary disposable battery cannot normally be recharged.

renewable energy
A type of energy, such as wind or solar power, that is made without burning fossil fuels such as coal, gas, or oil.

retina
The light-sensitive surface inside the human eyeball.

rotor
A moving blade, shaped like an aerofoil, used in an aircraft, wind turbine, or similar device.

S **satellite**
An object, such as a spacecraft, that moves in orbit around a planet. The Moon is a natural satellite of Earth.

sensor
A mechanical, electrical, or electronic device on a machine designed to respond to a change in the environment around it.

servo motor
An electric motor that can be rotated in small steps so it moves something (like a robot arm) with high precision. A servo motor is also known as a stepper motor.

shim
A thin layer of material that separates different parts.

shock absorber
A hydraulic component on a vehicle's suspension that uses a fluid-filled piston to absorb energy and smooth out bumps in the road.

software
The programs stored in a computer that control how it operates. See also hardware.

solar power
A type of energy made from the Sun's light or heat. Solar power can be used to heat something or to make electricity.

spoiler
A curved wing at the front or back of a car designed to deflect airflow and improve the car's handling or performance.

sprocket
A gear wheel.

starboard
The right side of a ship or aeroplane.

streamlining
A way of designing vehicles so that air moves over them more easily. By reducing drag, streamlining helps to increase speed and reduce fuel consumption.

supercomputer
An extremely powerful computer typically used to solve difficult scientific problems such as weather forecasting.

suspension
The mechanical system underneath a car that uses hydraulics and springs to cushion passengers from bumps in the road.

T **Teflon**
An extremely slippery material used as a protective material in spacesuits and as a coating in nonstick frying pans.

thermogram
A photograph showing patterns of heat given off

by objects. A conventional photograph shows the light that objects reflect, whereas a thermogram shows the infrared energy they give off.

transformer
An electrical device that increases or decreases the voltage of an electrical supply.

transistor
A small component that can work as an amplifier (current booster) or switch in an electronic circuit.

transmitter
An electrical device that produces radio waves and beams them through the air. See also receiver.

turbine
A machine similar to a windmill that spins around in a moving gas or liquid, capturing some of its energy. A wind turbine captures the energy from the moving airstream we call wind.

turbocharger
A device attached to the exhaust of a car or aeroplane that boosts the power created by the engine.

type
Pieces of metal or plastic used to print letters, numbers, or other characters in a printing press.

U **ultrasonic**
A sound with a frequency (pitch) too high for humans to hear.

ultraviolet
A type of invisible electromagnetic radiation similar to light, but the waves that carry it are shorter and carry more energy. Sunlight contains harmful ultraviolet light that we block out with suncreams and sunglasses.

upload
The process of copying files from your computer to the Internet.

USB
Universal serial bus. A standardized connection on a computer that can be used to attach and power printers, webcams, disc drives, and other devices (known as peripherals).

V **velocity**
The speed at which an object moves in a particular direction.

video
A way of permanently recording pictures filmed with a camera onto a tape or disc.

virtual reality
A computer-generated model of a real or imaginary world inside which a person can move around.

voltage
The amount of electrical force produced by something like a battery.

W **watt**
The amount of energy that something uses or produces in one second.

wave
A back-and-forth or up-and-down movement that carries energy from one place to another.

webcam
A small digital camera, usually connected to a computer with a USB lead, that sends pictures live (in real time) over the Internet.

Wi-Fi
Wireless Fidelity. A way of connecting computer systems together without wires over medium ranges (typically up to 100m or about 300ft).

wireless
A way of sending information or connecting electronic devices by using radio waves instead of cables.

INDEX

ACKNOWLEDGMENTS

The publisher would like to thank the following: Chris Bernstein for indexing; Kieran Macdonald for proofreading; Johnny Pau and Rebecca Wright for additional design; Claire Bowers and Rose Horridge in the DK Picture Library; Rachael Hender, Jason Harding, Rob Quantrell, and Stanislav Shcherbakov at Nikid Design Ltd; Chris Heal, FBHI; Nicola Woodcock.

The publisher would also like to thank the following manufacturers for their kind cooperation and help in producing the computer-generated artworks of their products:

Pendolino Train – Alstom Transport

Ariane 5 – ESA/CNES/ARIANESPACE

ENV Fuel Cell Bike – Seymourpowell/Intelligent Energy

Vestas Wind Turbine – Vestas

Freeplay Radio – Freeplay Energy PLC

KEF Muon speakers – KEF and Uni-Q are registered trademarks. Uni-Q is protected under GB patent 2 236929, U.S. patent No. 5,548,657 and other worldwide patents. ACE technology is protected under GB patent 2146871. U.S. patent No.4657108 and other worldwide patents.

Breitling Watch – Breitling

Steinway Piano – courtesy of Steinway & Sons

Gibson Electric Guitar – Gibson Guitar, part of the Gibson Guitar Corporation which is Trademarked - www.gibson.com

Lego Robot – MINDSTORMS is a trademark of the LEGO Group

London Eye – conceived and designed by Marks Barfield Architects. Operated by the London Eye Company Limited, a Merlin Entertainments Group Company.

Canon Camera and Canon Inkjet Printer – Canon UK Ltd. For more information please visit www.canon.co.uk

The publisher would like to thank the following for their kind permission to reproduce their photographs:

(Key: a-above; b-below/bottom; c-centre; f-far; l-left; r-right; t-top)

The Advertising Archives: 142br, 156bc, 210br; **Alamy Images:** Alvey & Towers Picture Library 25br; BCA&D Photo Illustration 99cr; Blackout Concepts 44cl; Bobo 99tl; Martin Bond 168tl; Richard Broadwell 90ftl; David Burton 105bl; Buzz Pictures 68b; ClassicStock 31tl; David Hoffman Photo Library 210t; Danita Delimont 118bl; Ianni Dimitrov 196-197c; Chad Ehlers 31tr; Andrew Fox 112tl; geldi 237r; Sean Gladwell 156br; Peter Huggins 79bl; ImageState 241tl; Jupiter Images/ BananaStock 95r; Vincent Lowe 33br; Mary Evans Picture Library 240tr; Eric Nathan 156bl; David Osborn 51br; Photofusion Picture Library 157tl; John Robertson 196b; Howard Sayer 128-129; Alex Segre 156cl; Shout 38bl; Skyscan Photolibrary 112-113c; Charles Stirling 119cr; Stockbyte 99tr; John Sturrock 221cl; The Print Collector 157cr; The Stock Asylum, LLC 173bl; David Wall 31cr, 186c; Zak Waters 136tl; **Anoto:** 200t; **Auger-Loizeau:** 198t; **Anthony Bernier:** 23; **British Library:** 204t, 205t; **Camera Press:** Keystone 186t; © **CERN Geneva:** 219cb; **Corbis:** 30t, 187tl; Piyal Adhikary 21crb; Bettmann 45bl, 120cl, 219ca; Stefano Bianchetti 186bl; Iñigo Bujedo Aguirre 151cl; Construction Photography 127cr; Jerry Cooke 234tl; Andreu Dalmau 44-45c;

Arko Datta 120-121c; DK Limited 241tr; Najlah Feanny 227br; Owen Franken 105cr; Stephen Frink 226cl; Chinch Gryniewicz 104b; Tim Hawkins 45t; Amet Jean Pierre 73br; Bembaron Jeremy 166-167c; Lake County Museum 187bl; Jonny Le Fortune 197t; Lester Lefkowitz 37bc; Jo Lillini 16b; Araldo de Luca 150br; Stephanie Maze 36bl; Tom & Dee Ann McCarthy 38br; Moodboard 226cr; NASA 8; Hashimoto Noboru 31b; Alain Nogues 67cr; David Pollack 161br; David Reed 21bl; Reuters 179tc; Bob Rowan 226br; Zack Seckler 105t; The Art Archive 226tl; Sunny S. Unal 197b; John Van Hasselt 166br; Martin B. Withers 137tr; Jim Zuckerman 38tr; **DK Images:** Rowan Greenwood 50cl; NASA 246b; National Motor Museum, Beaulieu 20bc; Robert Opie Collection, The Museum of Advertising and Packaging, Gloucester, England 218br; **Eyevine Ltd:** 241br; Floris Leeuwenberg 235; New York Times/Redux/ 163t, 210-211c; Redux 161tr; **2004 Funtime Group:** 187cl; **Getty Images:** 3D Systems Corp 242bl; 21tl, 36br, 73t, 120tl, 127t, 211br; AFP 21tr, 51cl, 59bl, 173t, 187br, 235br; Altrendo images 59br, 105br; Alejandro Balaguer 44tr; Peter Cade 100l; Cousteau Society 59t; Adrian Dennis 182tr; Michael Dunning 12-13; Tim Flach 108bl; Bruce Forster 143tl; Marco Garcia 72cr; Garry Gay 160; Catrina Genovese 205br; Gavin Hellier 30-31c; Hulton Archive 67fbr, 98bl, 151cr; Koichi Kamoshida 181r; Brian Kenney 126tl; Dennis McColeman 66fbl; Roberto Mettifogo 161bl; Hans Neleman 112br; Patagonik Works 207tr; Andrew Paterson 231tr; Mark Ralston 156-157c; Chris M. Rogers 187cr; Mario Tama 227cb; The Bridgeman Art Library 151t, 204bl; Time & Life Pictures 50br, 51bl, 72br; David Tipling 80bl; Roger Viollet 104l; **Reaksmy Gloriana:** 227ca; **Impact Photos:** Yann Arthus-Bertrand 90bl; **KEF Audio:** 142t; **The Kobal Collection:** 178-179bc; **Lebrecht Music and Arts Photo Library:** 166bc, 167cr, 167tl, 167tr; **Jennifer Maestre:** 161tl; **Mary Evans Picture Library:** 20bl, 36c, 50bc, 66bc, 66bl, 166tl, 218bl; **Maxppp:** 72t; **Milepost:** 30l; **Myst:** 157bc; **NASA:** 53br, 55r, 67br, 93t; Dryden Flight Research Center Photo Collection 50t; **NHPA/Photoshot:** Stephen Dalton 218-219c; **PA Photos:** 45cl, 120bl, 172t, 234b, 235t; **Panos Pictures:** Mark Henley 104-105c; Abbie Trayler-Smith 137tl; **Reuters:** Kimberley White 221tl; **Rex Features:** 20tr, 20-21c, 37t, 45cr, 47br, 72l, 73bl, 73cl, 119br, 121b, 137br, 143br, 143cr, 205bl, 218bc, 219br; Everett Collection 178cr; Eye Ubiquitous 211bl; Richard Jones 211cl; Alisdair Macdonald 39; David Pearson 156t; Chris Ratcliffe 193b; Sunset 86b; Sutton-Hibbert 197cb; Ray Tang 185tl; Times Newspapers 185tr; E. M. Welch 227tr; **Science & Society Picture Library:** 72bl, 78bc, 150bc, 151bl, 196t, 210bc, 210bl, 219bl, 226bc, 227bl, 235tr; **Science Photo Library:** 37br, 44bc, 58b; Steve Allen 38tl; Andrew Lambert Photography 79br, 140br; Julian Baum 112bl; Jeremy Bishop 211tr; Martin Bond 91cr; Andrew Brookes 150-151c; Tony Buxton 67t; Conor Caffrey 78c; Martyn F. Chillmaid 99br; Thomas Deerinck 78tc; Martin Dohrn 113cl; Carlos Dominguez 98tr; Michael Donne 240tl; David Ducros 60b; P. Dumas 197ca; Ray Ellis 127b; Pascal Goetgheluck 78-79c; Roger Harris 179tr; James Holmes 205cr; J. Joannopoulos / Mit 220-221; Cavallini James 79t; Jacques Jangoux 37bl; Ted Kinsman 98cr, 113bl; C.s. Langlois 143tr; Living Art Enterprises, Llc 107t; Jerry Mason 221tr; Andrew Mcclenaghan 79cr; Tony Mcconnell 110t; Peter Menzel 179tl; Cordelia Molloy 211cr; NASA 57r, 90fcla,

112c, 113t, 119bl; Susumu Nishinaga 118br; David Nunuk 113br; Sam Ogden 224tl; P.baeza, Publiophoto Diffusion 118-119c; David Parker 178b, 204-205c; Alfred Pasieka 155br, 161c; Detlev Van Ravenswaay 66c; Jim Reed 113cr; David Scharf 98-99c; Heini Schneebeli 137cr; Simon Fraser / Welwyn Electronics 220t; Pasquale Sorrentino 76t; Volker Steger 126-127, 221br, 226-227c; George Steinmetz 58-59c, 91br; Bjorn Svensson 78bl; Andrew Syred 103tr, 188-189; Sheila Terry 44bl; Jim Varney 219t; **Second Life** is a trademark of Linden Research, Inc. Certain materials have been reproduced with the permission of Linden Research, Inc. Copyright © 2001–2007 Linden Research, Inc. All rights reserved: 234-235c; **Sony Computer Entertainment:** 152tl; **Still Pictures:** 44cr; Mark Edwards 136tr, 136-137c; Danna Patricia 91tl; **StockFood.com:** 114l; **SuperStock:** Corbis 82-83; Swatch AG: 151b; **University of Calgary / Dr Christoph Sensen:** 158t; University of Washington: 229r; **US Department of Defense:** 40l, 45br; USGS: EROS 67c, 67ca; **Yamaha:** © 2007 Yamaha Corporation 167br

Jacket images: *Front:* **DK Images:** 2008 The LEGO Group/ MINDSTORMS is a trademark of the LEGO Group

All other images © Dorling Kindersley

For further information see: www.dkimages.com